The Essential

SPECIAL EDUCATION GUIDE

for the

Regular Education Teacher

ABOUT THE AUTHOR

Edward Burns received a Ph.D. from the University of Michigan in 1971, and is currently Professor Emeritus at the State University of New York, Binghamton, New York. His areas of specialty include special education and psychoeducational assessment, assistive technology, the interpretation and compliance of the Individuals with Disabilities Education Act amendments, and educational statistics. He has written numerous articles in such journals as *Educational Technology, Journal of School Psychology, Journal of Learning Disabilities, Reading Research Quarterly, Journal of Special Education* and the *American Journal of Mental Deficiency*. He is also the author of 11 books including *IEP-2005 Writing and Implementing Individualized Education Programs* (Thomas, 2006), *The Special Education Consultant Teacher* (Thomas, 2004), and *A Handbook for Supplementary Aids and Services* (Thomas, 2003). He is currently involved in issues relating to IDEA compliance and the overrepresentation of minorities in special education.

The Essential

SPECIAL EDUCATION GUIDE

for the Regular Education Teacher

By

EDWARD BURNS, Ph.D.

Professor Emeritus
State University of New York
at Binghamton
Binghamton, New York

CHARLES C THOMAS • PUBLISHER, LTD.
Springfield • Illinois • U.S.A.

Published and Distributed Throughout the World by

CHARLES C THOMAS • PUBLISHER, LTD.
2600 South First Street
Springfield, Illinois 62704

© 2007 by CHARLES C THOMAS • PUBLISHER, LTD.

ISBN 978-0-398-07754-9 (hard)
ISBN 978-0-398-07755-6 (paper)

Library of Congress Catalog Card Number: 2007010073

Printed in the United States of America
UB-R-3

Library of Congress Cataloging-in-Publication Data

Burns, Edward
    The Essential special education guide for the regular education teacher / by Edward Burns.
        p. cm.
    ISBN 978-0-398-07754-9 (hard) -- ISBN 978-0-398-07755-6 (pbk.)
    1. Special education--United States--Handbooks, manuals, etc. 2. Children with disabilities
--Education--United States--Handbooks, manuals, etc. 3. Inclusive education--United States
--Handbooks, manuals, etc. 4. Teachers--In service training--United States--Handbooks, man-
uals, etc. I. Title

LC3981.B87 2007
371.900973--dc22

                                                      2007010073

PREFACE

The Individuals with Disabilities Education Act (IDEA) of 2004 has placed a renewed emphasis on the importance of the regular classroom, the regular classroom teacher and the general curriculum as a primary focus of special education. Every individualized education program requires goals "to meet the child's needs that result from the child's disability to enable the child to be involved in and make progress in the **general education curriculum**." In order to achieve these goals supports for school personnel must be provided so that children with disabilities **can be involved in, and make progress in, the curriculum** and participate in nonacademic activities.

Special education is not, and has never been, conceptualized as a place where children are placed in order to provide services in a separate location. The presumed placement for every child is the regular classroom; and the goal for every child with a disability is to enable regular classroom participation to the maximum extent possible.

The purpose of this book is to provide a guide for achieving this fundamental goal: to enable children with disabilities to participate in the regular classroom and the general curriculum to the maximum extent appropriate. The role of the classroom teacher in the determination of classroom needs and curriculum involvement to maximize regular classroom participation is essential. Indeed, the goal is to decrease the need for special education, and to increase the ability of every child with a disability to function as independently as possible in the regular classroom. This cannot be achieved without the participation of the regular classroom teacher in the identification of real classroom needs, in the planning of individualized education programs, and in the inclusion of children with disabilities in all aspects of the general curriculum.

This book contains over 100 topics that deal with real issues and concerns regarding the regular classroom, the classroom teacher and the special education process. These concerns range from requirements for referring a child for an individual evaluation, the participation of classroom teachers in IEP meetings, inclusion and mainstreaming, and various legal requirements relating to the 2004 Individuals with Disabilities Education Act amendments, Section 504 of the Rehabilitation Act of 1973, and the No Child Left Behind act. In addition, a variety of additional topics are discussed that have a direct bearing on the regular classroom teacher's involvement in the education of children with disabilities such as classroom-based assessment, school discipline, IEP responsibilities, classroom accommodations, aide training and supervision, and how to advocate for all necessary classroom supplementary supports and services. The ultimate purpose of this book is to provide real information, based on current law and regulations, that will benefit the classroom teacher and enable the successful participation of children with disabilities in the regular classroom and general curriculum.

E.B.

CONTENTS

PART III: REFERRAL, RTI AND STANDARDS

PART IV: ASSESSMENT

PART V: IEP ESSENTIALS

PART VI: INDIVIDUAL ACCOMMODATIONS

PART VII: CLASSROOM BEHAVIOR

PART VIII: SERVICES

The Essential

SPECIAL EDUCATION GUIDE

for the

Regular Education Teacher

Part I
High Expectations

Research and experience has shown that the education of children with disabilities can be made more effective by high expectations, and ensuring their access to the general education curriculum in the regular classroom, to the maximum extent possible.[1]

1. A SERVICE AND NOT A PLACE

High expectations and access to the general curriculum will allow children with disabilities to meet developmental goals and, to the maximum extent possible, the challenging expectations that have been established for all children.[2]

When Congress approved the Individuals with Disabilities Education Act (IDEA) amendments in 2004 the law (Public Law 108-446) was introduced by several findings concerning the importance of regular classroom participation, appropriate services, independence, and high expectations.[3] All educators should be guided by the phrase that **special education is a service, not a place**. The meaning of this is that the needs of children with disabilities are best met by providing appropriate services, having high expectations for all children, and using the general curriculum and the regular education classroom as the benchmark for educational success and participation. The needs of children with disabilities are not best met by assuming that a placement in a restrictive environment, in and of itself, is in any way "appropriate." The following are several Congressional findings that characterize the philosophy of IDEA and the emphasis on the general curriculum and regular classroom participation:[4]

> **Regular classroom participation:** Before the enactment of IDEA in 1975, the educational needs of millions of children with disabilities were not being fully met because children did not receive appropriate services, were excluded from regular classroom participation, children were not identified, and many parents were forced to seek help outside of the school system.
>
> **Improving educational results:** Since the enactment of IDEA the law has been successful in ensuring children with disabilities have access to a free appropriate public education and in improving educational results for children with disabilities.
>
> **Low expectations:** The implementation of special education has been impeded by low expectations and an insufficient focus on research showing proven methods for teaching and learning for children with disabilities.
>
> **Special education is a service:** Coordinating the law other agencies and school improvement efforts to ensure that such children benefit from

such efforts and that special education can become a service for such children rather than a place where such children are sent.

Regular classroom support: Providing appropriate special education and related services, and aids and supports in the regular classroom, to such children, whenever appropriate.

Reduce labeling: Providing incentives for whole-school approaches, scientifically-based early reading programs, positive behavioral interventions and supports, and early intervening services to reduce the need to label children as disabled in order to address the learning and behavioral needs of such children.

What does this mean for the classroom teacher? Have high expectations for children with disabilities. Children with disabilities should not be simply "in the classroom" but participate in the general curriculum and classroom activities. Of course, the participation of children with disabilities in the classroom is always followed by the phrase "to the maximum extent appropriate," but the appropriate level of participation cannot be achieved without high expectations.

The key to special education is...? The key to successful special education is not the special education teacher and not special education classes, but the ability to participate in the regular classroom under the direction of the regular classroom teacher. The purpose of special education, the purpose of the special education teacher and special education classes is to achieve the goal of maximizing regular classroom participation. Having high expectation is the first step toward achieving this goal.

What can the classroom teacher do? Provide reasonable accommodations and encourage curriculum participation. Collaborate with special education and related service personnel. Help identify classroom needs and generalize skills learned in nonclassroom settings to meet regular classroom needs.

2. THE SPECIAL EDUCATION PROCESS

The FAPE Mandate: A Free Appropriate Public Education

Special education is a process that is designed to provide a child with a disability a free and appropriate public education; special education is not a place where children with disabilities are educated because this assumes that appropriate is synonymous with a special environment. The appropriate placement for a child with a disability is where a child can participate in the general curriculum to the maximum extent appropriate; and the determination of this appropriate placement always begins with the regular classroom.

The regular classroom teacher plays an important role in all phases of the special education process. The classroom teacher is an important source of data for understanding classroom needs of a child with a disability prior to referral; the classroom teacher provides important information and observational data during the full and individual evaluation; the classroom teacher contributes to the development of the IEP; the classroom teacher is essential for the implementation of the IEP; and the classroom teacher is obviously important for determining the extent a child can be educated with nondisabled students.

▼ **"Procedural flaws do not automatically require a finding of a denial of a free appropriate education, but procedural inadequacies that result in the loss of educational opportunity clearly result in the denial of a free appropriate education."**[5]

Prereferral

The key to the referral component in the special education process is response-to-intervention (RTI). The RTI approach to specific learning disabilities has re-emphasized the importance of the regular classroom teacher in the determination a specific learning disability by ensuring that every child has received high quality, research-based general education instruction prior to referral for special education. Just as important, RTI is viewed as a way to reduce the number of overreferrals and misclassifications in special education. The IDEA requires that "a child shall not be determined to be a child with a disability if the determinant factor for such determination is lack of appropriate instruction in reading, including in the essential components of reading instruction (as defined in section 1208(3) of the Elementary and Secondary Education Act of 1965)."[6]

Reducing the Need to Label

Providing incentives for whole-school approaches, scientifically based early reading programs, positive behavioral interventions and supports, and early intervening services to reduce the need to label children as disabled in order to address the learning and behavioral needs of such children.[7]

Referral

The classroom teacher is often the pivotal person when a referral for special education is made. To this end the referral should be comprised of three elements: **First,** the **reason for the referral.** The classroom teacher's obligation is not to identify the disability but to describe a child's academic performance and classroom behavior. The team of qualified professionals and the parents determine the existence of a disability following the full and individual evaluation. **Second,** the classroom teacher should provide a description of the various **classroom interventions** that have been attempted. For disabilities such as deaf-blindness, deafness, and disabilities that have a pronounced effect on educational performance, the extent of classroom interventions will be limited. However, for specific learning disabilities which account for almost 50 percent of all disabilities the classroom teacher should describe the child's response to high quality, systematic instruction and school-wide efforts to accommodate the child without special education. **Third,** the classroom teacher should describe **contact with parents** concerning classroom performance. If a disability is suspected, parents might have important medical information concerning their child or useful strategies or accommodations that have been effective in other settings or at home.

> ▼ The referral should always describe special levels of
>   classroom performance, special behaviors, and
>   include specific examples of academic work.

Referral Guidelines

Before you refer a child be sure that you have considered each of the following:

1. **The specific reason for the referral.**
2. **Examples of classroom work.**
3. **Attempted classroom interventions.**
4. **Possible classroom accommodations.**
5. **Needed classroom support.**
6. **Parent input.**

Evaluation

The initial evaluation must be conducted within 60 days of receiving parental consent for the evaluation.

The purpose of the full and individual evaluation will often require an observation of the child in the regular classroom...and for specific learning disabilities this observation is mandated. Classroom data is absolutely essential for a full and individual evaluation. The best evidence concerning what a child can and cannot do in the regular classroom is not a peripheral test (viz., an IQ test) but samples of classroom work, classroom tests and quizzes, observational classroom data, etc. The classroom teacher also provides important information for the determination of appropriate accommodations by reporting on the effectiveness of interventions and/or strategies that have been used or the need for additional accommodations and supports.

Eligibility

The classroom teacher is often a part of the team that determines whether or not a child has a disability. If the IEP Team and the evaluation team are one and the same, the classroom teacher will be involved in the decision that determines the child's disability and the need for special education. These are two separate decisions: **First**, does the child have a disability under IDEA? **Second**, does the child need special education? To receive services under IDEA the answer to both these questions must be yes. If a child has a disability, but does not need special education, services can be provided under Section 504. If a child has educational needs, but does not have a disability, services must be provided using school-wide resources (e.g., limited English proficiency, remedial reading, child study team assistance, etc.).

IEP Team

A meeting to develop an IEP for a child is conducted within 30-days of a determination that the child needs special education and related services.[8]

The classroom teacher is a member of the IEP Team if the child is, or may be, participating in the regular education environment. The participation of the classroom teacher as a member of the IEP Team is important for several reasons. First, the classroom teacher has essential expertise with respect to the general education curriculum. Second, the classroom teacher is often best able to determine the extent a child can be educated with nondisabled students or, at least, provide important information for this participation. Third, the classroom teacher has an important role in the determination of successful classroom participation and performance. The data and observations that the classroom teacher collects for all children enables the IEP Team to determine the extent academic performance is affected for a child with a disability by considering test performance, quizzes, classroom participation, work samples, homework, and so forth.

IEP

At the beginning of each school year, each public agency must have in effect, for each child with a disability within its jurisdiction, an IEP.[9]

If the evaluation team determines that a child has a disability and needs special education, an IEP must be developed. The IEP Team must convene and develop the IEP within 30 days after the qualified group of professionals and the parents have determined that a child has a disability and needs special education. The IEP is not developed prior to the meeting, nor is it developed following the meeting. The IEP is developed at the meeting so that members can actively participate in the consideration of present levels of academic performance and appropriate accommodations, goals and services. OK, this is not always done. If a completed IEP appears at the meeting, read the IEP (yes, at the meeting), and provide input concerning the classroom goals, services, accommodations and supports that you believe are necessary for the child to succeed in the classroom.

What if...

What if, at the IEP meeting, you are ignored and one or more members drone on about an seemingly endless list of test scores. Somewhere, somehow, ask for two minutes to discuss specific classroom performance, specific behaviors, specific reading and other needs that should be address to enable successful classroom performance. Do this and you will have done your job as a team member.

3. NCLB FOR THE CLASSROOM TEACHER

To close the achievement gap with accountability,
flexibility, and choice, so that no child is left behind.

Almost 50 percent of all children receiving services under IDEA have disabilities relating to reading. For many other disabilities reading can be an important educational need, an area that is impacted by the disability, or the disability itself (in the case of Specific Learning Disabilities). For example, a child with emotional needs might not have a reading disability but reading might be affected by behavior that precludes instruction or limits the ability to participate in regular classroom activities.

The Elementary and Secondary Education Act (ESEA) amendments, also known as No Child Left Behind (NCLB) or Public Law 107-110, includes loads of useful information for the classroom teacher. The regulations allow schools to use money received under IDEA to develop and implement early intervention services such as **scientifically-based literacy instruction** for children who are not currently identified "but who need additional academic and behavioral support to succeed in a general education environment."[10] Ah, but what does "scientifically based" actually mean? The answer can be found in the NCLB act:[11]

http://www.ed.gov/policy/elsec/leg/esea02/index.html

SCIENTIFICALLY-BASED READING RESEARCH

The term "scientifically based reading research" means research that applies rigorous, systematic, and objective procedures to obtain valid knowledge relevant to reading development, reading instruction, and reading difficulties, and includes research that

1. employs systematic, empirical methods that draw on observation or experiment;

2. involves rigorous data analyses that are adequate to test the stated hypotheses and justify the general conclusions drawn;

3. relies on measurements or observational methods that provide valid data across evaluators and observers and across
   multiple measurements and observations; and

4. has been accepted by a peer-reviewed journal or approved
   by a panel of independent experts through a comparably
   rigorous, objective, and scientific review.[12]

The classroom teacher provides important assessment information required by NCLB by evaluating a child's learning based on systematic observations, performing academic tasks that are part of their daily classroom experience, and "to improve instruction in reading, including classroom instruction." The classroom teacher also contributes to the assessment process by identifying strengths and weaknesses, determining classroom reading difficulties, "and helping to determine possible reading intervention strategies and related special needs."[13]

About Laws and Regulations

You need a scorecard to keep track of the various laws and regulations. For special education the basic law is the Individuals with Disabilities Education Improvement Act amendments (IDEA) that was signed by the President in 2004. These amendments represent one of a series of major amendments to the first special education law enacted in 1975 or the Education of All Handicapped Children Act (Public Law 94-142). Public Law 101-476 (in 1990) changed the name of the law to IDEA (and also changed the word **handicap** to **disability**), and added the categories of **autism** and **traumatic brain injury** to the list of IDEA disabilities. If you are ever asked why there has been a dramatic increase in the number of children with autism, mention that autism wasn't an "official" disability until 1990. Prior to that time children with autism were identified as having speech or language impairments, mental retardation, emotional disturbance, and so forth.

Public law 108-446 is the 446th law passed by the 108th Congress. Eventually every public law is codified in the United States Code (USC). The law passed by Congress and the version in the USC are almost identical except for the numbering. The law passed by Congress is numbered in the 600s, while the codified version is found in Title 20 and the numbering is in the 1400s (e.g., 20 USC 1414). Thus, section 614(d)(1)(B) in the law lists the requirements for the IEP Team, and this same section is 1414(d)(1)(B) in the USC. Actually, it takes a while for the law to be codified so if you want to know the current law, stick with the law passed by Congress.

Finally, there is one additional set of legal guidelines that must be considered. Within a year or so the Office of Special Education and Rehabilitative services under the Department of Education develops the regulations for the law in the Code of Federal Regulations (CFR). The regulations expand and explain the law (or more likely simply repeats the law). One item in the regulations, but not in the law, is a listing of the specific definitions for each of the 13 disabilities. For the classroom teacher this maze of laws and regulations is important if you are trying to make some sense out of what is required or what you are <u>told</u> is required by the IDEA. Want to know all about IEP Team attendance requirements? Download a copy of the regulations at

http://www.ed.gov/policy/elsec/leg/esea02/index.html

and go to Section 321 (or **§ 300.321 IEP Team.**). This same information can be found in the law passed by Congress in 2004 in section 614(d)(1)(B)&(C). What to use: the Law or the regulations for the law? Most schools tend to rely on the regulations as the best interpretation of the law. Bottom line for teachers: download a copy of the regulations and use this to answer any and all questions about definitions, IEPs, requirements for the classroom teacher, and everything from specific learning disabilities to due process questions. Want to know about school **discipline** that is permissible for a child with a disability? Search the PDF (Portable Document Format) file for the regulations and 80 items will appear ranging from comments about discipline to the word "discipline" actually cited in the regulations.

Legal Tidbits for the Classroom Teacher

AYP: Adequate Yearly Progress Supplemental educational services are provided when a fails to make adequate yearly progress for three consecutive years.

Chapter I: Now called Title I

CFR: Code of Federal Regulations

FEOG: Full Educational Opportunity Goal

IDEA: Individuals with Disabilities Education Improvement Act of 2004. I suppose the correct acronym should be IDEIR but IDEA is a lot easier to pronounce

IEP: Individualized Education Program

LEA: Local Educational Agency

National School Lunch Program: The number of students participating in the National School Lunch Program is often used to measure the poverty level of a school district. For 2006, $37,000 is the annual income cutoff for reduced price meals and $26,000 for free meals.

NCLB: No Child Left Behind act of 2001 (NCLB), Public Law 107-110.

Section 504: Much cited law (based on Section 504 of the Rehabilitation Act of 1973) which prohibits discrimination based on disability, and often used to provide accommodations when specially designed instruction is not necessary.

SES: Supplemental Educational Service" which is intended to provide "high-quality, research-based instruction."

Title I Schoolwide Program: designed for schools where at least 40 percent of students are considered low income.

Title I: The name of this section or "Title" of NCLB is Improving the Academic Achievement of the Disadvantaged.

4. CLASSROOM PARTICIPATION

Teachers should be relieved of irrelevant and unnecessary paperwork burdens that do not lead to improved educational outcomes.[14]

There are two areas relating to classroom participation that must be considered: (1) physical classroom participation, and (2) general curriculum participation. A child with a severe disability or multiple disability might be able to physically sit in a regular classroom but gain little from classroom instruction or participate in the general curriculum. This will occur for an extremely small percentage of children with disabilities. Many children who are classified as mentally retarded, children who have IQ's in the 50 to 70 range, will not only benefit from social interaction with nondisabled children but also from the academic stimulation. For children with severe disabilities, or children who require specialized services, the question is not full inclusion but the appropriate amount of regular classroom participation.

To understand the real difference between classroom and curriculum participation consider the case of a child with emotional disturbance who is placed in a self-contained classroom. Also assume that the school and the parents are in agreement that this placement is the most appropriate and least restrictive placement. For this child two questions must be answered: To what extent will the child participate in the regular classroom, and to what extent will this child participate in the general curriculum? Regarding the extent of classroom participation this might be one hour a day, 10 minutes a day, or 30 minutes a week. No matter the type of disability or the alternative placement, the extent a child can and will participate in the regular classroom must be considered.

In addition to the time a child spends in the regular classroom, the extent of participation in the general curriculum must be considered. If a child is in the fourth grade, and able to achieve fourth grade goals, the child should be provided with the same curriculum that is provided to children who are not disabled. What is not wanted is for a special education teacher to develop a list of fun activities, or to otherwise create a new curriculum, with no regard for the general curriculum. If a child requires an alternative setting, the ability of the child to participate in the general curriculum must also be considered. To this end input from (and planning with) the classroom teacher is extremely important in that special education must be aligned to the general curriculum as much as possible. Regular education teachers must have input into the curriculum provided to children with disabilities when that curriculum is aligned with the general curriculum either in part or in total.

Ignoring the general curriculum is a disservice to children with disabilities and IDEA. Example: the regular biology class has students dissecting, bisecting, whatever while the special education teacher holds up a picture of a plant. Students with disabilities must not only have access to the general curriculum but to the regular classroom teacher's expertise.

The Unique Benefits of the Regular Classroom

"A second factor courts should consider in determining whether a child with disabilities can be included in a regular classroom is the comparison between the educational benefits the child will receive in a regular classroom (with supplementary aids and services) and the benefits the child will receive in the segregated, special education classroom. The court will have to rely heavily in this regard on the testimony of educational experts. Nevertheless, in making this comparison the court must pay special attention to those unique benefits the child may obtain from integration in a regular classroom which cannot be achieved in a segregated environment, i.e., the development of social and communication skills from interaction with nondisabled peers."[15]

5. THE MAXIMUM EXTENT APPROPRIATE

To be very honest, special education is not about special education. Special education is about **specially designed instruction** to enable regular classroom participation to the maximum extent appropriate. Special education provides support for regular classroom participation rather than an alternative to the regular classroom. The goal is not "special education," in and of itself; and most certainly the goal of special education is not to remove a child from the regular classroom. The ultimate goal of special education has always focused on regular classroom participation and involvement in the general curriculum to the maximum extent appropriate. True, participation in the classroom or curriculum cannot always be achieved, in total or in part, which is why the term **maximum extent appropriate** is often used.

The "Maximum Extent Appropriate" Standard

First, provide appropriate services, accommodations and supports in the regular classroom.

Second, if removal from the regular classroom is required, select the least restrictive alternative setting.

Third, if a child requires an alternative setting, determine the extent the child is able to participate in the regular classroom and in the general curriculum.

---

34 CFR §300.38 Special Education

What is special education? The regulations for IDEA defines special education as meaning "specially designed instruction, at no cost to the parents, to meet the unique needs of a child with a disability, including (1) Instruction conducted in the classroom, in the home, in hospitals and institutions, and in other settings; and (2) Instruction in physical education."

6. LAWYERS

When is a lawyer not wanted? At a resolution meeting on behalf of the school unless the parent is accompanied by an attorney.[16]

Philadelphia lawyers are probably no different than lawyers elsewhere...I think. Apparently the first "Philadelphia lawyer" of record was Andrew Hamilton who, in 1945 or thereabouts, defended a printer who criticized British policy and won on the premise that the truth could not be libel. Makes sense to me. For whatever reason this nobility of purpose has been lost so that now a Philadelphia lawyer is less a fighter for truth and freedom than a person who is exceptionally knowledgeable in the intricacies of the law and legal loopholes, or simply someone who is unscrupulous and more interested in money than ethics. Are lawyers, Philadelphia or otherwise, important in special education. Oh, yes! Most judges are lawyers who have actually guided the development and interpretation of special education law; lawyers can accompany parents to impartial hearings; and parents generally rely on lawyers when marching off to a district or appellate court for redress and remedy. The current special education law has given courts the discretion to award reasonable fees to the **prevailing party** who is the parent of a child with a disability. Thus, parents must prevail (win) to receive reasonable attorney fees. But the law also has a provision for schools to receive a reasonable fee against the attorney of a parent for a complaint that is frivolous, unreasonable, or without foundation, or for an action (due process hearing) that was presented to harass, cause unnecessary delay, or to increase the cost of litigation.[17]

But Do You Need a Lawyer?

If you are a regular classroom teacher, generally, no. Most often, no. The regulations for 1997 require that schools (1) must provide special education and related services to a child with a disability in accordance with the child's IEP; and (2) make a good faith effort to assist the child to achieve the goals and objectives or benchmarks listed in the IEP.[18] Well, so much for the 1997 regulations on accountability in that this section was removed ("unnecessary" it seems) from the new regulations.

In an event, if you are a regular classroom teacher, you are expected to comply with the child's IEP. Regulations or no, make a "good faith" effort to comply with the law. A good example of what can happen when a teacher does not put forth a good faith effort is the case of a 16-year-old with a learning disability. One of the IEP accommodations for this student was oral testing which did not seem like a good idea to the student's history teacher who ignored the IEP and the parents (he apparently went deer hunting rather than meet with the parents), and continued testing using written tests. The student failed because IEP accommodations were ignored and this noncompliance resulted in $30,000 in compensatory and $30,000 in punitive damages because "as a direct and proximate result of the negligence and/or intentional acts and omissions of the Defendants, the Plaintiff in addition to receiving zero credits for history was subjected to embarrassment and shame within the school community."[19] This is harsh language.

For all children with disabilities the classroom teacher must be involved in decisions concerning individual needs, placement, classroom goals and collaborative strategies. As the classroom teacher you do not pick and choose what students will participate in your class; you cannot choose what accommodations to use or ignore. Many students will require very little help and some will obviously require more individual attention. For a student with a disability some needs will be the result of the disability and other needs will be similar to the needs of children who are not disabled. Special education provides the help and support for disability-related needs; and the classroom teacher helps meet the regular education needs of children with disabilities just as the varying learning needs of children without disabilities are met.

As a classroom teacher you should be familiar with each child's IEP in your classroom. If a child requires Braille, you don't give the child a printed version of a test. If you teach secondary social studies, and a student is reading at the first grade level and the IEP stipulates a reader, a printed version of a test would likely be inappropriate. If an accommodation is in the IEP, don't ignore it. This does not mean that you will need to abandon your class in order to read a test to a student or test a student in Braille. This is one of the explicit purposes of classroom supports. What you can't do, what you shouldn't do, is simply ignore the IEP and disassociate yourself from meeting a child's academic needs. Often meeting these needs requires little more than a willingness to include all children in the general curriculum and a belief that having high expectations is central to special and regular education.

7. TEACHER COMPLAINTS

In every school, at every level, there will be conflicts. In some schools these conflicts are few and in others... not so few. Life can be difficult, especially when the classroom teacher must balance the responsibility of school employee with that of legitimate concerns for students. The regular education teacher must serve a variety of roles. First and foremost, the regular education teacher has a responsibility to the school to implement school rules, policies and the desired regular curriculum. For every child the regular education teacher also has a responsibility to provide every student with an appropriate education.

What happens when you believe your school is not providing a child with an appropriate education? Consider this court case involving three teachers who were vocal advocates of special education, IEPs and the concept of an appropriate education. The teachers believed the middle school principal was less than supportive of special education. Apparently the intrepid teachers complained to the principal, the administration and then the media. There seems to be no question the principal was ignorant of the purpose, rules and basic precepts of special education, but to what extent can a teacher oppose even the most noncompliant administrative fiat?

A decision by the 8th court of appeals (*Fales v. Garst* (8th Cir. 2001) attempted to determine whether the speech of a public school teacher is protected by the First Amendment. Said differently, can an unhappy teacher, unhappy with decisions that are contrary to IDEA, complain to all regarding the perceived shortsightedness and noncompliance of these decisions? This free speech question for public school teachers is answered (so say this court of appeals) by inquiring "whether the speech may be described as 'speech on a matter of public concern.' If so, the court balances the teacher's interest in speaking against her employer's interest in promoting the efficiency of the public service it performs through its employees." In this case the court of appeals found that the complaints of the teachers did center around special education topics (viz., care and education) of public concern, but that the "speech itself caused the workplace turmoil, here it is beyond peradventure that the plaintiffs' speech caused the school upheaval."

As a result the court ruled in favor of the "interest of efficient administration of the middle school" and not free speech. The moral of all of this is to be somewhat temperate in speech and avoid causing workplace turmoil.

"But I'm Not Tenured!"

What if the school does something that is blatantly contrary to IDEA, the regulatory requirements for IDEA, and the development of a reasonably calculated plan? Also assume that the person responsible for these inadequacies is a self-serving idiot. What to do? Do you march in his or her office and loudly proclaim his or her self-serving idiocy? Or do the same in the teacher's lounge? On a nearby street corner?

First, who is in charge? Follow the chain of command as it were. If IEPs are not accessible, talk to the director of special education. Often there is a problem because the person in charge isn't even aware of a problem.

Second, talk to a colleague. When problems occur the experience of others for dealing with a similar problem can be useful. Don't just complain but seek out ideas and solutions. Complain too much and people will avoid you.

Third, seek professional help. Not necessarily the mental help type of help (well, maybe, maybe not) but more teacher union type help. For example, the United Federation of Teachers has a complaint form for teachers regarding special education issues.[20] One section concerns specific IEP complaints and includes potential concerns relating to location, required number of periods per week, group size (i.e., larger than specified on IEP, cancellation of mandated service to provide class coverage, collaborative team teaching class. This, however, should be a last resort and make every effort to find a amicable and civil resolution to the problem.

> ▼ More often than not the key to resolving problems
> is to seek a collaborative solution that best
> accommodates the needs of the child, the classroom
> teacher and nondisabled students. A contentious,
> adversarial and litigious environment might provide
> a solution but also considerable resentment.

Life will not be perfect and as a classroom teacher you are not and should not be solely responsible for special education decisions, IEP decisions, placements, etc. If you perceive a problem or a case of clear-cut noncompliance, you are one voice. Be civil, address the problem, and the law. Don't yell; don't stomp your feet; follow the chain of command (which generally does not include teacher-lounge gossip). Discuss the problem with the special education teacher, then the director/chairperson of special education, and the principal. Most importantly, have your say at the IEP meeting. Again, you are not the compliance officer for IDEA so to say that a certain action is noncompliant is your opinion of noncompliance. You might think a child is not mentally retarded, or that a child should be in a self-contained classroom (or not), but the IEP Team and not the regular education teacher makes these decisions.

What if the action taken by the school affects your workload and your sanity? For example, eight children with disabilities are placed in your classroom with minimal support. If you are a new teacher, hopefully you had sense enough to ask questions about the composition of the classroom before taking the job. If you are a second-year teacher without tenure, this type of situation should be considered at the IEP meeting (another reason to attend IEP meetings). If placements are inappropriate for lack of classroom support, these inadequacies should be raised when the placements are made or discussed during evaluation or IEP Team meetings. Be nice. Schools are more likely to axe a "not nice" teacher with legitimate complaints than someone who makes a legitimate effort to be collegial. Nice is cheap and you don't need a lawyer or a union.

If you are a tenured teacher, you certainly can be more vocal, but tenured or not, you should attempt to do "right thing." Well, the right thing might not actually be right or even possible, but you need to do what you need to do. Would an administrator hold advocating the rights of a child against? Maybe not, maybe so. Unless you are absolutely desperate for a job and prepared to lead an absolutely miserable life, you sometimes need to take a stand. Hey, maybe even a bit of yelling and screaming might be in order. In any case, a "don't-cause-upheaval" rule is a really good idea.

8. CLASSROOM TEACHER PARTICIPATION

There are several requirements in IDEA that specifically apply to regular classroom teachers in the special education process. First and foremost, a classroom teacher is part of the IEP Team so that "not less than one regular education teacher" is a member of the team if the child is, or may be, participating in the regular classroom.[21] As a member of the IEP Team the regular education teacher helps to identify needs, and to select appropriate classroom goals, services, and accomodations. In addition, the regular education teacher must, to the extent appropriate, be involved in the determination of appropriate positive classroom behavioral interventions and supports and other strategies for the child, and necessary supplementary aids and services, program modifications, and support for school personnel.[22]

How do you do this? What you observe in the classroom, what you collect in terms of classroom work, and your assessment of a child's learning needs should provide an important basis for behavioral interventions, the determination of supplementary aids and services, reasonable accommodations, and needed classroom support. Next, play an active role in the IEP meeting. The purpose of special education should be to enable regular classroom and general curriculum participation. This cannot be achieved without input from the regular classroom teacher. Indeed, one of the primary reasons for special education failure is a disregard for input from the regular classroom teacher.

9. DISABILITIES IN THE REGULAR CLASSROOM

What types of disabilities might result in a classroom placement, either full or part time? Every IDEA disability category, including deaf-blindness and mental retardation, is represented in regular classroom, ranging from token inclusion to 100 percent inclusion. As shown by the table below, specific learning disabilities account for over 48 percent or almost half of all children receiving services under IDEA. The five high incidence disabilities (specific learning disability, speech or language impairment, mental retardation, emotional disturbance, and other health impairments) account for 92 percent of all children with disabilities, while the remaining eight categories account for approximately 8 percent.

There have been several trends that have impacted children with disabilities in the regular classroom: The number of children identified with specific learning disabilities has decreased slightly from 2001. There has been a slight decrease in the mental retardation category. The Autism category has increased 20 percent from 98,589 in 2001 to 118,669 in 2002. The number of children in the Other Health Impairment category has shown an increase of 15 percent from 2001 to 2002 (as a result of ADHD being added to the OHI definition 1997). The following table shows the number of children served under IDEA as of 2002.[23]

Table 1. Number of Children 6 to 21 Receiving IDEA Services

Disability	2002	%
Specific learning disabilities (SLD)	2,878,146	48.30%
Speech or language impairments	1,112,119	18.66%
Mental retardation	591,440	9.92%
Emotional disturbance	481,069	8.07%
Other health impairments (OHI)	392,671	6.59%
Multiple disabilities	131,682	2.21%
Autism	118,669	1.99%
Orthopedic impairments	74,065	1.24%

Hearing impairments	71,964	1.21%
Developmental delay	58,265	0.98%
Visual impairments	26,113	0.44%
Traumatic brain injury	21,479	0.36%
Deaf-blindness	1,600	0.03%
All disabilities	5,959,282	100.00%

10. REGULAR AND SPECIAL EDUCATION

*To ensure that regular education teachers have the necessary
skills and knowledge to provide instruction to students
with disabilities in the regular education classroom.[24]*

Regular Education

Only by clearly understanding the importance of regular education, the general education curriculum and the role of the regular education teacher can a foundation for the development of an appropriate education for children with disabilities be developed. A primary goal of special education is to educate children with disabilities with children who are not disabled and that "removal of children with disabilities from the regular educational environment occurs only when the nature or severity of the disability of a child is such that education in regular classes with the use of supplementary aids and services cannot be achieved satisfactorily."[25]

No matter the disability or the extent of the disability, the frame of reference is always the regular classroom and the general education curriculum. Regular participation in the classroom is not always possible, and a small percentage of children might require a very specialized curriculum. But every child with a disability is entitled to participate in the regular classroom and in the general curriculum to the maximum extent appropriate.

▼ **Core academic subjects means English, reading or
language arts, mathematics, science, foreign
languages, civics and government, economics, arts,
history, and geography.[26]**

Nondisabled Students

Nondisabled students are an essential element of the special education equation. The task is to enable children with disabilities to participate with nondisabled students to the maximum extent appropriate. This does not mean that the law or the courts envision special education as a way to by-pass the needs of regular classroom students or to otherwise allow special education to have a negative impact on students. In this regard the regular classroom teacher must provide information concerning the ability of a child to participate in the classroom, to help the IEP Team make appropriate placement decisions and to best meet the leaning needs of all children in the classroom. Indeed, if a child prevents others from learning, this can be a factor to mitigate against regular classroom participation.

Regular Education Teacher

The IDEA has long recognized the important role of the regular education teacher in special education. The regular classroom teacher is a member of the group that determines whether a child has a specific learning disability "if the child is, or may be, participating in the regular education environment."[27] The regular education teacher is a member of the IEP Team and participates in the development of the IEP, including the identification of appropriate positive behavioral interventions and supports, supplementary aids and services, program modifications, and support for school personnel.[28]

The regular classroom teacher has the expertise that is crucial for a child with a disability to achieve satisfactorily in the regular classroom. The regular classroom teacher provides the framework for structuring the curriculum, selecting appropriate materials, reaching curriculum goals, for achieving the sequential benchmarks within the general curriculum, and for achieving the high expectation envisioned by IDEA that are often necessitated by state-wide assessments.

✓	**Classroom Participation Checklist**
☐	Participation in group activities?
☐	Social participation?
☐	Participation in the academic curriculum?
☐	Seat work activities?
☐	Participation in tests and quizzes?
☐	Ability to respond in group activities?
☐	Ability to follow classroom rules?
☐	Ability to work with one or more students?
☐	Ability to work independently?
☐	Participation in nonacademic activities?
☐	Homework and other assignments?

Not allowing a child with a disability to participate under the direction of the regular education teacher (as when all services are provided by a special education teacher or aide) defeats a fundamental purpose of special education which is to allow children with disabilities to be educated **with** nondisabled children. This does not mean the regular education teacher is the *de facto* special education teacher, and therefore must devote an inordinate amount of time to a small number of children. What this does mean is that for children with disabilities in the regular classroom, children who require specially designed instruction via a certified special education teacher, the regular education teacher is part of the team that enables successful classroom and curriculum participation.

11. THE GENERAL EDUCATION CURRICULUM

The general education curriculum is defined as "the same curriculum as for nondisabled children."[29]

Prior to the first version of IDEA in 1975 (P.L. 94-142) special education was often little more than a place for children with disabilities outside of the regular classroom. There was no curriculum other than the activities initiated by the special education teacher and these were often tangentially related to the general education curriculum (if that). Sometimes the special education teacher stressed the academic curriculum, or more likely parts of some academic curriculum, but not necessarily the general education curriculum used by nondisabled children in the school. More likely than not the curriculum was a unique collection of activities to enlighten, entertain and otherwise occupy the time of the children in alternate special education classroom placements. Even if a teacher had high expectations there was rarely a connection to the academic curriculum used in the school, and even less of a connection to the implementation of a sequential curriculum from one year to the next.

The general education curriculum is defined as "the same curriculum as for nondisabled children."[30] As much as possible children with disabilities should participate in the general education curriculum. This is mandated by IDEA and the No Child Left Behind Act which requires "challenging academic content standards, coherent and rigorous content that encourage advanced skills and are aligned with the State's academic content standards."[31]

The importance of the general curriculum is never more prominent than in the development of a child's **IEP** which requires:

Present levels: A statement of the child's present levels of academic achievement, including how the child's disability affects the child's involvement and progress in the general education curriculum.

Goals: A statement of measurable annual goals including academic and functional goals, designed to meet the child's needs that result from the child's disability to enable the child to be involved in and make progress in the general education curriculum.

Services: A statement of the services, program modifications or supports for school personnel that will be provided for the child to be involved in and make progress in the general education curriculum and to participate in extracurricular and other nonacademic activities.

Accommodations: A statement of any individual appropriate accommodations that are necessary to measure the academic achievement and functional performance of the child on State and districtwide assessments.[32]

> ▼ **The appropriate education for children who are not disabled requires instruction in the regular classroom, provided by the regular classroom teacher, and involving the general curriculum. This is also the presumed placement, the presumed teacher, and the presumed curriculum for children with disabilities.**

12. "ADEQUATE" APPROPRIATE EDUCATION

"Thus, a determination that a child with disabilities might make greater academic progress in a segregated, special education class may not warrant excluding that child from a regular classroom environment."[33]

In *Roncker v. Walter*, the parents wanted an inclusive placement for their child who was identified as mentally retarded. The school district did not believe that mainstreaming would be beneficial as did the district court. Upon appeal the appellate court for the sixth district indicated that the school did not adequately consider supplementary aids and services and that mainstreaming can outweigh "educational reasons" for a segregated placement so that "in a case where the segregated facility is considered superior, the court should determine whether the services which make that placement superior could be feasibly provided in a nonsegregated setting. If they can, the placement in the segregated setting would be inappropriate under the Act" (p. 1063).[34]

Not "Best" but "Adequate

The standard for special education is not "best," not "superior" but "adequate." This is an essential element of *Hudson v. Rowley* in which the school had complied with the regulations and the evidence established the child in question was receiving an "adequate" education because classroom performance was above average and the child was advancing "easily from grade to grade."[35]

"Adequate" might seem an unusual standard but not if you consider that the purpose of an "adequate" standard is to emphasize the importance of a regular classroom education. What we want for a child with a disability, what we want for all children, is to succeed in the classroom and pass from grade to grade.

REQUIREMENT WITH RESPECT TO REGULAR EDUCATION TEACHER.

A regular education teacher of the child, as a member of the IEP Team, shall, to the extent appropriate, participate in the development of the IEP of the child, including the determination of appropriate positive behavioral interventions and supports, and other strategies, and the determination of supplementary aids and services, program modifications, and support for school personnel.[36]

13. AN "INAPPROPRIATE" EDUCATION

Special education in the regular classroom is not assigning a full-time aide to a child with a disability under the guise of an appropriate education. Aside from the fact that aides must be **trained and supervised**, an appropriate education involves participation and general curriculum to the maximum extent appropriate.

So what is inappropriate? Here's a short list:

- **Not providing the general curriculum in a special classroom.**

- **Not providing the general curriculum in the regular classroom (e.g., assigning teaching responsibilities to a one-to-one aide).**

- **Not providing opportunities for a child with a disability to participate with nondisabled children.**

- **Not providing meaningful goals.**

- **Not providing reasonable accommodations.**

- **Not providing the least restrictive placement.**

- **Not providing necessary services.**

- **Not enabling participation in statewide assessments.**

- **Not providing transition services.**

14. DISABILITIES AND RETENTION

The Supreme Court opined in *Hudson v. Rowley* that "if the child is being educated in regular classrooms, as here, the IEP should be reasonably calculated to enable the child to achieve passing marks and advance from grade to grade."[37] Do children with disabilities generally pass from grade to grade? Well, not as much as we would like. For nine year old children with disabilities, 4 percent are in the fourth grade, 61 percent in the 3rd, 31 percent in the 2nd, and 2 percent in the 1st grade as shown in Table 2.

Table 2. Grade Levels of Elementary and Middle School Children with Disabilities.[38]

Grade	Age								
	6	7	8	9	10	11	12	13	14
1st	88	86	32	2					
2nd		10	60	31	2				
3rd			4	61	35	5	1		
4th				4	58	38	6		
5th					2	50	34	4	1
6th						5	53	45	14
7th							5	45	83
8th								4	3

One reason why retention is a frequent occurrence for children with disabilities is that the classroom teacher has limited or no input into the IEP process. An obvious goal should be exactly what the Supreme Court directed: "to enable the child to achieve passing marks and advance from grade to grade." The IEP Team might focus on specific disability-related goals but the classroom teacher must focus on what the child must do to pass from grade to grade. Sometimes specifics (the trees) get in the way of more general needs (the forest) such as passing from grade to grade. Of course, not passing from one grade to the next is a complicated matter. Factors such as the child's age, ability level, disability, motivation are a few of the many factors that must be considered. However, having high expectations for all children means that we want all children to receive an adequate education, to demonstrate competency, and pass from grade to grade. Some children will not be able to succeed at grade level, but there is much that can be done to improve the passing rate of children with disabilities.

▼ **Another factor in the academic success of these students is that many of their teachers do an outstanding job of individualizing instruction and modifying curriculum and tests.**

What to Do?

Consider passing criteria at the IEP meeting, what the child must do to pass from grade to grade, and what prevents a child from passing. Too often the classroom teacher attends the IEP meeting but does not actively participate in the development of the IEP. An IEP that enables classroom participation cannot logically be developed without input from the classroom teacher concerning classroom performance, classroom needs, and what interventions/strategies may or may not be effective. When IEP goals are being developed, the classroom teacher should help identify goals that will enable classroom participation. To select appropriate services, accommodations and supports the classroom teacher can provide input concerning such factors as attendance, grades and classroom work, and provide specific examples of classroom behavior.

Teachers Do an Outstanding Job

Many students identified as having learning disabilities are not failing to achieve commensurate with their age level and are passing from grade to grade at the same rate as their peers. Yet these same students are still in need of special education and related services in order to benefit from education. This is true for students with above average intelligence as well as students with average intelligence. The reason these students are achieving and passing is because parents are spending countless hours helping their children with homework, reviewing material and studying for tests. Parents also spend a great deal of money year after year on tutors thereby providing services themselves. Another factor in the academic success of these students is that many of their teachers do an outstanding job of individualizing instruction and modifying curriculum and tests. These children are not failing because they are not being allowed to fail. Parents and teachers are giving this type of support because they understand the devastation that comes with failure.[39]

Part II
LRE and Inclusion

IN GENERAL. – To the maximum extent appropriate,
children with disabilities, including children in
public or private institutions or other care facilities, are
educated with children who are not disabled, and special
classes, separate schooling, or other removal of children
with disabilities from the regular educational environment
occurs only when the nature or severity of the disability
of a child is such that education in regular classes with
the use of supplementary aids and services cannot be
achieved satisfactorily.[40]

15. LEAST RESTRICTIVE ENVIRONMENT

The concept of Least Restrictive Environment (LRE) is usually given lip service, or simply ignored, but this basic tenet of special education clearly outlines the importance of the regular classroom. The law does not require inclusion, does not mention mainstreaming; what is required is the least restrictive environment for every child with a disability.

To the maximum extent appropriate, children with disabilities, including children in public or private institutions or other care facilities are educated with children who are not disabled. This does not mean that children with disabilities are trooped into regular classes in order to proclaim mainstreaming (this is more akin to *pretend mainstreaming*), dumped into regular classes with little or no support, or physically included in regular classes with no expectation for real participation in classroom or curriculum activities.

Special classes, separate schooling, or other removal of children with disabilities from the regular educational environment occurs only when the nature or severity of the disability of a child is such that education in regular classes with the use of supplementary aids and services cannot be achieved satisfactorily.[41] The key to special education involves supplementary aids and services that include special education, accommodations and supports for the regular classroom teacher.

Behavior and LRE

"A third factor the court should consider in determining whether a child with disabilities can be educated satisfactorily in a regular classroom is the possible negative effect the child's inclusion may have on the education of the other children in the regular classroom. While inclusion of children with disabilities in regular classrooms may benefit the class as a whole, see supra n. 24, a child with disabilities may be 'so disruptive in a regular classroom that the education of other students is significantly impaired.'"[42]

The (note the *italic*) least restrictive environment is the regular classroom, but "environment" also includes the physical environment, the curriculum, other students in the classroom and the regular classroom teacher. The reason for being in the regular classroom is to participate in the general curriculum and to be educated **with** (and an extra emphasis on "with") children who are not disabled. To participate in the general curriculum, and to be educated with children who are not disabled, the regular classroom teacher plays a vital role. The regular classroom teacher provides curriculum expertise; the regular classroom teacher provides an inclusive educational environment; and the regular classroom teacher helps determine and incorporate appropriate supplementary aids and services.

> ▼ **The classroom teacher helps provide a child with the least restrictive environment by encouraging participation in the general curriculum, by collaborating with special education personnel to enable classroom participation, and by identifying reasonable accommodations and classroom supports that will result in successful classroom performance.**

Is Every Accommodation Permissible

What if the classroom teacher is presented with an IEP that contains an accommodation that seems to invalidate the test? Must the teacher permit the use of this accommodation? This is not an easy question to answer. On the one hand, in a memorandum from Washington State to School Officers neither the State or school "can limit the authority of the IEP team to select individual accommodations and modifications in administration needed for a child with a disability to participate in State and district-wide assessments of student achievement." However, if the IEP Team selects accommodations that invalidate a test this might affect the determination of benefits such as promotion or a high school diploma.[43]

Is every accommodation permissible? Yes, if an accommodation is made by the IEP Team and included in the IEP, the accommodation should be implemented regardless of whether or not the accommodation invalidates a test. However, if an accommodation invalidates a test as per State guidelines, especially if the test results in an unfair advantage, the State might discount the test. By the same token, an IEP Team might decide that literacy is no longer necessary because of the availability of assistive technology and other accommodations (e.g., a reader, scribe), but abandoning literacy can have dire life consequences for a child, and result in other areas of noncompliance (e.g., not considering the literacy needs of a child, not providing appropriate services and accommodations).

16. THE SPECIAL EDUCATION MYTH

A good way ("good" meaning effective not good "good") to remove a child from the classroom is take the high and altruistic road. A child is not removed because providing services is a matter of inconvenience, but because the child can be helped in a **special** class, where a **special** teacher can use **special** techniques to help the **special** child. Lots of **special** here. But the law is not about **special** and never has been; the law is about that pesky "enabling a child to participate with nondisabled children" mandate. The purpose of special education is to enable participation with nondisabled children, and not about special classes, special teachers or special techniques. To this end the role and importance of the classroom teacher has often been ignored and devalued. Only when the classroom teacher is inextricably involved in the special education process will special education achieve its ultimate purpose of enabling successful participation in the general curriculum with appropriate services, supports and accommodations.

There is nothing special that occurs in special education classes that make these settings wonderful places to be, highly effective, and where the needs of children with disabilities can be best met. The placement of children with disabilities in special classes is not the first but the last resort. Studies (those proverbial studies) have repeatedly shown that children with disabilities do better academically in regular classes than children placed in special classes or schools. This is why the law places such a great emphasis on the regular classroom and the general curriculum. The fact is that the curriculum provided in special classrooms or special school placements is more likely than not disjointed and might only remotely resemble the general curriculum (if at all), and participation with nondisabled children will be extremely limited.

Are there no special techniques? As a matter of fact there are. A child who is deaf will certainly need to develop an alternative mode of communication or at least special skills (e.g., speech reading, fingerspelling, sign language); a child who is blind might require extensive instruction in Braille; and a child with cerebral palsy might require an assistive communication device. All these do require special expertise and special instruction. However, for the majority of children with disabilities, and certainly for children with behavioral problems, the special techniques and specialized instruction are designed to enable participation in the general curriculum.

The Real Expert

The best place to provide the general curriculum is the regular classroom; the real expert in the general curriculum is the regular education teacher (even for children having special language needs such as Braille or AT); and the best techniques for providing the general curriculum are those used in the regular classroom with appropriate accommodations.

17. TOKEN GESTURES

Although broad, the requirement is not limitless. States need not provide every conceivable supplementary aid or service to assist the child.[44]

In the case of *Daniel v. State Board of Education* involving a child with Down syndrome, the appellate court determined that "the Act does not permit states to make mere token gestures" when providing supplementary aids and services.[45] For the classroom teacher this does not mean attention must be given to one child "to the detriment of her entire class," or to modify the regular curriculum beyond recognition. What supplementary service does mean is the school must provide serious support to enable regular classroom participation and not make "token gestures."

Classroom teacher goal: Help all children participate in the classroom and in the curriculum. This is the law; this is fair; and this is really a good thing.

In <u>Daniel</u> we are told that

- **States need not provide every conceivable supplementary aid or service to assist a child with a disability.**

- **The Act does not require regular education instructors to devote all or most of their time to one child.**

- **A teacher need not modify the regular education program beyond recognition.**

- **A teacher need not act as a special education teacher in a regular education classroom.**

- **A teacher should not focus all attention on one child to the detriment of the entire class.**

- **A classroom teacher need not modify the regular education curriculum to the extent that a child is not required to learn skills normally taught in regular education.**

18. CLASSROOM PLACEMENT CHECKLIST

Integrating a handicapped child into a nonhandicapped environment may be beneficial in and of itself. Thus, our inquiry must extend beyond the educational benefits that the child may receive in regular education.[46]

Before a child's placement is determined following the development of an IEP several factors should be considered. In the checklist shown below the regular classroom plays a prominent role in almost all placement decisions. Most importantly, regular classroom participation should be considered for every child with a disability. Several of the factors shown below have special import for the classroom teacher such as providing support, training aides, and enabling participation in the general curriculum. Finally, many of the factors shown below should be school policy such as ensuring that every child with a disability receives specially designed instruction, either directly or indirectly, via a certified special education teacher.

	The presumed placement for every child is the regular classroom.
	Every child is entitled to the least restrictive educational placement.
	The least restrictive placement is selected from a continuum of placements.
	The term "maximum extent possible" is the mandate concerning the extent of regular classroom participation.
	Children with disabilities should not be "dumped" into the regular classroom with no or minimal support. This is simply wrong, inappropriate and against the law.
	All children with disabilities must receive either direct and/or indirect services by a certified special education teacher.
	An aide does not provide special education unless trained and supervised.
	The goal of special education is to enable children to participate in all regular classroom activities.

	The regular classroom should not be a de facto special education class by means of tracking students with needs into one classroom.
	The regular education teacher must receive support.
	The regular education teacher must be part of the special education process.
	The special education teacher must understand the importance of the regular education teacher's expertise and the goal to enable children to participate in the general curriculum.
	The purpose of special education is not to create a "special" curriculum apart from the general curriculum.
	Some children with disabilities will have extensive needs that require the development of basic communication, social, physical and self-help skills. These needs must be addressed, but the role of the regular classroom is constant: to enable participation to the maximum extent appropriate.
	The regular education teacher is expected to help "all children" participate in the classroom and in the general curriculum.

19. INCLUSION AND MAINSTREAMING

The Courts like the term mainstreaming as do college and university folk who write Pollyannaish treatises about the wonderfulness of mainstreaming. Mainstreaming, like inclusion, is not mentioned in the law or the regulations. Often mainstreaming is built on the myth that all children with disabilities require special classes/teachers and that children are "mainstreamed," as appropriate, into regular classes. This is backward and contrary to the law. What IDEA does require is that children are placed in the least restrictive environment, and then placed in a more restrictive environment only when needed. One reason for a separate placement might be unsuccessful classroom performance even with appropriate classroom supports, services and accommodations.

Is there a requirement that all children must participate in the regular classroom? No. This has been addressed in the various regulations and by several court cases. The statutory mandate (special education law or IDEA) requires that every placement be based on need, the child's IEP, and as least restrictive as possible.

Court cases have addressed several situations in which participation in the regular classroom may or may not be appropriate, and provide general guidelines for testing the ability to participate in the regular classroom. In *Daniel v. State Board of Education*, the question concerned a child's participation in a regular education prekindergarten classroom.[47] Because of the "constant attention" the child needed, and failure to master basic skills, the decision was made to place the child, Daniel, in a special education early childhood classroom. Upon appeal the Fifth Circuit Court raised several question that must be asked when removing a child from the regular classroom:

- ☛ **Were supplementary aids and services provided?**
- ☛ **Were the supplementary aids and services sufficient?**
- ☛ **What are the academic and nonacademic benefits of mainstreaming?**
- ☛ **What effect does mainstreaming have on other students?**[48]

In *Greer v. Rome City School*, the issue was the placement of a child with Down syndrome in a regular education class.[49] Upon appeal the court cited several factors when determining whether education in the classroom may be achieved satisfactorily which included educational benefits, the effect on other children and cost, especially if cost impact the educational benefits provided other children. As cited in Greer "if the cost of educating a handicapped child in a regular classroom is so great that it would significantly impact upon the education of other children in the district, then education in a regular classroom is not appropriate."

Inclusion and Noncompliance

If including children with disabilities in the regular classroom means to enable children with disabilities to participate with nondisabled children to the maximum extent appropriate, **inclusion** is a philosophical and procedural cornerstone of special education. If inclusion is interpreted to mean a regular classroom placement for all children with disabilities, this form of inclusion is noncompliant with IDEA. One hundred percent inclusion is not mandated; 100 percent occurs less frequently than desired; but 100 percent inclusion is not only feasible but possible for every IDEA disability ranging from specific learning disabilities to multiple disabilities, mental retardation, traumatic brain injury and autism.

As shown by the following table for students ages 13 to 17 many students with disabilities, including multiple disabilities (4%), mental retardation (7%) and deaf-blindness (12%), are included in the regular classroom 100 percent! For all disabilities 100 percent inclusion does occur. However, 100 percent inclusion will not be successful without the cooperation and collaboration of the classroom teacher. Meaningful inclusion, whether 100 percent or not, means meaningful inclusion in the general curriculum and meaningful participation in other classroom activities.

Table 3. Percentage of Students with Disabilities Ages 13 through 17 Included in the Regular Classroom 100%[50]

100% Inclusion			
Disability	%	Disability	%
Speech/Language Impairment	50	Emotional Disturbance	22
Visual Impairment	47	Traumatic Brain Injury	20
Other Health Impairment	34	Autism	13
Hearing Impairment/Deafness	33	Deaf-Blindness	12
Specific Learning Disability	32	Mental Retardation	7
Orthopedic Impairment	30	Multiple Disabilities	4

If every child with a disability is placed in the regular classroom, and placements have not been based on individual need but rather on a steadfast philosophy that inclusion is mandated for every child, the placements are inconsistent with IDEA, the regulations and the basic principle of "least restrictive environment." Understand that an inappropriate environment, whether the regular classroom or a residential setting, is a restrictive environment.

> ## The Key to 100% Inclusion
>
> **The key to 100% inclusion is the designation of consultant teacher services whereby a certified special education teacher provides direct and indirect services in the regular classroom. Direct services include direct teaching by the special education teacher to both disabled and nondisabled children. Indirect services includes planning, curriculum modifications, accommodations, aide supervision and all other activities that will support success by a child with a disability in the regular classroom.**

So you are at a meeting and a zealot lectures on the need for 100 percent inclusion. No exceptions. Complete total inclusion. This is a noble idea but this is not IDEA, undermines the law, opens the door for legal mayhem and noncompliance. The law, the IDEA, requires the least restrictive environment. Period. The regular classroom is one environment, and not necessarily "the" least restrictive for all children. The least restrictive environment is determined by providing supplementary aids and services in the regular classroom and, if these services are not successful, using the continuum of services to select the appropriate mix of educational environments.

> ▼ **The determination of the most appropriate educational placement is not based on the quality of the segregated placement, or the perceived superiority of the placement, but the first consideration is whether appropriate services could be feasibly provided in regular education classroom.**[51]

Other Strange Ideas about Inclusion

Possibly as a way to segregate under the guise of mandated inclusion, **concentrated inclusion** has emerged to give respectability to segregative placements. Concentrated inclusion is one of the more serious perversions of IDEA. The term concentrated inclusion involves including a large number of children *with disabilities in a single classroom.* For example, a regular education teacher is responsible for five children with disabilities and 15 who are not disabled which is above the 10 percent guide for the number for children who should be in the same classroom. Obviously, as the number of children with disabilities increases, the opportunity to participate with nondisabled children in the curriculum and classroom decreases.

The goal is not to concentrate children with disabilities in one classroom for bureaucratic reasons; nor is the goal to group children because a teacher has "experience," to simplify scheduling, to otherwise track students, or to provide a "special" curriculum. The mandate is simply this:

> **To the maximum extent appropriate, children with disabilities, including children in public or private institutions or other care facilities, are educated with children who are not disabled.**

Inclusion has always implied the participation of a child with a disability in the regular classroom with nondisabled children. Paradoxically, the word has somehow been reinvented as a type of tracking system (at best) or even semi-self-contained classroom (at worst). Thus, a classroom comprised of 20 students consists of 10 who have disabilities and 10 who are not disabled. The high proportion of children with disabilities in one classroom is bureaucratically efficient but hardly complies with either the spirit (and much less the letter) of the LRE mandate. Don't let zealots, either for or against inclusion, bully for the misplacement of children with disabilities into so-called "regular classrooms" by grouping these children into certain classes or otherwise creating de facto special education classes under a misrepresentation of inclusion.

Tests for Inclusion

How do we determine this every elusive level of "appropriate"? One important test for mainstreaming involved Rafael Oberti who was identified as having mental retardation (Down syndrome). The parents of Rafael wanted a regular kindergarten placement while the school thought that, because of Rafael's behavior, an out-of-district placement would be appropriate. The court of appeals agreed with the district court decision that the school's approach to Rafael's behavior was "woefully inadequate" and that there was no real educational or management plan. Schools do this a lot. The school district was then ordered to "develop a more inclusive program for Rafael in compliance with IDEA for the upcoming school year."[52]

▼ **The goal of real inclusion and real mainstreaming is to find what the courts have referred to as "the appropriate mix of educational environments."[53]**

There are two prongs to the Oberti test:

First: Whether the child can be educated in the regular classroom with supplementary aids and services. When making this determination the school should take into consideration three factors:

a. **whether the school district has made reasonable efforts to accommodate the child in a regular classroom;**
b. **the educational benefits available to the child in a regular class, with appropriate supplementary aids and services, as compared to the benefits provided in a special education class; and**
c. **the possible negative effects of the inclusion of the child on the education of the other students in the class.**

Second: If a child must be removed from the regular classroom (supplementary aids and services were not successful), has the school included the child in school programs with nondisabled children to some degree? This decision to place a child is not binary, and not a decision between regular and special education, but entails providing an appropriate **mix of regular and special education**.

The Appropriate Mix

Thus, the school must take intermediate steps where appropriate, such as placing the child in regular education for some academic classes and in special education for others, mainstreaming the child for nonacademic classes only, or providing interaction with nonhandicapped children during lunch and recess. The appropriate mix will vary from child to child...[54]

Real Mainstreaming

The concept is simple: children with disabilities should be educated in regular classrooms unless supplementary aids and services are unsuccessful.

Children are not placed in special classes and then mainstreamed into regular classes. Mainstreaming is a useful invention but one that is easily misinterpreted. The IDEA requires that the least restrictive environment be given careful consideration at the time of the initial placement at the IEP meeting. Children with disabilities do not earn the right to participate in regular classes; children with disabilities belong in regular classes and the presumed placement for every child with a disability is the regular classroom. If you recommend a child for an individual evaluation because you believe that a child might have a disability, the purpose of this recommendation should be to enable the child to receive an appropriate education in the regular classroom. The purpose of the evaluation, and then special education if the child has a disability, is not to remove the child from the regular classroom and then mainstream the child when appropriate, but to provide appropriate services and supports to enable successful regular classroom participation.

Does this always happen? Absolutely not! Children are removed from the regular classroom for all sorts of reasons under the guise of "special education" when, in fact, the goal is first and foremost to remove the child from the regular classroom. Below is a sampling of ways in which children are not provided with the least restrictive environment.

Misclassification: A child does not have a disability under IDEA but does have academic needs. This could be the result of economic disadvantage, lack of instruction or cultural factors, lack of motivation, truancy, one or more of these factors, or a combination thereof. None of the above are IDEA disabilities. Misclassification is costly, wrongly identifies children as having disabilities, and takes away resources from children with real disabilities.

The "No IEP" decision: If the placement is not based on the IEP, the placement is not in compliance with IDEA. This can be an easy one to spot, especially when a placement is made at the beginning of the IEP meeting. If the placement is made before the IEP is developed, the placement is obviously not based on the IEP. Yes, there actually is a regulation (34 CFR 300.116) that states that placements must be made by the parents and a group of persons knowledgeable about the child, the placement must be considered at least annually, and **the placement is based on the child's IEP.**[55] More about placement criteria later.

The "All Children with Disabilities" placement decision: When all children with disabilities are placed in a certain setting, be assured that the decision is not based on individual need but disability. All children with specific learning disabilities do not need the exact amount of resource room help; all children with emotional disturbance do not need a separate placement; all children who are identified as having emotional disturbance do not need a segregated placement. This is a no-no.

The real "presumed placement": Often the presumed placement is any place but the regular classroom. Not exactly what the law has in mind. Always, always, always, the presumed placement is the regular classroom. Only when supplementary aids and services are not successful can a child be removed from the regular classroom. This can be a sneaky type of placement decision. The regular classroom and regular classroom participation are not considered, but the placement decision begins with the special education setting...because this is the real presumed environment.

No supplementary aids and services: If supplementary aids and services are not considered, or what the child needs to be successful in the regular classroom, the placement decision is tainted. For the classroom teacher this means that the regular classroom is the benchmark for determining educational success with appropriate services, supports and accommodations.

Non-FAPE placements: The purpose of special education is to provide children with disabilities a free appropriate public education with an emphasis on *appropriate*. If the IEP is not reasonably calculated, if the regulations for IDEA are ignored, an appropriate placement cannot follow.

Residential school placements: Residential schools are notorious for completely ignoring the concept of LRE. More often than not if a child is in a special school or residential placement, participation in regular classroom or in the general curriculum is unlikely. Why so? Mainstreaming children in regular classroom who have been placed in residential/special schools is inconvenient and bureaucratically messy. No, there is no law or regulation that takes into account bureaucratic inconvenience.

▼ **Placing excluded children within a mainstream setting does not of itself achieve inclusion. Inclusive education must be underpinned by key principles and practice.**[56]

20. VARIATIONS OF INCLUSION

Including Tourette syndrome in the definition of other health impairment may help correct the misperception of Tourette syndrome as a behavioral or conduct disorder and prevent the misdiagnosis of their needs.[57]

For many students with disabilities the question is not behavior that warrants discipline but behavior that differs from the norm. For example, Tourette syndrome can involve humming, whistling, throat clearing, tics or, more rarely, inappropriate utterances/obscenities (**coprolalia**). Although Tourette syndrome can require special education (under the Other Health Impairment category), often accommodations and in-service training, school counseling, peer education, positive reinforcement plans classroom support, and use of related personnel (e.g., psychological services) can meet a child's needs in the regular classroom.

But before you begin to imagine that your class will be filled with children identified as having Tourette syndrome be aware that Tourette is considered a "rare disease" and affects less than one in 2,000. Considering that not all children with Tourette will exhibit coprolalia (less than 10%), the likelihood that you will have a child shouting obscenities in your classroom because of Tourette is really quite small. But the point is not one of rarity but rather the limits of inclusion.

The 9th Circuit Court of Appeals developed a test for mainstreaming *(Sacramento City Unified School District v. Rachel H.)* that consisted of four parts.

1. **the academic benefits of placement in a mainstream setting, with any supplementary aides and services that might be appropriate;**

2. **the nonacademic benefits of mainstream placement, such as language and behavior models provided by nondisabled students;**

3. **the negative effects the student's presence may have on the teacher and other students; and**

4. **the cost of educating the student in a mainstream environment.**

The court used these four criteria to decide that that the inclusion of a child with Tourette syndrome and ADHD had a negative impact on other students in that the child had become dangerously aggressive, attacked two students, assaulted a school staff member and "frequently taunted other students with name-calling and profanity, and that on several occasions he made vulgar and insulting comments to teachers, " and "also directed sexually-explicit remarks at female students."[58]

What to Do for a Child With Tourette Syndrome?

- **Reduce stress as much as possible**
- **Provide frequent breaks**
- **Consider the need for assistive technology (e.g., computer, writing aids)**
- **Discuss possible accommodations with parents**
- **Provide extra time because of motor needs**
- **Create a variety of participatory activities**
- **Focus on positive reinforcement**
- **Remember: Tics do "come and go"**
- **Arrange seating near teacher**
- **Give shorter assignments**
- **Structure activities**
- **Model how to respond to Tourette-related behavior**
- **Test in a separate location**

What we can learn from Tourette syndrome is that the classroom teacher must be provided with the necessary in-service and classroom support to enable a child to successfully participate in the regular classroom. The problem occurs when the classroom teacher is not part of the process, has no idea what the IEP entails, and is provided with little or no actual support. Whether the problem is emotional disturbance, ADHD, Asperger's syndrome, or Tourette syndrome, classroom success cannot be achieved without the participation and cooperation of the classroom teacher.

Although Tourette syndrome is relatively uncommon, other classroom behaviors can occur that will push the concept of inclusion to the edge. After all, for those who advocate full inclusion, are there no limits to a child's behavior that might require removal from the regular classroom? From a strictly legal point of view a child can be removed from the regular classroom for violation of a violation of a school code for up to 10 days or for up to 45 days for substance abuse or bringing a weapon to school. If the disability is not the cause of the violation, the student can be disciplined like other students. If the disability is determined to be the cause of the violation, the school must develop a plan and make the necessary changes in the IEP.

Reverse Mainstreaming

Reverse mainstreaming describes programs, classes and settings that are designed to allow children without disabilities to participate in classes for children with disabilities. Reverse mainstreaming is most frequently associated with children ages 3–5. The 25th Annual report to Congress indicates that 8,209 children in this age group are reverse mainstreamed. The following are the top ten states for reverse mainstreaming.[59]

KANSAS	2,339
OHIO	1,270
CONNECTICUT	1,103
IDAHO	1,037
UTAH	440
OREGON	247
IOWA	208
WEST VIRGINIA	199
NORTH CAROLINA	194
WASHINGTON	165

"Neverstreaming"?

There is reverse mainstreaming (placing children without disabilities with children who are disabled) and now **neverstreaming**. The idea is that by providing high quality and effective instruction we can avoid special education and mainstreaming altogether. Thus, the term **neverstreaming**. Good idea, bad word.

21. ESSENTIAL LAWS AND REGULATIONS FOR THE CLASSROOM TEACHER

IEP meetings: Not less than one regular education teacher of such child (if the child is, or may be, participating in the regular education environment).[60]

IEP participation: A regular education teacher of the child, as a member of the IEP Team, shall, to the extent appropriate, participate in the development of the IEP of the child, including the determination of appropriate positive behavioral interventions and supports, and other strategies, and the determination of supplementary aids and services, program modifications, and support for school personnel.[61]

IEP review and revision: A regular education teacher of the child, as a member of the IEP Team shall participate in the review and revision of the IEP of the child.[62]

IEP accessibility: Accessibility of child's IEP to teachers and others. Each public agency must ensure that the child's IEP is accessible to each regular education teacher, special education teacher, related service provider, and other service provider who is responsible for its implementation.[63]

Teacher observations: As part of an initial evaluation (if appropriate) and as part of any reevaluation under this section, the IEP Team and other qualified professionals, as appropriate, shall review existing evaluation data on the child, including evaluations and information provided by the parents of the child; current classroom-based, local, or State assessments, and classroom-based observations; and observations by teachers and related services providers.[64]

22. FAPE

Since the enactment of IDEA the law has been successful in ensuring children with disabilities and the families of such children access to a free appropriate public education and in improving educational results for children with disabilities.[65]

Everything in special education centers about this phrase: **F**ree **A**ppropriate **P**ublic **E**ducation or **FAPE**. Children are evaluated so that they can be provided with FAPE if a disability is determined. An IEP is developed to provide FAPE. Teachers participate in the evaluation and IEP development to provide FAPE. Services and accommodations are designed to provide FAPE. Placement decisions are made to provide FAPE. Children are reevaluated to provide FAPE.

When FAPE is not the deciding factor, the special education process has been compromised. When determining whether or not a child has a disability, remember that an appropriate classification is not based on economic disadvantage, cultural factors, or lack of instruction. When developing the IEP, determine what services and accommodations are necessary to provide an appropriate education. An IEP might be developed but, if goals are meaningless and accommodations poorly considered, a child's education will suffer, and possibly suffer more if nothing had been done! Finally, when considering the educational placement, determine what is needed for success in the regular classroom.

Primum Non Nocere ("Do No Harm")

There is a problem in medicine called "iatrogenesis" which means something like "brought forth by a healer." Two prescribed drugs cause an interaction that produces a harmful reaction; using poorly sterilized syringes. In other words, under the guise of "help," an individual is caused harm by those responsible for the individual's care.

Educators take note: "Do no harm."

The FAPE mandate is satisfied, according to the *Supreme Court in Hudson v. Rowley,* when the State provides personalized instruction and sufficient support to allow a child with a disability to benefit educationally. The instruction provided must be free, meet the State's educational standards, approximate the regular education, and comport with the child's IEP. "If the child is being educated in regular classrooms, as here, the IEP should be reasonably calculated to enable the child to achieve passing marks and advance from grade to grade (see pp. 187–204)."[66]

Regular Classroom FAPE Checklist

FAPE Checklist	
☐	Have the regulations been followed?
☐	Are the services supervised?
☐	Do services meet individual needs?
☐	Are services provided in the least restrictive environment?
☐	Have appropriate classroom accommodations been provided?
☐	Have appropriate classroom supports been provided?
☐	Do services and instruction meet State standards?
☐	Does instruction "comport" with the child's IEP?
☐	Is the IEP "reasonably calculated" to provided educational benefit

If you feel that a child is not receiving FAPE, what to do? This depends on whether you suspect the child of having a disability or whether the child has already been identified as having a disability.

For a child suspected of having a disability:

- Consider classroom accommodations.
- Provide school-wide remediation (e.g., reading, speech).
- Discuss the child's needs with the regular education team.
- Discuss possible strategies and interventions with the parents.

• Seek input from the child study team if available.

• Request a consultant teacher or mainstreaming specialist.

For a child who has been identified as having a disability:

• Be specific.

• Evaluate the child's IEP.

• Identify needs that are not being met.

• Identify what you think is an appropriate placement.

• Identify the child's educational progress or lack thereof.

• Discuss the problem with the chairperson of the IEP Team.

• Remember that FAPE is the responsibility of the school and not the sole responsibility of the classroom teacher.

23. MORE LRE

A child with a disability is not removed from education in age-appropriate regular classrooms solely because of needed modifications in the general education curriculum.[67]

The fact that special education is a service and not a place reemphasizes the importance of the regular classroom and the basic purpose of special education: to enable children with disabilities to be educated with nondisabled children. After a child has been determined to have a disability and needs special education, an individualized plan is developed to provide these services and accommodations. After a disability has been determined what is not done is to decide the child's placement. This is discriminatory in that the placement would then be based on disability rather than need. The first consideration is always services and then where these services can best be provided. The order for considering disability, IEP content and placement is extremely important:

First, disability is determined.

Second, the IEP is developed.

Third, the placement is decided based on the child's IEP.

The Regulations for Placement Decisions[68]

In determining the educational placement of a child with a disability, including a preschool child with a disability, each public agency must ensure that –

(a) The placement decision –
(1) Is made by a group of persons, including the parents, and other persons knowledgeable about the child, the meaning of the evaluation data, and the placement options; and
(2) Is made in conformity with the LRE provisions of this subpart, including Sec. Sec. 300.114 through 300.118;

(b) **The child's placement –**
  (1) **Is determined at least annually;**
  (2) **Is based on the child's IEP; and**
  (3) **Is as close as possible to the child's home, unless the parent agrees otherwise;**

(c) **Unless the IEP of a child with a disability requires some other arrangement, the child is educated in the school that he or she would attend if nondisabled, unless the parent agrees otherwise;**

(d) **In selecting the LRE, consideration is given to any potential harmful effect on the child or on the quality of services that he or she needs; and**

(e) **A child with a disability is not removed from education in age-appropriate regular classrooms solely because of needed modifications in the general education curriculum.**

After the IEP has been developed and placement is being determined, the IEP Team must select the Least Restrictive Environment. *Brown v. Board of Education* made it abundantly clear that "education is perhaps the most important function of state and local governments" and "it is doubtful that any child may reasonably be expected to succeed in life if he is denied the opportunity of an education. Such an opportunity, where the state has undertaken to provide it, is a right which must be made available to all on equal terms."[69] However, special education is empowered to do exactly what the Brown decision clearly denounced as inappropriate: the removal of children from regular education.

Special education is able to justify this potential segregation (or partial segregation) of children with disabilities by the LRE mandate. Children are not simply removed from the regular classroom because of a disability; children are first provided with supplementary aides and services to allow satisfactory achievement in the regular classroom. If these supplementary aids and services are not successful, the least restrictive environment where the child can succeed is determined.

The regular classroom is the presumed placement for every child with a disability, and the regular classroom is **generally** the least restrictive environment. The least restrictive environment does not simply refer to a place, but a philosophy of maximizing a child's potential, participation with nondisabled children, and the development of independent skills to the maximum extent. A child would not be in the least restrictive environment who is able to participate in the general curriculum but is deprived of this participation by virtue of the placement. For example, a child's disability is emotional disturbance and the child's behavior limits participation in the regular classroom for most of the school day. If the placement for this child results in a curriculum other than the general curriculum, when participation in the general curriculum is entirely possible, the placement would be unduly restrictive. This, of course, is exactly what occurs when a child is removed to a special school where the general education curriculum is a remote consideration. When this occurs, the ability to reintegrate into the general curriculum becomes much more difficult in that the alternative placement and different curriculum can exacerbate a child's academic needs. Being deprived of the general education curriculum is hardly appropriate for reintegration into the general curriculum.

> ▼ **Improving educational results for children with disabilities is an essential element of our national policy of ensuring equality of opportunity, full participation, independent living, and economic self-sufficiency for individuals with disabilities.**[70]

24. THE CONTINUUM OF PLACEMENTS

The appropriate mix will vary from child to child and, it may be hoped, from school year to school year as the child develops.[71]

For every child with a disability the first task, a task required by law and the LRE clause, is to provide supplementary aids and services to enable participation in the regular classroom. If the child's behavior, educational needs or disability are such that removal from the regular classroom is necessary, the least restrictive placement must be selected which is accomplished by considering the continuum of alternative placements.[72] As shown below the continuum of alternative placements begins with the regular classroom and ends with very restrictive placements that are completely apart from the regular classroom.

Instruction in regular classes

Supplementary services (e.g., resource room)

Itinerant teacher

Special classes

Special schools

Home instruction

Instruction in hospitals and institutions

The above continuum can be deceptive for two reasons. First, the continuum suggests a discrete series of placements such that a child is either in a regular classroom, resource room, special classroom, etc. The continuum of placements shown above is not a series of discrete placements but simply illustrates the various types of placements that can be used in combination with one another to formulate the overall least restrictive placement. Determining this overall mix when arriving at the least restrictive placement is accomplished by "placing the child in regular education for some academic classes and in special education for others, mainstreaming the child for nonacademic classes only, or providing interaction with nonhandicapped children during lunch and recess."[73]

The real key to understanding the continuum of placements is the determination of the "appropriate mix." The idea is not a regular classroom, or a

61

resource room, or a special class, but the mix of placements that allows a child to spend the maximum amount of time appropriate in each of the various placements. The choice is not between a regular classroom placement or a special class but rather how much time can the child participate in the regular classroom with supplementary aides and services. For one child the mix might be 80 percent regular classroom, 20 percent outside of the regular classroom; for another child the mix might be 100 percent in the regular classroom; while a third child might require services that are provided 100 percent outside of the regular classroom.

▼ **"We note that these experts challenged the School District's view that readiness for mainstreaming or inclusion could successfully be developed within a segregated setting and argued that it is illusory, and perhaps even pretextual, to contend that segregation can breed readiness for inclusion."**[74]

A second reason why the continuum of placements can be deceptive is that participation in the regular classroom does not simply mean physical participation but actual participation in classroom activities, and the opportunity to participate in all nonacademic and extracurricular activities (including meals, recess periods, etc.). One child might be "included" in the regular classroom but denied access to the general education curriculum, while a second child is in a resource room but actively participates in the general education curriculum. The first child might spend more time in the regular classroom but actually this regular classroom placement might be more restrictive than the child placed in a resource room or a special education classroom for a part of the day.

The Multidimensional Continuum

Special education should enable participation in the regular classroom and participation in the general curriculum. As discussed above a child might be able to spend 20 percent of the day, or 36 percent or 94 percent of the day in a regular classroom with supports and services (what we call supplementary aids and services). Likewise, the ability to participate in the general curriculum might range from 0 percent to 100 percent. This is the tricky part: one child might be placed in the regular classroom the entire day but only participate in the general curriculum 30 percent or 50 percent. Another child might not be able to participate in the regular classroom but is able to participate in the general curriculum 100 percent (e.g., for a child with severe emotional problems). This is the true concept of a multidimensional continuum of placement/curriculum environments. As shown in the below figure a "true" continuum embraces a continuous range of possibilities involving curriculum and classroom participation.

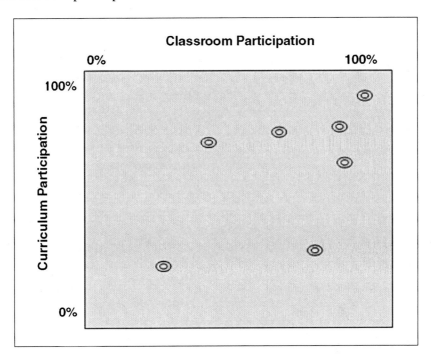

▼ The regulations (34 CFR 300.39) define special education as including instruction conducted in the classroom, in the home, in hospitals and institutions, in other settings, and instruction in physical education. The regulations also describe the continuum (see 34 CFR 300.115) as alternative placements that include instruction in regular classes, special classes, special schools, home instruction, and instruction in hospitals and institutions.

25. PLACEMENT DECISIONS

The guidelines for educational placements begin with a consideration of a child's ability to achieve satisfactorily in the regular classroom. A common misunderstanding is to confuse disability and need, and not to realize that accommodations to the general curriculum is not the criterion for an alternate placement. Regarding classroom modifications and placements the regulations are explicit: "a child with a disability is not removed from education in age appropriate regular classrooms solely because of needed modifications in the general education curriculum."[75]

Every placement must be based on need as delineated in the IEP and not disability. If all children with a certain disability, or all children with disabilities, receive the same placement, disability rather than need would be the determinant factor for placements and this is clearly not in compliance with IDEA.

Placement Decision Guidelines

The following are several guidelines concerning placement decisions that are especially important for the regular classroom placements (and the regular classroom teacher).

❐ **Placements are based on the child's IEP. As part of the IEP Team the regular classroom teacher must contribute to the development of the IEP in terms of what a child needs to be successful in the regular classroom. And what a child needs will be defined by needed goals to achieve, needed services, needed accommodations and, most importantly, needed supports.**

❐ **The placement decision is made by a group of persons, including the parents, and other persons knowledgeable about the child, the meaning of the evaluation data, and the placement options.[76]**

❐ **The regular classroom is the presumed placement for every child with a disability. This is especially important for the vast majority of children receiving services under IDEA.**

❐ **Supplementary aids and services are provided to enable regular classroom participation.**

❑ A child is provided with an alternative placement when education in the regular classroom cannot be achieved satisfactorily.

❑ Alternative placements must be as least restrictive as possible and must consider the extent of regular classroom participation.

❑ Placements must be determined at least annually. The concept of "at least annually" means that if a placement is overly restrictive or otherwise inappropriate, the decision must be revisited. Placement decision are not unchanging, and although a child might be restricted from regular classroom participation one year, the intent of special education is to provide services that will increase independence and eventual classroom participation. Note for the classroom teacher: if you have a child with a disability in your classroom less than 100% of the school day, and the child is able to succeed without specially designed instruction, recommend a full-time regular classroom placement or even declassification.

❑ Placements must be as close as possible to the child's home, unless the parent agrees otherwise.

❑ Unless the IEP of a child with a disability requires some other arrangement, the child is educated in the school that he or she would attend if nondisabled, unless the parent agrees otherwise.[77]

❑ In selecting the least restrictive environment, consideration is given to any potential harmful effect on the child or on the quality of services that he or she needs. For example, a child's behavior might prevent services from being provided if the behavior requires frequent removal from the classroom.[78]

❑ Children with disabilities are entitled to participate in nonacademic and extracurricular services and activities, including meals, recess periods with nondisabled children to the maximum extent appropriate to the needs of that child.[79]

❑ A child with a disability is not removed from education in age appropriate regular classrooms solely because of needed modifications in the general education curriculum.[80]

26. DISABILITY AND PLACEMENT

*The South Dakota IEP includes a "reintegration plan" section that details
"what strategies are required to appropriately address reintegration."*

The following data from the 26th Annual Report to Congress shows the
strong connection between disability and placement. For children identified as
mentally retarded over 52 percent received placements outside of the regular
classroom (more than 60% of the day outside of the regular classroom).[81] The
fact is that most children classified as mentally retarded do not exhibit a pattern
of severe retardation, or retardation for which there is a specific identifiable
cause (e.g., Down syndrome), but are children who fall into that vague "cultural-
familial" retardation category. Indeed, only 5.9 percent of students in this category require a restrictive placement (separate, residential, hospital or home).

Table 4. Children with Disabilities Served in Different Educational Environments

Disability	< 21%	21–60%	> 60%	Restrictive
Speech	86.96	7.53	4.69	0.81
Visual	52.53	17.32	16.56	13.58
OHI	49.55	31.38	15.26	3.82
SLD	46.89	38.59	13.48	1.05
DevDel	46.28	32.39	19.69	1.63
Orthopedic	45.76	22.2	27.52	4.53
Hearing	43	19.29	23.65	14.05
ED	28.78	23.03	30.65	17.55
TBI	28.45	34.77	27.84	8.95
Autism	24.67	17.82	45.52	11.98
Deaf-Blind	17.64	20.05	32.16	30.14
MD	11.59	17.31	46.84	24.27
MR	10.95	30.53	52.61	5.90

Telltale Signs of an Inappropriate Placement

• The IEP meeting begins with a completed IEP.

• The placement is made prior to developing the IEP.

• The discussion centers about placement and not needs.

• Children are placed without considering the regular classroom.

• Children are placed without considering supplementary aids and services.

• Placements are not based on the IEP.

• Children are placed based on disability and not need.

27. DISABILITY AND ACHIEVEMENT

Can children with disabilities succeed in the classroom? This depends, in part, on the disability and the severity of the disability. For children with speech or language impairments 34 percent are in the low range in passage comprehension (0–20 percentile range), while 66 percent of students with specific learning disabilities, and 88 percent identified as children with mental retardation are in this low range. By and large all children with disabilities do better in mathematical skills (calculation, applied word problems) which is simply an indication of the importance of language in the determination of disabilities. The following table shows how the various disabilities rank with respect to reading comprehension and mathematics skills (calculation and applied word problems).[82]

Table 5. Rank Order of Different Disabilities with Respect to Passage Comprehension and Mathematics Skills

Disability	Reading Comp.	Math
Speech/language	1	1
Visual impairments	2	2
Orthopedic impair.	3	6
Other health impair	4	7
Autism	5	3
Emotional dist.	6	4
Hearing impair.	7	9
Traumatic brain injury	8	5
Specific Learning Dis.	9	8
Multiple disabilities	10	10
Mental Retardation	11	11

28. SELF-CONTAINED CLASSROOMS

The regular classroom teacher should provide input relating to participation in the general education curriculum in self-contained classrooms. This can be done at team meetings, curriculum meetings, school-wide meetings, workshops, in-service, etc. The self-contained classroom curriculum should not be independent of the general education curriculum.

The regular classroom teacher and self-contained classroom teacher should have a planned curriculum based, as much as possible, on the general education curriculum. For children who require specialized curriculum objectives, the general curriculum should provide the model for developing alternative indicators. One way to coordinate regular and self-contained curriculum objectives is to include the special educator in all school curriculum meetings. A more hands-on approach is for the regular classroom teacher to spend some time in the self-contained classroom setting. Not a lot; just a little time. If a consultant teacher is available, the consultant teacher might take over the class so that 30 minutes or so can be spent in the self-contained classroom. The regular classroom teacher can provide information concerning the implementation of the general curriculum in the self-contained classroom, and the degree of regular classroom participation feasible for students in the self-contained setting.

> ▼ **Every self-contained special education classroom should be part of a team process in which regular classroom teachers can provide input concerning curriculum, regular classroom activities, and district-wide/State-wide tests.**

For children who require a full-time alternate placement, the classroom teacher should be a valued resource for replicating the general education curriculum as much as possible. The classroom teacher can provide guidance concerning activities, materials, tests, projects, etc. that might be used in the alternate setting. If a child requires an alternate setting because of emotional disturbance, this does not mean that the child cannot participate either, whole or in part, in the general curriculum.

Placement in an alternate setting should not exclude a child from as much regular classroom participation as possible. If regular classroom participation by self-contained classroom students is minimal, justifiably or not, the regular classroom teacher might work in cooperation with a consultant teacher or resource room teacher to meet with the students in the self-contained class periodically to maintain a connection with the regular classroom via the regular classroom teacher.

29. OPTIMIZING PARTICIPATION

The regular education classroom should be comprised of primarily nondisabled children. This is not intended to restrict access to the regular classroom but to ensure that children with disabilities are educated with nondisabled children. If all children with disabilities are tracked into one class, or a large proportion of one class consists of children with disabilities, the regular classroom is no longer a regular education classroom.

How many children with disabilities should be in the regular classroom? Although there are several guidelines, this is not an easy question to answer. In addition to the total number of children with disabilities in a specific regular classroom, factors such as the type of disability, severity, and required support must also be considered. However, a general rule of thumb is that the number of children with disabilities who should be in a given regular classroom should be in the 10 percent range[83] or a percentage of the total number of children with disabilities in the school (see Burns, 2003, p. 149). If the percent of children with disabilities in the school is 10 percent, this should be the number in the regular classroom; if the number of children with disabilities is 20 percent of all children, the percentage in the regular classroom should be 20 percent. The population estimate for children between the ages of 6 to 21 in the U.S. is 65,845,492, and the number of children with disabilities is 5,893,038 which is 8.95 percent.[84]

The Department of Education in the Annual Report to Congress operationally defines a regular classroom placement as one in which a child is removed from the regular classroom no more than 21 percent of the day. The 26th Annual Report to Congress indicates 4.32 percent of children in regular classrooms have been identified as a child with a disability. Of this percentage approximately 2.02 percent have specific learning disabilities and 1.46 percent speech or language impairments. These data suggests that a percentage between 5 percent and 10 percent is a reasonable range for the percent of children in the regular classroom with disabilities, and that 10 percent is not far off the mark for the maximum number of students with disabilities who should be in regular classrooms. Obviously, when the overall percentage of children with disabilities is above 10 percent, this will affect the number of children with disabilities in specific regular classrooms.

Table 6. Percent of Children with IDEA Disabilities in Regular Classroom Placements

Disability	N	% of Regular Classroom
Specific Learning Disability	1,331,239	2.02%
Speech/Language Impairment	960,645	1.46%
Other Health Impairment	193,411	0.29%
Emotional Disturbance	138,010	0.21%
Mental Retardation	63,536	0.10%
Orthopedic Impairment	33,710	0.05%
Hearing Impairment	30,610	0.05%
Autism	29,176	0.04%
Multiple Disabilities	15,093	0.02%
Developmental Delay	26,887	0.04%
Visual Impairment	13,416	0.02%
Traumatic Brain Injury	6,077	0.01%
Deaf-Blindness	271	0.00%
Total	2,842,081	4.32%

As was already said allowances must be made for the type of disability, severity, required support services, and the availability of regular classes. A child with cerebral palsy and extensive assistive technology needs might suggest that fewer children with disabilities would be in the same class, while a percentage well above 10 percent might be appropriate for children with less extensive disabilities. Likewise, behavior is an important concern so that one child with serious emotional needs might be the appropriate number for a regular classroom.

"Studenti Inseriti"

In a 1994 report by Carol Berrigan, Center on Human Policy (Syracuse University),[85] the equivalence of inclusion in Italy was referred to as "studenti inseriti" or the insertion of students with disabilities in the regular classroom. "Studenti inseriti" implies "that a student is simply and naturally a part of the class and not just a fulfillment of the law." The report goes on to state that the maximum number of all students in an integrated class is 20, and the maximum number of students with disabilities is two. Hmm...the 10 percent maximum seems to be catching on!

If you are a regular classroom teacher in the United States, and students with disabilities are being placed in your classroom, take note of the number of students with disabilities in your classroom and the total number of students. If there are more than 25 students, and four or five students with disabilities, discuss the possibility of reducing this number so that proportion of students with disabilities to the total number of students falls within the 10 percent guideline. This is good for you, good for the class, and good for children with disabilities. If you have 30 students in your classroom, and 15 have disabilities, not only does this stretch the concept of inclusion but obviously detracts from the level of participation with nondisabled students.

30. AUTISM AND THE CLASSROOM TEACHER

There is considerable concern among parents and school officials over the increase in autism over the last 15 years. The following graph shows the number of children receiving IDEA services for autism and other health impairments (OHI). The general increase for autism is actually somewhat less than OHI. For OHI much of the increase is due to the fact that ADD/ADHD was included in the definition of OHI in IDEA-1997 by stipulating that a child could be OHI because of "limited strength or alertness as a result of heightened alertness to environmental stimuli."

The increase in autism can also be contributed, in part, to the newness of the definition in that autism was added to the list of IDEA disabilities in 1990. Prior to 1990 autism was included in speech or language disorders, multiple disabilities, mental retardation or whatever other category that would result in IDEA services.

A second reason for the increase in autism has been the change from a relatively specific disorder involving language, social skills and overly structured (stereotypic) behavior to a spectrum disorder that ranges from traditional criteria to Asperger's syndrome which places more emphasis on social criteria and structured behavior.

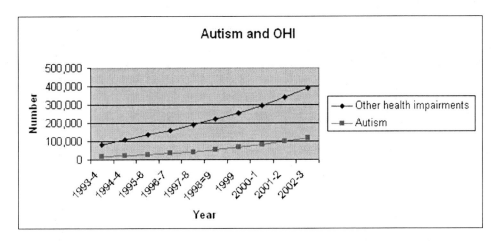

The IDEA definition of autism is concerned with three factors: (1) language, (2) social ability, and (3) "resistance to change" (e.g., repetitive activities). Autism is defined in the IDEA regulations as meaning a developmental disability significantly affecting **verbal and nonverbal communication** and

social interaction, generally evident before age three, that adversely affects a child's educational performance. Other characteristics often associated with autism are engagement in **repetitive activities and stereotyped movements, resistance to environmental change or change in daily routines**, and unusual responses to sensory experiences. Finally, autism does not apply if a child's educational performance is the result of emotional disturbance. Also, a child who manifests the characteristics of autism after age three could be identified as having autism if the criteria for autism are satisfied.

Many psychologists use the *Diagnostic and Statistical Manual* (4th edition) or DSM-IV criteria for autism which provides greater specificity in terms of the types of behaviors that a child exhibit the various areas within the spectrum of autism.

✓	DSM-IV Criteria, Pervasive Developmental Disorders (299.00 Autistic Disorder)
☐	Impairment involving nonverbal behaviors (e.g., eye-to-eye gaze)
☐	Failure to develop peer relationships
☐	Not sharing enjoyment, interests, or achievements with others
☐	Lack of social or emotional reciprocity
☐	Delay lack of spoken language with no alternative communication
☐	Ability but child does not initiate or sustain a conversation
☐	Stereotyped and repetitive use of language or idiosyncratic language
☐	Lack of varied make-believe play or social imitative play
☐	Preoccupation with stereotyped and restricted patterns of interest
☐	Inflexible adherence to routines or rituals
☐	Repetitive motor mannerisms (e.g., hand or finger flapping, tapping)
☐	Persistent preoccupation with parts of objects
	Total Number Checked from Above
☐	Delays in at least one of the following areas prior to age 3: (1) social interaction, (2) language, or (3) symbolic or imaginative play
☐	No significant delay in cognitive development or in the development of age-appropriate self-help skills

Autism and Classroom Participation

The classroom teacher can do much to enable a child with autism to participate in the classroom. The first task is to encourage communication; talk to the child. This can require a modicum of persistence but the goal is purposeful communication; that is, the child responds to a verbal prompt or initiates meaningful communication. Next, provide opportunities for the child to participate in group activities as much as possible. Other children are wonderful communication models and can serve as peer coaches for enhancing classroom communication and participation.

For the classroom teacher inclusion becomes problematic when there is little or no classroom support, and the special education teacher has little to do with the general curriculum. As noted by Ann Dybvik inclusion "demands a higher degree of coordination and planning among regular and special-education teachers, yet few school systems allot the time and resources to promote these exchanges."[86] Successful inclusion, especially for autism, is tantamount to successful collaboration, and the goal of this collaboration is success in the classroom and general curriculum.

What to Do?

- Discuss possible needs and interventions with parents.

- Familiarize yourself with the child's IEP.

- Help identify social behaviors that might require measurable annual goals.

- Include children in as many different social situations as possible. This is more a question of simply "including" and not necessarily "teaching."

- Enlist the entire class as part of the overall remedial plan (especially involving language and social activities).

- Be aware of the content of an existing Behavioral Intervention Plan (or BIP).

- Discuss with the special education teacher possible classroom strategies.

- Make the curriculum accessible to the child.

- Provide situations in which the child can participate in the classroom.

- Structured classrooms can reduce the perceived chaos of many children with autism.

31. LOW-INCIDENCE DISABILITIES

Low-incidence disabilities include multiple-disabilities (131,682), hearing impairments (71,964), orthopedic impairments (74,065), visual impairments (26,113), autism (118,669), deaf-blindness (1,600), traumatic brain injury (21,479) and developmental delay (58,265).[87] Where specific learning disabilities accounts for almost 50 percent of all children with disabilities, these eight disabilities account for 8 percent of children with disabilities receiving IDEA services. A classroom teacher may never experience a child in the classroom with a low-incidence disability, but each of these disabilities presents unique problems concerning regular classroom participation. However, we do know that on those occasions when a child with a low-incidence disability is in the regular classroom, the classroom teacher plays a vital role by focusing on each of the following:

Communication: This does not require a vast amount of communication, but any rapport between a child with extensive needs and the classroom teacher, and between the child and nondisabled students, is one of those unique benefits of regular classroom participation. Example: a child tries to communicate and we don't have any idea what the child is trying to say. What not to do is to nod, smile and get away as quickly as possible. For all we know the child is saying that he/she needs help, but the response is a nod, smile and a quickly departing teacher. Communication is not always easy, not always comfortable, and not always effective, but give it a try.

Levels of academic performance: If a child is not able to identify sight words, expecting that the child will use a communication device to write an essay is hardly realistic. Identify what the child is able to do, and then build on that ability. If a child is able to identify 10 sight words, a goal might be to identify 20 or 30 words. If the child can comprehend 40 percent of what is read, a reasonable goal might be to comprehend 75 percent. On the other hand, for a child whose reading comprehension is zero percent, a goal might be to comprehend 40 percent or 50 percent. Levels of performance vary and so to must corresponding goals.

Feedback: Provide feedback or acknowledge success whenever possible. A periodic "very good" takes but a second. Most children with disabilities don't need constant one-to-one help, but a little guidance from the classroom teacher is essential for real inclusion.

Intentionality: For students with severe disabilities reward intentionality, attempts to participate in the curriculum, attempts to be actively involved in classroom activities. What not to do is to reward random behavior, or simply accept all behavior as meeting the "high expectation" criterion.

Traumatic Brain Injury (21,479)

Traumatic brain injury (TBI) accounts for approximately .32 percent of all children with disabilities (compared to 48.29% for children with specific learning disabilities). Traumatic brain injury is defined as meaning **an acquired injury to the brain caused by an external physical force, resulting in total or partial functional disability or psychosocial impairment**, or both, that adversely affects a child's educational performance. Traumatic brain injury applies to open or closed head injuries resulting in impairments in one or more areas, such as cognition; language; memory; attention; reasoning; abstract thinking; judgment; problem-solving; sensory, perceptual, and motor abilities; psychosocial behavior; physical functions; information processing; and speech. Traumatic brain injury does not apply to brain injuries that are congenital or degenerative, or to brain injuries induced by birth trauma.[88] Common causes of TBI include falls, motor vehicle accidents, colliding with an object, and assaults. Symptoms of TBI include balance problems, blurred vision, body numbness or tingling, difficulty speaking, difficulty swallowing, difficulty with thinking skills, dilated pupils, dizziness, headache, inappropriate emotional responses, lethargy, poor judgment, poor attention span, slurred speech, and vomiting.[89]

A related disability to TBI is Acquired Brain Injury that affects the entire brain. Causes include injuries to the chest, electrical shock or lightening strike, trauma to the head, heart attack, stroke, aneurysm, infectious disease, meningitis, AIDS, brain tumors, hypo/hyperglycemia, hepatic encephalopathy, seizure disorders among other causes.[90]

Classroom inclusion: Traumatic brain injury is the one disability that might be related to the educational environment in that falls, motor vehicle accidents and sports-related injuries can result in TBI. Traumatic brain injury can result in a variety of needs relating to speech and language, behavioral disorders and motor functioning so the classroom teacher must be prepared to work with a variety of special education and related service providers. Although TBI can vary in terms of severity, there are several overall strategies that can be used in the classroom.

Focus on understanding. If an older student has been in an automobile accident and language/cognition are seriously involved, a teacher (based on knowing the student before the accident) might assume that understanding is intact and that only the ability to communicate is involved. In fact, the student's ability to process language might be seriously affected. The best practice is to look for some means to know that the student understands the content, task, question, etc. This is not necessarily an easy task but without understanding the task little learning will take place. Outlining material, structuring lessons, structuring the environment can all help the TBI student better cope with what might be a confusing and overwhelming environment.

A catastrophic reaction is an extreme response to an activity, event, criticism, etc. A student with TBI might be frustrated or overwhelmed and the response is anger or an emotional outburst. The best practice is prevention. Look for signs of frustration then take a break. Be aware that long-involved activities might be frustrating. What to do? Take a break; shorten the length of tasks; use more frequent tasks; do something else; no big deal.

Orthopedic Impairments (74,065)

Orthopedic Impairment means a severe orthopedic impairment that adversely affects a child's educational performance. The term includes impairments caused by a congenital anomaly, impairments caused by disease (e.g., poliomyelitis, bone tuberculosis, etc.), and impairments from other causes (e.g., cerebral palsy, amputations, and fractures or burns that cause contractures).[91]

Classroom inclusion: An assistive device or service is often required in the classroom by a child with an orthopedic impairment. Also, AT devices or services should be designed to enable participation in the general curriculum, and this often requires time and personnel to convert curriculum material to an AT compatible format. A child with extremely limited movement, does not necessarily have limited cognitive capacity. If a child can only move a finger to activate a switch, and the child's cognitive ability is normal, the child can learn to read, write and participate fully in the general education curriculum with obvious and absolutely necessary AT services. Intentionality is the essence of an effective educational program. Banging on a keyboard, with no other intent than to bang on a keyboard, must be molded into the meaningful and intentional use of the device to communicate.

Multiple Disabilities (131,682)

Multiple Disabilities is defined as meaning **concomitant impairments** (such as mental retardation-blindness, mental retardation-orthopedic impairment, etc.), the combination of which causes such severe educational needs that they cannot be accommodated in special education programs solely for one of the impairments. Multiple disabilities does not include deaf-blindness.[92]

Classroom inclusion: Sometimes we just don't know the cause of a child's disability because of the apparent existence of several disabilities. Often a child with multiple disabilities will have a variety of educational needs so that extensive specialized instruction will be a necessity. For the classroom teacher there should be a willingness to include a child with a multiple disability in the regular classroom to some degree in that these children are often the least likely to be included in regular classes. Thus, only 11.59 percent of children with multiple disabilities are included full-time in the regular classroom. Because of the learning needs of a child with multiple disabilities, many children will require extensive classroom support, often in the form of a one-to-one aide. The classroom teacher, however, must encourage as much as possible independent behavior on the part of the student, and provide guidance concerning curriculum content. If a learning theme centers about Thanksgiving, a language board might be used to engage the student in Thanksgiving-related concepts. For example, using clip art a simple 2X2 language board might be used to present concepts and a means to respond.[93]

Assistive Technology Activities

Microsoft has several accessibility options that can be useful for certain students with disabilities but also provide an opportunity to demonstrate to nondisabled students the concept of assistive technology accommodations. By going to the start menu (at the bottom of the screen) and selecting Control Panel and then Accessibility Options, a variety of options will be displayed including a screen magnifier and an on-screen keyboard.

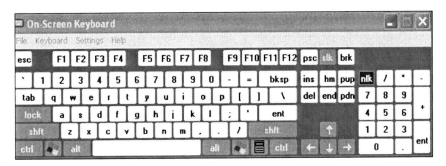

More Technology for the Classroom

For Microsoft Word (especially for newer versions of Word) there is a very useful Speech option under the Tools menu. When displayed this will allow text-to-speech, speech-to-text, a writing pad option and access to the on-screen keyboard. Of course, the purpose of text-to-speech is not to eliminate the need for print and Braille literacy but this technology can be a useful tool for some students. For the classroom teacher the Microsoft Word Speech option is excellent for experimenting with various assistive technology options such as speech recognition and "teaching" the computer to recognize your speech prior to using the speech recognition option.

Assistive Technology and the IEP

The need for assistive technology devices and services must be considered by the IEP Team. However, this is one area where a list of devices and services would not be appropriate in that an "*assistive technology device* means any item, piece of equipment, or product system, whether acquired commercially off the shelf, modified, or customized, that is used to increase, maintain, or improve the functional capabilities of a child with a disability."[94] Consider that an abacus, arm stabilizer, slant desk, puff switch, arm support, bold-lined paper, page turner, FM amplification system, speaker phone, humidifier, light pointer, stand table, visor, walker, closed circuit television, communication board, writing aids, wheelchair lifts, calculators, bookholder, back supports, Braill 'n Speak, Kurzweil reader, and one-handed tools are all assistive technology devices. The list is truly endless. Every item is a potential assistive technology device if it "is used to increase, maintain, or improve the functional capabilities of a child with a disability."

What to Do?

Consider what the child needs. For the classroom teacher consider what will enable the child to participate in the general curriculum. Often the classroom teacher can help in the selection of appropriate assistive technology devices and services by providing input concerning academic performance, and providing observation data concerning devices that are effective.

Remember that need should determine the appropriate device and service and not vice versa. Also, consider both high technology (e.g., computers, synthesized speech), and low technology (e.g., lined paper, visor, reading window) devices and services. For all devices and services the ultimate purpose is not to simply make the service or device available, but to ensure that assistive technology is used to really meet a child's language and academic needs. Providing a child with a $5,000 augmentative communication device, but not a sequential program for using the device, serves no purpose other than to create a fiction that technology, in an of itself, is all that is necessary to meet a child's needs.

32. VISUAL IMPAIRMENTS

Visual impairment including blindness means an impairment in vision that, even with correction, adversely affects a child's educational performance. The term includes both partial sight and blindness.[95]

Of the 26,113 receiving IDEA services because of visual impairments, over 52 percent are included in the regular classroom on a full-time basis. Of these children 85 percent to 90 percent use traditional print materials (including large print) rather than Braille. Children with visual disabilities easily participate in all aspects of the curriculum. Although some support will be needed for curriculum modifications (e.g., large print), the focus for the classroom teacher should be to promote independent classroom work and active participation in all classroom activities and in all aspects of the general curriculum. Ensure that curriculum materials are available in large print, Braille, assistive technology, and so forth, when specified in the IEP.

In addition to participation in the general education curriculum, the American Council of the Blind has identified several core curriculum areas that must be considered for every child who is blind: (1) orientation and mobility (teaching the child to understand spatial position and travel independently); (2) daily living skills (training to live independently, including maintaining clothing, preparing meals, cleaning, and managing money); (3) blindness-specific computer training (use of an audible screen reader, large print magnification or a Braille display, keyboard skills, access games, word processing, and other programs); and (4) Braille instruction (teaching the child to read using the Braille system).

Braille In the Classroom

The classroom teacher can use a variety of fun activities to introduce Braille to nondisabled students. The American Foundation for the Blind has developed several game-related activities for the classroom including the following:[96] (1) using 12-inch balloons to write Braille letters, (2) using a six-hole muffin tin to write Braille letters, (3) having each child write their name in Braille, (4) transcribing Braille words to written words, and (5) using a Braille card to identify Braille letters. The Braille alphabet is readily available on the Internet such as the Braille card offered by the National Braille Press:[97]

Braille Alphabet

The six dots of the braille cell are arranged and numbered:

	1	4
	2	5
	3	6

The capital sign, dot 6, placed before a letter makes a capital letter.

The number sign, dots 3, 4, 5, 6, placed before the characters a through j, makes the numbers 1 through 0. For example: a preceded by the number sign is 1, b is 2, etc.

a	b	c	d	e	f	g	h	i	j
k	l	m	n	o	p	q	r	s	t
u	v	w	x	y	z	Capital Sign	Number Sign	Period	Comma

NATIONAL BRAILLE PRESS INC.
88 ST. STEPHEN STREET
BOSTON, MA 02115
www.nbp.org

Free stuff: Free Braille and fingerspelling fonts are available on the internet and are useful for making a variety of games and learning activities for the regular classroom. The Texas School for the Blind and Visually Impaired has an excellent font resource page at

http://www.tsbvi.edu/Education/fonts.html

Classroom Vision Problems

Educational performance that is affected by a sensory impairment must be discerned during the evaluation process. Thus, a child would not be identified as having a specific learning disability, if educational performance was the result of a visual impairment. For the classroom teacher, before suggesting that the problem is a specific learning disability, consider behaviors that might suggest a more basic underlying cause such as visual acuity.

Vision Problem Checklist		
☐ Awkwardness	☐	Holds material in unusual position
☐ Can't see television	☐	Itching eyes
☐ Closes one eye	☐	Light sensitivity
☐ Reading difficulty	☐	Loses place when reading
☐ Complains of blurred vision	☐	Moves head while reading
☐ Comprehension problems	☐	Pink eye
☐ Covers one eye with hand	☐	Poor eye-hand coordination
☐ Difficulty seeing at night or in poor lighting	☐	Red/crusty eyelids
☐ Disinterest in reading	☐	Rubs eyes
☐ Dizziness	☐	Skips material when reading
☐ Double vision	☐	Squints
☐ Drooping lids	☐	Swelling eyelids
☐ Excessive blinking	☐	Tilts head
☐ Eyes hurt	☐	Tires easily when reading
☐ Eyes turn in and out	☐	Uses to finger as guide
☐ Headaches	☐	Watery eyes

▼ Assistive technology does not always the best solution, especially with respect to Braille literacy. As noted by the National Braille Press, "while tape recorders and talking computers are handy and important sources of information for blind people, only Braille allows for complete command of written language."[98]

Library of Congress: Braille and Books on Tape

Students who are blind or who have and other physical disabilities are eligible for the loan of library materials through the National Library Service for the Blind and Physically Handicapped (NLS). Eligibility criteria include the following:

1. Blind persons whose visual acuity, as determined by competent authority, is 20/200 or less in the better eye with correcting lenses, or whose widest diameter of visual field subtends an angular distance no greater than 20 degrees.

2. Other physically handicapped persons are eligible as follows:
    a. Persons whose visual disability, with correction and regardless of optical measurement, is certified by competent authority as preventing the reading of standard printed material.
    b. Persons certified by competent authority as unable to read or unable to use standard printed material as a result of physical limitations.
    c. Persons certified by competent authority as having a reading disability resulting from organic dysfunction and of sufficient severity to prevent their reading printed material in a normal manner.[99]

Deaf-Blindness (1,600)

Deaf-blindness means **concomitant hearing and visual impairments,** the combination of which causes such severe communication and other developmental and educational needs that they cannot be accommodated in special education programs solely for children with deafness or children with blindness.[100]

Classroom inclusion: Children in this category have extensive learning needs, but participation in the classroom is a real goal. The good news: 17.6 percent of children identified as having deaf-blindness are included 100 percent of the day in the regular education classroom. General strategies: (1) include a child with deaf-blindness in classroom activities; (2) communicate with the child; make an attempt; (3) be open to the need for special training in the classroom such as by a mobility specialist; (4) be organized so that a student with deaf-blindness is better able to find materials independently; (5) enlist the entire class in developing communication skills based on the child's relevant mode of communication (e.g., sign language, communication device.

Deaf-Blind Alphabet

One method to communicate with a student who has deaf-blindness is to use the forefinger to write block letters on the palm of another student's hand. Although in all likelihood you will not have students with deaf-blindness in your classroom, the deaf-blind alphabet is an excellent activity for understanding how students with extensive hearing and visual needs communicate.

33. SOCIAL SECURITY AND DSM-IV DISABILITIES

The IDEA disabilities tend to be somewhat general by definition, and disabilities such as ADD/ADHD are downright impossible to define using IDEA criteria. What to do? One option is to refer to the DSM-IV manual (which obviously emphasizes disabilities with a psychological basis) or social security disabilities which tend to be functional and very useful in terms of the variety of disabilities covered and the specific diagnostic criteria used. The following are the social security guidelines for Attention Deficit Hyperactivity Disorder:[101]

> **112.11** *Attention Deficit Hyperactivity Disorder:* **Manifested by developmentally inappropriate degrees of inattention, impulsiveness, and hyperactivity.**
> **The required level of severity for these disorders is met when the requirements in both A and B are satisfied.**
> **A. Medically documented findings of all three of the following:**
> **1. Marked inattention; and**
> **2. Marked impulsiveness; and**
> **3. Marked hyperactivity;**
>
> and
>
> **B. For older infants and toddlers (age 1 to attainment of age 3), resulting in at least one of the appropriate age-group criteria in paragraph B1 of 112.02; or, for children (age 3 to attainment of age 18), resulting in at least two of the appropriate age-group criteria in paragraph B2 of 112.02.**

If you have a child in your classroom and you are unsure of the disability or how the disability was diagnosed, Social Security guidelines provide information that is useful and to the point. For example, for HIV the following guideline is provided:

> **For a child 24 months of age or older, a serum specimen that contains HIV antibodies. HIV antibodies are usually detected by a screening test. The most commonly used screening test is the ELISA. Although this test is highly sensitive, it may yield false positive results. Therefore, positive results from an ELISA must be confirmed by a more definitive test (e.g., Western Blot, immunofluorescence assay).**

Part III
Referral, RTI and Standards

Any State educational agency, State agency, or local educational agency that receives assistance under this part shall establish and maintain procedures in accordance with this section to ensure that children with disabilities and their parents are guaranteed procedural safeguards with respect to the provision of a free appropriate public education by such agencies.[102]

34. PREREFERRAL TEAMS

The best practice for prereferral interventions is to use a team approach for developing strategies for successful classroom performance prior to referral for special education.

The classroom teacher needs support before the need for special education is determined. This is necessary to reduce referrals by meeting student needs without special education.

Many schools use a prereferral or Child Study Team (CST) approach to ensure that every child is provided with appropriate classroom and school-wide interventions, and that there is justification for an actual referral for an individual evaluation. The Child Study Team is a problem-solving process by which school personnel (teachers, team members, specialists) collaborate to determine strategies and interventions that will best meet a child's needs within the framework of the regular classroom, the general curriculum and suing available school resources. Idaho requires a Prereferral Team "process to problem solve and plan general education modifications and instructional interventions (e.g., teaching strategies, curriculum adaptations, scheduling, cooperative learning) to ensure that referrals to consider special education evaluation are appropriate."[103] The Prereferral Team is composed primarily of school personnel, and parent involvement "is valuable," but parents are not required to be part of the team.

In Ohio a "differentiated referral" which "means the planning, implementation and evaluation of interventions conducted prior to referral for multifactored evaluation," while the referral for special education is a multifactored evaluation.[104] North Dakota relies on a Building Level Support Team (BLST) to provide support to the regular education teacher. This is "a structured problem-solving process that is used by educators and parents to develop interventions for a student who is experiencing difficulty in classroom achievement or behavior."[105]

A prereferral team or child study team process is not mandated by IDEA and therefore has many and wide-ranging forms and responsibilities. The Child Study Team (CST) can be referred to as a Child Assistance Team (CAT), Child Service Team (CST), Instructional Support Team (IST), Student Assistance Team (SAT), Student Study Committee (SSC), Student Study Team (SST), Teacher Academic Team (TAT). The CST is most often an informal collaboration among school personnel to resolve school problems and implement school-wide interventions without special education. Often the CST provides initial input concerning classroom strategies and interventions, and, if these are not effective, the CST makes a referral for a full and individual evaluation.

The CST can also be a preliminary step that is required prior to referral for special education. In Alabama, before a child is referred for special education, prereferral intervention strategies must be implemented in the general education program and monitored by the Building Based Student Support Team (BBSST) for at least six weeks or longer. Following this period the BBSST must make a determination that the interventions were unsuccessful. As is the case with many prereferral programs this rule can be waived for a child with intensive needs that require immediate attention.[106]

35. REFERRAL PROCESS

The referral process begins with a request for a full and individual evaluation to determine the existence of a disability and the need for special education.

The timeline required by each state for the evaluation and determination of disability varies from "a reasonable period of time"[107] to a period less than 60 days as is the case in Washington (the state) where the school district must fully evaluate the child and make a decision 35 days after receiving consent.[108] In Virginia the timeline is 65 business days after the referral is received to the initial evaluation.[109] The timeline for the individual evaluation can also be linked to the referral-to-placement process. Alabama has a ninety day time-line from the date a written referral is received to a placement "regardless of any scheduled interruptions in the scholastic year."[110] In Texas the time from referral to evaluation is 60 days, and 30 days from evaluation to IEP meeting.[111] Idaho allows 60 days from consent to IEP implementation (but 30 days to assessment information and IEP development and placement).[112] The moral of all these timelines is to be familiar with the specific procedures and timeline requirements for your state.

▼ **In Virginia a referral a child study committee can determine the need for an evaluation but the committee shall not:**
   a. **Deny or delay the parent's or parents' right to a due process hearing to contest the decision not to evaluate;**
   b. **Deny or delay the parent's or parents' right to make another referral in the future; or**
   c. **Delay the evaluation of a child who is suspected of having a disability.[113]**

Making a Referral

Before a child can receive special education services or accommodations under IDEA the local educational agency (LEA) "must conduct a full and in-dividual initial evaluation." The referral for an evaluation can be made by either the parent of a child, or a State educational agency, other State agency, or local educational agency.[114] Most often the referral for an individual evaluation will be initiated by the parent and/or teacher, but a referral is sometime made by a State agency or other interested party.

In Illinois, a referral "may be made by any concerned person...a child, or an employee of the State Board of Education."[115] In Massachusetts, a referral can be made by "a parent or any person in a care giving or professional position concerned with the student's development."[116] In New York, a referral for a child suspected of having a disability is made in writing to the chairperson of the Committee on Special Education or to the building administrator by a parent, a professional staff member, licensed physician, judicial officer, a designee of a public agency with responsibility for welfare, health or education of children, or a student over 18 or an emancipated minor eligible for services.[117]

Referral Content

The referral is a formal request for a full and individual evaluation, and a statement as to why the request is being made. The request should not be to determine a specific disability, but to determine whether behavior or educational performance have been impacted by a disability. The first element of every referral should be the documentation of the specific behavior or skills that affect educational performance. There is a specific reason or specific behaviors that somehow suggest that the regular classroom and/or general curriculum might not be appropriate. If the referral is made by a teacher, observations, reports, grades and samples of performance can be cited to document educational performance or the lack thereof. There is no need to include a wealth of test scores but to simply identify specific areas of academic concern or behavior that affect educational performance.

The referral is not a blank request for an initial evaluation to find a disability, any disability, using criteria and tests completely unrelated to the classroom. For example, there is no "test" to determine a specific learning disability, but rather classroom performance provides the basis for determining the disability. However, additional tests can be useful for supporting the existence of a specific learning disability (e.g., the Wechsler Individual Achievement Test).

Interventions

Identifying classroom interventions and accommodations, and the resulting success, is an essential element of the referral process for reducing overreferrals and misclassifications. Also, classroom interventions and accommodations used prior to the referral are useful for identifying needed assessments, potential

IEP goals and services, and effective IEP accommodations if a child requires special education. The classroom teacher is at the forefront of classroom interventions and strategies, and these interventions and strategies (and the resulting success) should be a part of every referral.

Parents

Parent involvement should be documented in the referral unless, of course, the referral is made by the parent. Parent input might relate to the cause or reason for the behavior, possible medical concerns, or what might be done to accommodate the child's needs with or without special education. Whether or not the behavior or problem exists at home, in nonschool settings, and what has been effective for addressing the need/behavior/need at home are all important areas for parent input. The IEP, and the entire special education process, is intended to be a partnership between parents and the school. Although the emphasis on due process can easily suggest that the thrust of IDEA is an adversarial relationship between parents and schools, IDEA has always emphasized the need for parental involvement in the evaluation process and in the development of the IEP. Advice for the classroom teacher: don't forget the parents. Parents are an excellent source of information; sometimes by what they say, do, or observe; and sometimes what that do not say, do, or observe.

Other Factors

The referral should also contain information relating to other factors that can affect educational performance that do not result from a disability, or at least factors that can confound the determination of a disability. Alabama requires that "information must be gathered as part of the referral to determine if there are any environmental, cultural, language, or economic differences that might mask a student's true abilities and thereby affect the student's performance in the areas evaluated." And "tests and evaluative materials selected and administered should be sensitive to environmental, cultural, linguistic, and economic differences."[118]

36. RTI (RESPONSE TO INTERVENTION)

Nonetheless, the implementation of special education has been impeded by low expectations and an insufficient focus on research showing proven methods for teaching and learning for children with disabilities.[119]

Response To Intervention (**RTI**) is the latest buzzword in special education. Why so? The primary reason why many feel that RTI is the missing link in special education is that this approach will prevent overidentification and the misclassification of students as having disabilities when, in fact, they do not. Also, RTI also provides an alternative approach to the IQ-achievement discrepancy model in the identification of specific learning disabilities. The specific learning disabilities classification is not intended for every child with academic needs, especially for children who have not received adequate instruction. As noted in the proposed regulations for IDEA "identification models that incorporate response to intervention represent a shift in special education toward the goals of better achievement and behavioral outcomes for students identified with SLD because the students who are identified under such models are most likely to require special education and related services."[120]

The Importance of Classroom Instruction

The House Report for P.L. 108-446 indicated discouragement with "the practice of overidentifying children as having disabilities, especially minority students, largely because the children do not have appropriate reading skills. Special education is not intended to serve as an alternative place to serve children if the local educational agency has failed to teach these children how to read. The bill updates language within the Act to contain a specific requirement that a child cannot be determined to be a child with a disability solely because the child did not receive scientifically based instruction in reading."[121]

A problem for schools, and certainly for parents, is the overidentification of children having specific learning disabilities. If a child does not have a disability but is provided with an array of services and accommodations, the result can limit participation in the general curriculum which, in turn, can prevent a student from receiving all the benefits of regular classroom participation. Inappropriately remove a child from the general curriculum, under the guise of remediation, and successful participation in the curriculum might be jeopardized.

Misclassification can stigmatize students (yes, being labeled mentally retarded would come under the category of stigmatization), and can prevent opportunities relating to courses, graduation and post-school opportunities. Just as important, providing special education services and accommodations for children who do not have disabilities can result in segregative practice such as when black children are wrongly identified as mentally retarded and then placed in a separate classroom/location (doesn't that phrase "separate but equal" come to mind).

The law is clear: When making the determination of eligibility a child cannot be determined to have a disability if the determinant factor is (1) lack of appropriate instruction in reading, including in the essential components of reading instruction, (2) lack of instruction in math; or (3) limited English proficiency.[122] For specific learning disabilities learning problems that are primarily the result of environmental, cultural, or economic disadvantage are not included in the definition of a specific learning disability.

Every child should be given an opportunity to succeed in the classroom using research-based and systematic instructional techniques. Provide every child with an opportunity to succeed in the regular classroom. Identify specific educational needs, and then attempt to meet these needs without special education. The essence of RTI is data; data that is specific, and data that is used to systematically monitor growth and progress.

What to Do?

First, identify a present level of performance. The task is to identify what the child can and cannot do. For example, the child is able to comprehend information after reading material at the third grade level, but not material from a sixth grade social studies book.

Second, develop a set of instructional activities to improve performance.

Third, Provide systematic instruction to bridge this gap.

Fourth, collect data; monitor performance.

A child is in the second grade and has a very limited reading vocabulary when asked to read orally. A list of 220 sight-words is presented to the child (via flash cards) and the result reveals that the child is able to identify 22 words. A plan is developed whereby sight words are used in reduced vocabulary sentences/paragraphs/stories. Prior to each activity sight words are reviewed and new sight-words added. After four weeks the student is able to identify 72 sight-words. Response-to-intervention works!

Is RTI important? Congress certainly thinks so and believes that prereferral, early intervention and response-to-intervention will reduce misclassification and better serve all students:

> **Through the application of high quality instruction, delivered by well-trained individuals, local educational agencies will be able to differentiate between children that have different learning styles and children that have disabilities. The experience of some local educational agencies and States that have adopted other methods, such as "Neverstreaming" or "response-to-intervention" have demonstrated that scientifically based, rigorous assessment methods exist and should serve as models for other local educational agencies and States to follow.[123]**

37. THE ROWLEY STANDARD

If the child is being educated in regular classrooms, as here,
the IEP should be reasonably calculated to enable the child
to achieve passing marks and advance
from grade to grade.[124]

Hudson v. Rowley is often referred to as the Rowley standard. This "standard" is a two-step analysis (actually more) that requires consideration of the procedural merits of the problem (relating to the appropriateness of special education for a child), and then a sustentative analysis of the merits of the case. When evaluating an IEP the first step is to determine whether or not the procedures have been followed, and then to determine whether the IEP is reasonably calculated. Even if an IEP is reasonably calculated and excellent in all respects, the regulations must be followed. A school could not argue that parents were not needed at a meeting (a procedural requirement) because the resulting IEP (sustentative requirement) was reasonably calculated. This is the old cart-before-the-horse problem.

When the Courts Require No More[125]
(What the Rowley Mandate Requires)

First, has the State complied with the procedures set forth in the Act?

Second, is the individualized educational program developed through the Act's procedures reasonably calculated to enable the child to receive educational benefits?

Third, if these requirements are met, the State has complied with the obligations imposed by Congress and the courts can require no more.

"Does This Meet the Rowley Standard?"

We affirm the conclusion that the District was not required to
provide... an IEP that exceeded the Rowley standard.[126]

There is a huge amount of case law concerning special education, and many of the various decisions have helped determine the meaning of mainstreaming, the obligation of schools to provide FAPE, and basic guidelines concerning evaluation, disability and services. Of all the litigation relating to special education, *Hudson v. Rowley* is considered the legal standard for determining the appropriateness of special education.

Amy Rowley was a deaf student in the Hendrick Hudson School District in Peekskill, New York. The Committee for Special Education decided that an "appropriate" education for Amy required an FM hearing aid, a tutor one hour a day, and three hours of speech and language services a week. A determination was made by the IEP Team that an interpreter was not needed. Amy's parents thought that this denial of an interpreter was not "appropriate" and requested an impartial hearing. The hearing officer supported the school's contention that a qualified sign-language interpreter was not needed. Upon appeal the Second Court of Appeals concluded that the Amy was not provided with an appropriate education for lack of a qualified interpreter. The reason for this was the belief that because of the disparity between Amy's achievement and her potential she was not receiving a free appropriate public education. The appeal to the Supreme Court reversed this decision and provided the legal basis for a school's obligation regarding FAPE.[127]

HUDSON v. ROWLEY, 458 U.S. 176(1982)

The Act's requirement of a "free appropriate public education" is satisfied when the State provides personalized instruction with sufficient support services to permit the handicapped child to benefit educationally from that instruction. Such instruction and services must be provided at public expense, must meet the State's educational standards, must approximate grade levels used in the State's regular education, and must comport with the child's IEP, as formulated in accordance with the Act's requirements. If the child is being educated in regular classrooms, as here, the IEP should be reasonably calculated to enable the child to achieve passing marks and advance from grade to grade (see pp. 187-204).

For the Classroom Teacher

What does all this mean for the regular classroom teacher? A whole lot. The individualized program for every child with a disability should be reasonably calculated to enable "the child to achieve passing marks." This means "passing marks" in the regular classroom. This is not "passing marks" as determined by a special education teacher but by the regular classroom teacher. True, not all children will be able to achieve this standard. A very small percentage of children receive services and will require a very specialized program, but the goal for most children receiving IDEA services is to achieve successfully in the regular classroom. What is success? Passing marks...and so says the Supreme Court. Although a goal of all special education should be to maximize every child's potential, this is not the standard in special education. The reason for this is that if the goal were to maximize every learning experience for a child, one might conclude that one-to-one instruction, in a separate location, would be "appropriate." However, what all teachers must embrace is that special education is about a free appropriate public education to enable children with disabilities to participate with nondisabled children.

The Rowley standard also affirms the link between special and regular education. The instruction provided a child with a disability must meet the State's educational standards and most approximate instruction used in the regular grades. Special education is not a separate curriculum that is best accomplished apart from the regular classroom. Instruction in special education is predicated on State standards and the general curriculum.

A frequent misunderstood fact about special education is its underlying purpose. Special education is not and was never intended to be "better" than regular education. One misconception of special education is that for children receiving special services under IDEA that these services should maximize a child's potential. In other words, some believe that special education must have a higher standard than the education for children who are not disabled. This is not true. The standard is not the best education available, and not to maximize a child's potential, but to enable a child with a disability to participate with nondisabled children.

"Basic Floor of Opportunity"

The Rowley standard provides an excellent guideline for classroom teachers. Your job, indeed the job of special education, is not to maximize the potential of each child with a disability but to determine a child's needs and then provide a free appropriate public education. This is the business that should concern the classroom teacher: determining how a child with a disability with reasonable accommodation, services and supports can participate in the general curriculum.

More Hudson v. Rowley

In explaining the need for federal legislation, the House Report noted that "no congressional legislation has required a precise guarantee for handicapped children, i.e., a basic floor of opportunity that would bring into compliance all school districts with the constitutional right of equal protection with respect to handicapped children." Assuming that the Act was designed to fill the need identified in the House Report that is, to provide a "basic floor of opportunity" consistent with equal protection neither the Act nor its history persuasively demonstrates that Congress thought that equal protection required anything more than equal access. Therefore, Congress' desire to provide specialized educational services, even in furtherance of "equality," cannot be read as imposing any particular substantive educational standard upon the States.

The District Court and the Court of Appeals thus erred when they held that the Act requires New York to maximize the potential of each handicapped child commensurate with the opportunity provided nonhandicapped children. Desirable though that goal might be, it is not the standard that Congress imposed upon States which receive funding under the Act. Rather, Congress sought primarily to identify and evaluate handicapped children, and to provide them with access to a free public education.

38. REASONABLY CALCULATED IEPS

Develop a reasonably calculated IEP.

The guidance provided by the Supreme Court is relatively simple: develop a reasonably calculated IEP. However, there are a few things that can occur when developing an IEP...and not all are good.

The same placement for "all children" invariably means the placements are not in compliance with the law. If all children identified as having mental retardation, emotional disturbance, and so forth, are placed in self-contained classrooms, the disability rather than the "reasonably calculated" IEP is the basis for the placements. Every placement should be individually determined, and based on the services, goals, accommodations and supports outlined in the IEP. The IEP must dictate placement, and not disability.

The IEP chairperson begins the meeting with a completed IEP and the comforting words that this "of course, is not final." Yeah, right. No wonder parents hire lawyers. When presented with what looks like a completed IEP, the intent is that the IEP is indeed completed. What does the law say? In the development of the IEP, the IEP Team must consider the strengths of the child, the concerns of the parents, the results of the most recent evaluation, and the child's academic, developmental, and functional needs.[128] Obviously, if the IEP is developed prior to the IEP meeting, the parents concerns are not considered. Why would a school do this? To save time, to save money, and because the person(s) who allow this to happen (or require this to happen) are ignorant of the law, special education, and consider paperwork more important than a child's needs.

Meaningless goals are a primary culprit in the development of unreasonably calculated IEPs. These are easy to spot. Exceedingly picky goals (e.g., recognize short vowel sounds) that result in endless pages of goals that no one will actually use or ever revisit (as in an annual review). The apparent logic is that a thick IEP with an endless number of goals is a good substitute for a reasonably calculated IEP. Goals that can't be measured, such as the venerable "increase self-concept as determined by teacher observation," are augmented by the ever popular 85 percent level of success to make already vague goals totally bewildering.

You would think that if a thoughtful IEP were developed some thought would be given to the appropriateness of IEP content. Why accommodations sometimes seem to be selected out of thin air is a mystery. Accommodations should be specific and should be designed to meet a child's needs. If accommodations are thoughtlessly selected, such as providing "extended time" to every child with a disability, when a child might actually need shorter work (or test) periods or more breaks between work periods, the accommodations are based on disability and certainly not need. Often accommodations are frivolous such as "provide extra help when needed" or "assist with homework." These types of activities should be used with all children when needed. If a teacher must be instructed to provide a child with "extra help when needed," there are more serious problems with the provision of an appropriate education than the IEP accommodations.

The development of a reasonably calculated IEP is a goal only when the IEP is a real planning document. Many school administrators are adamant and righteous in the belief that special education is a placement and not a service (not withstanding Congressional mandate and the law). The school focuses on where a child will receive services as if the placement itself solves all problems. This is wrong. Appropriate services should be determined first; and then (following the development of the IEP) the place where these services are provided is determined.

For the Classroom Teacher

Help develop a reasonably calculated IEP by identifying

- **Specific classroom needs;**
- **Specific performance goals to succeed in the classroom (e.g., completing homework assignments, passing weekly quizzes, etc.);**
- **Goals that will enable participation in the general curriculum;**
- **Classroom/test accommodations that are effective;**
- **Services that will enable successful classroom participation; and**
- **Classroom supports that will promote success and enable independence.**

Reducing Services

The committee believes this can be accomplished by a number of means, including supporting teachers and other staff by providing high quality training and reducing paperwork burdens, encouraging more efficient and effective conflict resolution between parents and schools, providing earlier access to services and supports to children to reduce the need for IDEA services (Senate Report 108-185).[129]

39. NONCOMPLIANCE

If you need to know one word that relates to IDEA, "noncompliance" is a most excellent word. States and schools are notorious for not complying with the law. In theory, if a school is not in compliance after notice of noncompliance and a hearing, "the State educational agency shall reduce or shall not provide any further payments to the local educational agency or State agency until the State educational agency is satisfied that the local educational agency or State agency, as the case may be, is complying with that requirement."[130] This is the law, but a law that is largely ignored.

An excellent document for understanding the extent of noncompliance, and what can be done, is available from the National Council on Disability (NCD) entitled Back to School on Civil Rights at

http://www.ncd.gov/newsroom/publications/2000/backtoschool_1.htm

The NCD report on noncompliance indicates the following percentages for states not in compliance in key areas: general supervision (90%), transition services (88%), FAPE (80%), procedural safeguards (78%), LRE (72%), IEPs (44%), and protection in evaluation (38%). Why doesn't State departments of education intercede to demand that schools comply with the regulations? The answer to this is the first area of noncompliance: general supervision. Schools are often not held accountable by state agencies, and compliance will always be lax until state agencies "after reasonable notice and an opportunity for a hearing," finds that a local educational agency has failed to comply with a requirement, "the State educational agency shall reduce or shall not provide any further payments to the local educational agency or State agency until the State educational agency is satisfied that the local educational agency or State agency, as the case may be, is complying with that requirement."[131]

Schools and Noncompliance

The next time you are given an IEP for a child in your classroom evaluate the document with respect to specific content (e.g., evaluation data, beginning levels of performance) or what is included (e.g., meaningless goals). Consider present levels of performance, what the child actually does, and the meaningfulness of the measurable annual goals. Consider whether supplementary aids and services are provided and what supports, services and accommodations are cited to enable classroom success. If a placement outside the regular classroom was determined necessary, evaluate the extent of regular classroom participation and the input that you had in the determination of this level of participation.

What to do when faced with blatant noncompliance? IDEA decisions are made by a Team, not by one individual, and not by the classroom teacher. Collect data, attend meetings, and make your case. If a school is determined on noncompliance, and the parents agree, there is not a whole lot you can do (without jeopardizing your job, sanity, or both). Without tiptoeing into the murky area of insubordination, your job is to enable all children to participate in the classroom and general curriculum. Do this for a child with a disability and no more can be asked. One would hope that the information you provide will be used, that goals will be developed to enable participation, and that appropriate supports and services will be provided.

> ▼ Between 1997 and 2002 more than half of reports of
> noncompliance were the result of a failure to provide
> basic services, especially related services such as
> counseling, speech pathology, and assistive technology.
> Following the failure to provide basic services, the
> next major area of noncompliance involved a failure
> to meet IDEA procedural requirements involving
> paperwork, timelines, etc.[132]

Do schools consciously set about to engage in noncompliance? I don't think so. The problem is that school officials only know that IEPs must exist, and not to exist as a real plan to enable regular classroom participation. As a result bureaucratic need (e.g., to complete an IEP document) has taken the place of program effectiveness (i.e., IEPs that actually improve student performance).

40. THE PRESUMED PLACEMENT

Your classroom, the regular classroom, is the presumed placement for every child with a disability.

Even though IDEA does not mandate a regular classroom placement for every child with a disability, IDEA presumes that the first placement option considered by the IEP Team is the regular classroom with appropriate supplementary aids and services. Thus, before a child can be placed outside of the regular educational environment, **the full range of supplementary aids and services** that, if provided, would facilitate regular classroom success must be considered.[133]

These regulations for IDEA-1997 state that "IDEA presumes that the first placement option considered for each disabled student by the student's placement team, which must include the parent, is the school the child would attend if not disabled, with appropriate supplementary aids and services to facilitate such placement."[134] This is similar to the Senate Report (105-17) for IDEA-1997 that stipulates "the law and this bill contain a presumption that children with disabilities are to be educated in regular classes. Therefore, the legislation requires that the IEP include an explanation of the extent, if any, to which a child with a disability will not participate with nondisabled children in the regular class and in the general education curriculum including extracurricular and nonacademic activities."

▼ **Section 504 of the Rehabilitation Act of 1973 prevents discrimination, exclusion from participation, or being denied benefits by any program receiving financial assistance based solely on disability.**[135]

What does all this mean for the regular classroom teacher? First, the law (especially Section 504) is quite clear that schools should not discriminate against children with disabilities. Specifically, a child with a disability cannot "be excluded from the participation in, be denied the benefits of, or be subjected to discrimination under any program or activity receiving Federal financial assistance." This should not require the Office of Civil Rights (or a lawyer) to remind schools that restricting a child from an appropriate education is discriminatory, or that the development of a meaningless IEP, or placing a child based on disability, is not the purpose of special education.

41. COMPLAINTS

*Parents and schools should be given expanded opportunities to
resolve their disagreements in positive and constructive ways.[136]*

How to complain, that is the question. As the classroom teacher you might
be made painfully aware of the fact that a parent is unhappy with an accommodation, service or placement. Parents can complain but there is a procedure to the complaint process.

The first rule regarding complaints is to listen to parents and attempt to resolve complaints amicably. Communication between the classroom teacher
and parents is essential for children with disabilities. Much of the excessive
litigation and contentious climate that prevails in special education is the result
of poor communication. Parents are entitled an opportunity to present complaints, and a formal complaint by a parent should not be a surprise to the
classroom teacher. When a parent is dissatisfied with a special education service or placement, the classroom teacher might be asked to discuss the child's
participation in the classroom. This you should do in terms of specific levels of
academic performance, work samples, and overall classroom behavior. Be
positive. Discuss with the parent what the child needs to succeed. Listen to
the parents. Much of the litigation in special education could be avoided by
common courtesy and respect for parent input.

If a parent is considering a formal complaint, the complaint must include
basic information (viz., name, address, school), a statement of the problem (including facts relating to the problem) and a proposed solution. For the classroom teacher, when meeting with a parent, ask if there are any problems.
More importantly, ask what a solution to the problem might be. You may or
may not be able to provide a solution, but consider the parents complaint and
proposed solution. Who knows? The parent might have *the* answer.

What to Tell Parents?

The role of the teacher is certainly not to initiate complaints by the parent.
The role of the teacher is, as best as possible, to help resolve complaints and
problems. The classroom teacher can help parents define what the problem is
or the solution to the problem. One reason why parents often are not successful when complaining about a service (or lack thereof) is not having formulated what it is they want on behalf of the child. Help parents get beyond

"I don't like…" and focus on not only what the problem is, but what would be an acceptable solution.

The following lists several guidelines for the classroom teacher regarding parent complaints and the complaint process:

- **Focus on the problem and not personalities.**

- **Think solution, not just problem.**

- **Talk to the special education teacher or whoever is providing specially designed instruction**

- **If the complaint cannot be resolved, a mediation process is available and less contentious. Parents should know this.**

- **A due process hearing cannot be held until a notice has been filed.**

- **The complaint must include the following information:**
    1. **Name**
    2. **Address**
    3. **School**
    4. **The problem**
    5. **Proposed solution**

- **A school must respond to a complaint within 10 days.**

Response to a Complaint

The school must respond to every complaint, and the classroom teacher might have input concerning this response with relation to classroom performance, classroom accommodations and interventions, and classroom behavior and academic performance.

1. **an explanation of why the agency proposed or refused to take the action raised in the complaint;**

2. **a description of other options that the IEP Team considered and the reasons why those options were rejected;**

3. **a description of each evaluation procedure, assessment, record, or report the agency used as the basis for the proposed or refused action; and**

4. **a description of the factors that are relevant to the agency's proposal or refusal.**

Two-year Statute of Limitations

An important change in the IDEA compliant process is a two-year time period in which a complaint must be filed. The rationale for this time limitation is the belief by Congress that schools cannot effectively function under a never-ending threat of litigation.

IDEA-2004 615(6)

An opportunity for any party to present a complaint–

(A) with respect to any matter relating to the identification, evaluation, or educational placement of the child, or the provision of a free appropriate public education to such child; and

(B) which sets forth an alleged violation that occurred not more than 2 years before the date the parent or public agency knew or should have known about the alleged action that forms the basis of the complaint, or, if the State has an explicit time limitation for presenting such a complaint under this part, in such time as the State law allows, except that the exceptions to the timeline described in subsection (f)(3)(D) shall apply to the timeline described in this subparagraph.

Resolving Complaints

A goal of IDEA is to develop an environment that results in an appropriate education for every child by way of collaboration between parents and school. Unfortunately, special education is often anything but a collaborative effort. In order to resolve serious complaints (meaning complaints that might rise to the level of an impartial hearing) IDEA requires the following:

> Within 15 days of receiving notice of the parents' due process complaint, and prior to a due process hearing, the school must convene a meeting with the parents and the relevant member or members of the IEP Team who have specific knowledge of the facts identified in the due process complaint.

and

> The purpose of the meeting is for the parents of the child to discuss their due process complaint, and the facts that form the basis of the due process complaint, so that the LEA has the opportunity to resolve the dispute that is the basis for the due process complaint. [137]

42. NOTICE

For the classroom teacher: read the procedural safeguards notice for your school system so that you know what safeguards are available for every parent.

A copy of the procedural safeguards are given to parents "only 1 time a year," or upon initial referral or parental request for evaluation; when a complain is first filed; or when requested by the parent.[138] The IDEA also requires that the Procedural Safeguards Notice (PSN) provide "a full explanation of the procedural safeguards, written in the native language of the parents (unless it clearly is not feasible to do so) and written in an easily understandable manner." For the most part, the availability of the PSN is easier achieved than understandability in that the notice is often a gobblygook of legalese that defies understanding (or interest). If you are a classroom teacher, give the PSN a read and you might be surprised by the rights that are required by law and that schools *should* provide parents.

The PSN provides parents with important rights and due process procedures that relate to evaluation, identification and special education. The PSN provides "a full explanation of the procedural safeguards, written in the native language of the parents (unless it clearly is not feasible to do so) and written in an easily understandable manner."[139] Parents are entitled to an independent educational evaluation (IEE) if dissatisfied with the evaluation conducted by the school. Unless the school challenges the appropriateness of the evaluation by a hearing, this IEE is free and conducted by a qualified personnel consistent with the standards and criteria used by the school. Parents are entitled to examine all educational test information, records and other information relating to their child and to "and to participate in meetings with respect to the identification, evaluation, and educational placement of the child, and the provision of a free appropriate public education to such child, and to obtain an independent educational evaluation of the child."[140] If parents are dissatisfied with some aspect of the identification, evaluation or provision of services, parents can present a complaint with respect to any matter relating to the special education process (e.g., identification, evaluation, placement, etc.) that alleges a violation that occurred not more than 2 years before the school should have known about problem.[141]

The required content for PSN is shown below. For the classroom teacher the notice may involve you in several ways: (1) your input concerning classroom performance might be part of the prior written notice; (2) lack of parent consent might result in a child with a disability being in your classroom without IDEA services; (3) parents are entitled to review all records and reports which means that parents are entitled to review all your records and reports concerning their child; (4) parents can complain to the school or state regarding accommodations or services that might or might not occur in your classroom; (5) the child remains in his or her educational placement during a due process proceeding (more about pendency below); and (6) informal discussions, mediation and a formal due process proceeding can be used to resolve complaints.

Independent educational evaluation: An evaluation paid for by the school if the parent is dissatisfied with the evaluation conducted by the school.

Prior written notice: Notice must be given to parents prior to an action (e.g., evaluation, placement) by a school.

Parental consent: Separate consent must be given for an evaluation and for services.

Access to educational records: All educational records and reports relating to a child are available to the parent.

Complaints: The opportunity to present and resolve complaints, including the time period in which to make a complaint; the opportunity for the agency to resolve the complaint; and the availability of mediation.

Pendency: The child's placement during pendency of due process proceedings is the current educational placement where the IEP is being implemented. This could be the regular classroom, a resource room, or more restrictive educational setting.

Mediation: Mediation is intended to be less costly and litigious than a formal due process hearing but definitely an underused option.

Placement: Requirements are outlined for the unilateral placement by parents of children in private schools at public expense. Interestingly enough, there is considerable litigation in special education regarding parents seeking reimbursement for private school attendance because of the belief that the public school was not providing an appropriate education.

Due process: The due process specified in IDEA and the regulations includes everything from notice, to resolution, to the notorious due process hearing. Many feel that this section of the regulations (Subpart E) is overly lengthy but this should be read by one and all who are concerned with the realities of due process under IDEA.

Appeals: State-level appeals (if applicable in that State).

Higher-level complaints: Complaints to the State Department of Education.

Lawsuits: Civil actions, including the time period in which to file such actions There can be a time to go to court, but this can be costly and is certainly unnerving. What to do if you are requested to appear at an impartial hearing? Focus on your area of expertise, especially specific examples of academic performance and classroom participation.

Attorneys' fees: The regulation reads that the court "may award reasonable attorneys' fees as part of the costs to the prevailing party.[142]

43. PRIOR WRITTEN NOTICE

Sequence: Referral, Notice, Consent, Evaluation

The prior written notice (PWN) is an expansion of the referral for the full and individual evaluation. Whereas the referral is a brief documentation of the problem, attempts to accommodate the problem in the regular classroom, and parent involvement, the prior written notice is sent to parents and provides the basis for the parent's consent for an individual evaluation or services. The classroom teacher should be familiar with the prior written notice content in that unsatisfactory classroom performance might be the basis for an action (e.g., the reason why a child is being referred for an individual evaluation). To this end classroom reports, test scores, classroom behavior might be cited as the basis for a proposed action. The elements of a prior written notice are as follows:

Action: A description of the action proposed or refused by the agency. For example, an initial "action" might be notice that an individual evaluation is requested to determine whether a child is a child with a disability.

Explanation: An explanation of why the agency proposes or refuses to take the action and a description of each evaluation procedure, assessment, record, or report the agency used as a basis for the proposed or refused action.

Safeguards: A statement that the parents of a child with a disability have protection under the procedural safeguards of this part and, if this notice is not an initial referral for evaluation, the means by which a copy of a description of the procedural safeguards can be obtained.

Help: Sources for parents to contact to obtain assistance in understanding the provisions of this part. Yes, schools must actually provide parents with information concerning sources who can translate the law and regulations into understandable English such as a parent Resource Center or qualified school personnel (e.g., Director of Special Education). Think all schools do this? Think again.

Options: A description of other options considered by the IEP Team and the reason why those options were rejected; and

Relevance: A description of the factors that are relevant to the agency's proposal or refusal.[143]

44. PARENT CONSENT

For children in private schools or home schooled, schools may not override a lack of parent consent for an initial evaluation.

Consent for evaluation or services is extremely important, yet often misunderstood. Problems involving consent for evaluation or services often arise because parents have been left out of the loop, parent input is not sought or, when given, not really considered. When the parent is an ally, when parent input is valued, the ability of the classroom teacher to include the child in the classroom is much easier. OK, not all parent input will be valued but give it a try. Seek advice from parents; respect what parents want on behalf of their child. You might not always agree; you might vehemently disagree, but respect parent views.

Consent and Evaluation

The consent for evaluation is often the initial benchmark for the length of time in which the evaluation must be completed. The IDEA-2004 requires that a determination of disability is made "within 60 days of receiving parental consent for the evaluation, or, if the State establishes a timeframe within which the evaluation must be conducted, within such timeframe." This timeframe does not apply if a child transfers and consent had already been given, or if "the parent of a child repeatedly fails or refuses to produce the child for the evaluation."[144]

A Big Change in the Law

There has been an important change in the law regarding parent consent. First, a parent must give consent before an initial evaluation is conducted. This is not new, but how this should be interpreted certainly is. If the parent does not consent to an individual evaluation, the school "may" pursue to override lack of consent by mediation or a due process hearing, but the Department of Education believes that schools should only use the consent override in rare circumstances.[145] For children in private schools or home schooled, schools may not override a lack of parent consent for an initial evaluation.

Although a State can override lack of parent consent for an initial evaluation by the arduous due process procedures, schools are silly to go beyond

113

simple mediation. Why? Because as per IDEA-2004 parents can refuse services. What is the point of requiring an initial evaluation if services are going to be refused? There is actually one situation in which due process procedures for an initial evaluation might be necessary and that is when there is a lack of consent. A parent may not be against special education services but for some reason does not provide consent because the school cannot locate the parents or when parent rights have been terminated.

> ▼ **Not every test or evaluation is considered an initial evaluation so that consent is not required for screening that will help teachers find appropriate instructional strategies.**

Consent for Services

Consent for services is an entirely different matter. Not giving consent for services or refusing consent for initial services is different than for initial evaluations. If the parent refuses consent or does not respond to a consent request for initial special education services, the school is no longer required to provide a Free Appropriate Public Education, to convene an IEP meeting, or to develop an IEP. In short if, for whatever reason, there is not written consent for services, the school is not authorized to provide services or to seek a due process hearing to require parents to consent to services.

The wording "initial receipt of services" or "initial provision of services" means that parent consent is not required every time a service is provided. The **initial** consent is **the** consent. If a parent is unhappy with a service after initial consent, this should be discussed with the special education teacher, the IEP Team, or resolved via complaint, mediation or a due process hearing.

45. MEDIATION[146]

Parents and schools should be given expanded opportunities to resolve their disagreements in positive and constructive ways.[147]

What do you tell parents when they are unhappy with a special education service or lack thereof? If a parent has complaint, the best practice is encourage the parent to discuss the problem with the person/persons providing (or not providing) the service or accommodation. If a parent is unhappy with regular classroom participation, the first step is to meet with the regular classroom teacher and the special education teacher. If a child is in a restrictive placement, and the parent is seeking a regular classroom placement, the regular classroom teacher can provide information concerning classroom and curriculum activities, and what might be necessary for successful classroom participation.

The IDEA also has several other mechanisms for resolving complaints. If at all possible, issues should be resolved informally. This is why the participation of the regular classroom teacher is so important. If the problem centers about the regular classroom and the ability to participate in the classroom, the classroom teacher cannot be ignored in attempts to resolve the issue. If a problem cannot be resolved informally, there are several approaches that can be used that are less litigious than the formal due process hearing. First, the school can arrange for parents to meet with a "disinterested party" at a time and location that is most convenient for you. This person can also explain the use and purpose of the mediation process. Second, a mediation process can be used to reconcile problems between parent and school. If the problem involves the regular classroom, the classroom teacher should be a part of this process. Key concepts for the classroom teacher: the mediation process is voluntary, confidential, and results in a legally binding agreement.

Several of the essential mediation requirements are as follows:

- **Mediation is voluntary. A school cannot threaten to use mediation as a scare tactic to coerce a parent.**

- **The mediation is conducted by a qualified and trained mediator.**

- **Although mediation is a way to avoid a due process complaint (and an impartial hearing) schools cannot use remediation as a way to avoid such complaints.**

- The State must keep a list of mediators.

- A written, signed mediation agreement under this paragraph is enforceable in any State court of competent jurisdiction or in a district court of the United States.

- Discussions that occur during the mediation process must be confidential and may not be used as evidence in any subsequent due process hearing or civil proceedings arising from that dispute.

- Impartiality of mediator. An individual who serves as a mediator may not be an employee of the school that is involved in the education or care of the child; and must not have a personal or professional interest that conflicts with the person's objectivity.

Part IV
Assessment

All children with disabilities are included in all general State and district-wide assessment programs, including assessments described under section 1111 of the Elementary and Secondary Education Act of 1965, with appropriate accommodations and alternate assessments where necessary and as indicated in their respective individualized education programs.[148]

46. FULL AND INDIVIDUAL EVALUATION

Evaluation means procedures used to determine whether a child has a disability and the nature and extent of the special education and related services that the child needs.[149]

Understanding what assessments and evaluation measures to use during the conduct of a full and individual evaluation must begin with a clear understanding of the purpose of the evaluation. A primary function of the evaluation is a determination of disability so that information (e.g., medical records), specialists (e.g., psychologists, audiologists, physician) and specialized assessments (e.g., surveys, disability-specific assessments, audiological and visual assessments) must be selected to identify possible causes for a child's performance.

The educational needs of the child and the **Present Levels of Academic Achievement** define the impact of the disability on educational performance (which is a requirement for a determination of disability) and provides important educational information relating to specific educational needs (e.g., percent of reading comprehension with grade-level material). The following is a list of the various elements that the full and individual evaluation must address:

- **Whether the child is a child with a disability;**

- **The educational needs of the child;**

- **The present levels of academic achievement and related developmental needs of the child;**

- **Whether the child needs special education and related services;**

- **Whether any additions or modifications to the special education and related services are needed to enable the child to meet the measurable annual goals set out in the individualized education program of the child and to participate, as appropriate, in the general education curriculum;[150]**

- **The content of the child's individualized education program, including information related to enabling the child to be involved in and progress in the general education curriculum, or, for preschool children, to participate in appropriate activities.[151]**

119

• **A comprehensive evaluation that is sufficient to identify all of the child's special education and related services needs, whether or not commonly linked to the disability category in which the child has been classified.[152]**

• **The gathering of relevant functional, developmental, and academic information, including information provided by the parent, that may assist in determining.[153]**

State-wide Assessments and Disabilities

Academic accountability for all students, including students with disabilities, under No Child Left Behind has reaffirmed the importance of the general curriculum.

The underlying rationale for including students with disabilities in school and state-wide assessments is that "when students with disabilities are part of the accountability system, educators' expectations for these students are more likely to increase." In addition, when students with disabilities are excluded from school accountability measures "the rates of referral of students for special education increase dramatically."[154] Why? When there is no need to emphasize the general curriculum, the importance of the regular classroom is diminished. When schools are accountable for the academic performance of all students, the essential role of the regular classroom and the regular classroom teacher in special education becomes readily apparent.

For the Classroom Teacher

Are you expected to spend hours and hours determining classroom needs, developing interventions, etc.? No, you are the classroom teacher and not the special education teacher. However, as the classroom teacher devoting 10 or 15 minutes to determine what a child with a disability needs to be successful in the classroom is not an extravagant amount of time, and what you do determine should be the basis for effective IEP development and implementation.

Classroom Need Report
Primary classroom needs?
Examples of classroom work?

Examples of specific classroom behavior?
Provide information concerning effective accommodations.
What have been effective classroom interventions?
What goals will enable classroom success?
What supports are needed to be successful in the classroom?

47. GRADES AND REPORT CARDS

Improving educational results for children with disabilities is an essential element of our national policy of ensuring equality of opportunity, full participation, independent living, and economic self-sufficiency for individuals with disabilities.[155]

Grades and report cards provide an extremely important gauge for measuring classroom participation and success. A standardized test measures a student's relative performance, but standardized test scores are only indirect measures of classroom performance. A standardized test does not measure the activities, assessments, reports, and classroom participation that provides an overall index of classroom success. The requirement is to educate children with disabilities with children who are not disabled, and classroom grades and report cards often provide the best index for achieving this goal. Yes, your grades, evaluations and reports are likely just as, or even more important than a standardized test.

If a student is not successful in the classroom, this lack of success should be reflected in the report card. One area in which report cards are especially useful is in the determination of **strengths** and **weaknesses**. A student might have extensive learning needs in reading but classroom performance in science and social studies might be satisfactory. This is extremely important information in that this successful classroom performance indicates a capability for success. Classroom performance and grades might help indicate the need for test accommodations (or not). If a student is receiving good grades in algebra, science and social studies without test accommodations, specifying IEP test accommodations in these areas might be overly restrictive.

What to Do?

Report cards: Examine report cards, if available, for several years.

- **Are there consistent trends from one year to the next?**
- **Are there certain areas that are always low?**
- **Are there areas in which the student shows definite strengths?**
- **Bring a student's report card to the IEP meeting.**

122

Classroom progress: Discuss classroom progress and what the student needs to do to be successful in the classroom.

Reasons: Identify specific areas (e.g., not doing homework, daily quizzes) that affect classroom performance and grades.

Grades: Consider grades at the IEP meeting.

Improvement: Grades should be used to help understand classroom performance. At the IEP meeting focus on ways in which classroom performance (and grades) can be improved.

Progress: Consider graphing grades. The following shows grades of E=Excellent, S=Satisfactory and D=Developing has been changed to a three-point scale (3=Excellent, etc.). This simple quantification is easily used to determine the average grade for each marking period and overall performance of 1.8125 on a scale from 3 (high) to 1 (low).

Subject	P1	P2	P3	P4
Social/Learning	1	2	1	1
Reading	2	2	1	1
Writing	2	1	1	1
Science	3	2	2	2
Social Studies	3	2	2	2
Mathematics	2	3	2	2
Music	2	2	2	2
Physical Education	2	2	2	1
Average	2.5	2.375	1.75	1.625

The above grades are easily converted to a chart as shown below to highlight important trends. Bring the chart to the meeting which will make more sense to team members than a list of standardized test scores. In addition to overall trends, examine grades for trends in specific courses or marking periods, or trends over an extended period of time.

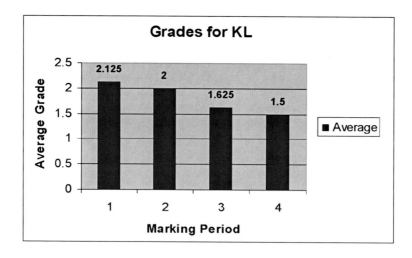

Important Grading Criteria

The following table shows what regular and special education teachers consider important grading criteria when evaluating secondary students in regular and special secondary classes.[156] As shown "daily class work" is an important criterion in all settings and this is an area where data is easily collected (use a simple portfolio of work samples, and date each sample). "Homework" might be considered of secondary importance to the special education teacher, but this is far from unimportant for the regular classroom teacher if not doing homework prevents success in the classroom.

Table 7. Grading Criteria Used By Regular and Special Education Teachers

Grading Criteria	Regular	Special	Grading Criteria	Regular	Special
Homework	62	48	Class participation	46	62
Tests	57	54	Standards	45	38
Attendance	57	76	Attitude/ behavior	36	64
Projects and activities	52	48	Portfolio	18	35
Daily class work	70	88	Compared to class	14	17

48. ASSESSMENT AND THE CLASSROOM TEACHER

The IEP must include a statement of any individual appropriate accommodations that are necessary to measure the academic achievement and functional performance of the child on State and district-wide assessments.[157]

The purpose of a full and individual evaluation is threefold: (1) to determine whether a child has a disability, (2) to determine the need for special education, and (3) to determine, if a child has a disability, the content of the IEP.[158] The following are essential assessment guidelines required by IDEA (and what they really mean):

1. Use a variety of assessment tools and strategies: ***don't just use IQ!!!***

2. Do not use any single procedure as the sole criterion: see above.

3. Use technically sound instruments: Most assessments are "technically sound." ***The real problem is what a test measures (validity).***

4. Assessments are not discriminatory on a racial or cultural basis. Give me a break...most tests, especially IQ tests, are racially/culturally biased.

5. Assessments are provided in the child's language or mode of communication: this should be obvious but often ignored when the child's language is other than English. ***Limited English Proficiency (LEP) English as a Second language (ESL) is not a disability, but this LEP/ESL can mask a disability or be misinterpreted as a disability.***

6. Evaluations are used for the purposes for which they are valid and reliable. So what is the exact use of IQ? Mostly to misplace students under the belief that a quantitative index means a valid index.

7. Evaluations are administered by trained and knowledgeable personnel. ***Read the manual.***

8. Assessments are given in accordance with instructions provided by the producer. ***Read the manual again.***

125

9. Assessments include those tailored to assess specific areas of educational need. ***This is really important when assessing a specific learning disability.***

10. Assessments are selected and administered so as best to ensure that if an assessment is administered to a child with impaired sensory, manual, or speaking skills, the assessment results accurately reflect the child's aptitude or achievement level or whatever other factors the test purports to measure, rather than reflecting the child's impaired sensory, manual, or speaking skills ***(unless those skills are the factors that the test purports to measure)***. This means that if you test reading, you do not read the test to the student. If you are testing spelling, you do not allow a child to use spellcheck. If you are testing the ability to write, you do not write/compose on behalf of the child. If reading a reading test is a permissible accommodation, you will not be able to assess reading ability or what might be needed to improve reading performance.

11. ***The child is assessed in all areas related to the suspected disability***, including, if appropriate, health, vision, hearing, social and emotional status, general intelligence, academic performance, communicative status, and motor abilities. I hope so.

12. ***The evaluation is sufficiently comprehensive to identify all of the child's special education and related services needs***, whether or not commonly linked to the disability category in which the child has been classified.

13. ***Assessment tools and strategies that provide relevant information*** that directly assist in determining the educational needs of the child. And ***relevant information*** means information that explains classroom performance and the ability to participate in the general curriculum.

Reevaluations

A change of placement requires a reevaluation if the school determines that the child's needs or services warrant a reevaluation or "the child's parents or **teacher** requests a reevaluation."[159] For the classroom teacher: If a child is in your classroom, and you believe that available data indicates that the child no longer needs special education, the IEP Team should consider the need for a reevaluation and the continuation of services. As the regular classroom teacher you might have important information concerning the need for special education, modification of services, or the need for classroom supports or accommodations. Remember that a child who does not need special education is not entitled to special education under IDEA (but is likely entitled to all needed services and accommodations under Section 504).

49. ACADEMIC ACHIEVEMENT

...to enable children with disabilities to meet the challenging State student academic achievement standards.[160]

The best "test" of academic achievement is determined by actual classroom performance. Standardized tests or diagnostic tests (especially in reading) are useful, but there is a tendency to ignore what the child actually does in the classroom, and to incorrectly assume that a test that marginally relates to actual classroom work will determine the problem. This is not so.

Consider a child who is not passing mathematics as reflected by the following scores on weekly tests: 47, 49, 51, 34, 24, 28. One approach to understanding these scores is to give another test (a test to understand a test) and somehow the various scores will reveal the cause of the problem. Of course, the second test (the diagnostic test) might not measure what was tested on the various quizzes, or the second test might measure **some** of the quiz material and **some** of what was done in the classroom. What we want to know is not information about unrelated concepts or skills, but why the student is not doing well on the quizzes.

In addition to the various test scores discussed at the IEP meeting, the classroom teacher can easily record scores on quizzes and classroom tests in an Excel spreadsheet, chart the results, and provide a useful and data-based graphic regarding classroom performance as shown in the below chart.

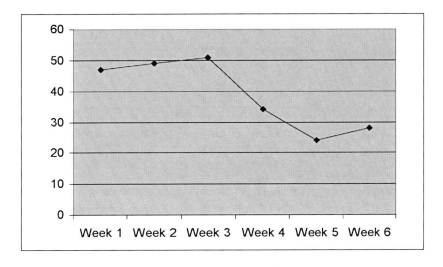

Rather than focusing solely on a variety of standardized tests at the IEP meeting, a better approach might be to highlight the quiz scores, consider reasons that might have impacted performance, **show an actual quiz**, then develop a plan to meet this specific classroom need. This is the essence of **Response to Intervention** or the use of "a process that determines if the child responds to scientific, research-based intervention."

Assume that the child study team (the "prereferral team") determines that the reason for poor quiz performance is a failure to complete homework assignments which is caused by a failure to understand the material. The systematic instruction might entail (1) working with parents to ensure that homework is completed, (2) several minutes (not hours of remediation but "several minutes") of individualized help to ensure that basic concepts are understood, and (3) providing daily classroom problems (in quiz format) to further ensure that the material is understood. The test for the effectiveness of this plan is whether or not performance improves. If performance improves, good plan; if performance does not improve, modify plan.

> ▼ **"If the student shows adequate progress with prereferral activities – modifications and interventions – a referral to consider a special education evaluation may be unnecessary. However, if modifications and interventions must be provided on an ongoing basis, or if the student shows limited or no progress, a referral to consider a special education evaluation is warranted."**[161]

Will this guarantee successful performance? Of course not, but this does represent the rudiments of a "reasonably calculated" plan to enable successful participation in the general curriculum prior to referral for special education. After six weeks of "systematic instruction" pre- and post-scores are easily compared as follows:

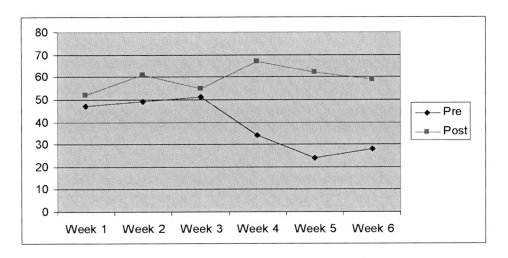

Improvement? A bit; not earth shaking, but improvement nonetheless. Enough improvement to suggest that the Child Study Team, the teacher, the parents and the child might be on a road to success, or at least enough success to see a light at the end of the tunnel.

If there is one area of assessment that is consistently ignored at IEP meetings it is real and documented areas of academic performance. These areas include data relating to

- **Grade book**
- **Attendance**
- **Basic reading skills**
- **Classroom behavior**
- **Essays**
- **Homework**
- **Informal reading inventories**
- **Observations**
- **Oral reading**
- **Projects**
- **Quizzes**
- **Reading comprehension**
- **Reading fluency**
- **Teacher ratings**
- **Tests**
- **Work samples**
- **Work sheets**

50. ANNUAL YEARLY PROGRESS

NCLB goal: to ensure that all students make Adequate Yearly Progress.

Yet another No Child Left Behind catchphrase: Annual Yearly Progress or AYP. Consider a child with multiple disabilities involving language, social and self-help skills. If this child is unable to communicate basic needs, can this child, should this child, participate in academic assessments? Well, the answer is that taking an academic assessment in this situation is not only meaningless but IDEA does not require regular assessments for all children with severe needs. Rather, IDEA requires schools to develop alternate assessments which are "are aligned with the State's challenging academic content standards and challenging student academic achievement standards."

Of the many criticisms of NCLB none is more controversial than the accountability system required by States to ensure that all students make Adequate Yearly Progress (the much used AYP acronym) which refers to "sanctions and rewards that the State will use to hold public elementary and secondary schools accountable for student achievement and for making AYP."[162] For students with the most significant cognitive disabilities proficiency can be based on the alternate academic achievement standards "provided that the number of those students who score at the proficient or advanced level on those alternate achievement standards at the LEA and at the State levels, separately, does not exceed 1.0 percent of all students in the grades assessed in reading/language arts and in mathematics."[163] The expectation is that this one percent cap will result in no more than nine percent of all children with disabilities taking alternate assessments.

The Role of the Classroom Teacher

Schools are required to provide alternate assessments that are aligned with the State's standards to measure the achievement of children with disabilities.[164] In Illinois a goal is to apply word analysis skills and recognize new words, while a corresponding alternate goal entails reacting to the sound of language and demonstrating understanding that pictures, symbols, signs, and objects have meaning.[165]

The classroom teacher should be aware of alternate assessments defined by the State, and how these assessments are measured and scored. A portfolio might be used to measure alternate assessment performance, and the classroom teacher can help identify items (e.g., classroom work/performance) that measure the various goals. Although a student might have a severe disability that limits participation in Statewide assessments, the classroom teacher will be able to provide input concerning the performance of all students in the classroom regardless of the extent of the disability.

A child participating in an alternate assessment will probably not be included in all general curriculum activities, but the classroom teacher can nonetheless provide input using a simple rubric to evaluate the activities in which the child is able to participate. For example, the extent of participation in a language arts activity might be evaluated by the following rubric.

1. **Able to perform with little help or cues** (over 90% independence)

2. **Requires occasional help** (over 70% independence)

3. **Student requires considerable help to achieve goal** (over 40% independence)

4. **Student requires a high level of help, prompts and cues to achieve goal** (less than 40% independence)

51. EVALUATION IN THE CLASSROOM

Appropriate instructional strategies for curriculum implementation shall not be considered to be an evaluation for eligibility for special education and related services.[166]

There is sometimes a belief that the regular classroom teacher is not able to evaluate students with disabilities. This is not true. What the classroom teacher cannot do is conduct an individual evaluation to determine eligibility for special education. If the classroom teacher suspects a disability, an evaluation cannot be administered for the specific purpose of determining the disability, or needed services and accommodations, without abiding by the various procedural rights entitled to every parent (e.g., prior written notice, etc.).

Screening

The law specifically states that "the screening of a student by a teacher or specialist to determine appropriate instructional strategies for curriculum implementation shall not be considered to be an evaluation for eligibility for special education and related services."[167] Implicit in this rule is an understanding that a teacher has a responsibility to evaluate and determine "appropriate instructional strategies." Of course, the effectiveness of appropriate instructional strategies in the classroom is also a part of the individual evaluation.

Full and Individual Evaluation

Before a full and individual evaluation is conducted, the school must give the parents prior written notice which includes an explanation "of each evaluation procedure, assessment, record, or report the agency used as a basis for the proposed" evaluation to determine eligibility for special education and the need for special education."[168] The classroom teacher is in a unique position to provide information to the evaluation team concerning a child's classroom needs and what accommodations have been effective for meeting these needs. The classroom teacher is certainly not responsible for the more detailed assessment of a child. Nonetheless, assessments used to determine instructional needs, assessments used with all children, grades, quizzes and observational reports and ratings are important in the overall evaluation of classroom performance.

Eligibility for Services

Two factors determine eligibility for services under IDEA: (1) meeting the criteria for one of the 13 disabilities listed in the regulations for IDEA, and (2) the need for special education. If either condition is not met, the evaluation team must determine that a child is not eligible for services, related services or **accommodations** under IDEA. If special education is not needed, a child cannot receive related services such as speech therapy, social work, physical therapy, and so on. When special education is not needed, but a child has a disability that requires an accommodation or service, the accommodation or service must be provided under Section 504.

Remember that disability is not synonymous with the need for services or accommodations. A child might have a disability and not need special education or accommodations; a child might have a disability and the parent might refuse services; or a child might have a disability and only need a related service (e.g., speech) or an accommodation (e.g., a special chair, desk, a humidifier).

Disability Determination

Who determines whether or not a child has a disability? This is determined by "a group of qualified professionals and the parent" following the completion of all evaluations and assessments. The determination of eligibility is drawn from a variety of sources and documented in an evaluation report and "carefully considered." The sources that must be considered include aptitude assessments, achievement tests, parent input, teacher recommendations, physical condition, social or cultural background, and adaptive behavior.

Is the classroom teacher ever a part of the team that determines disability? Very possibly. Often the IEP Team has a dual role of overseeing the individual evaluation, determining disability, and then developing an appropriate IEP. When this is the case, the classroom is part of the "qualified group of professionals" who make the determination of disability by virtue of being a member of the IEP Team. In New York, an individual evaluation of a referred student is made by a Committee on Special Education or CSE and includes "a variety of assessment tools and strategies, including information provided by the parent, to gather relevant functional, developmental and academic information about the student that may assist in determining whether the student is a student with a disability and the content of the student's individualized education program, including information related to enabling the student to participate and progress in the general education curriculum."[169]

52. SPECIFIC LEARNING DISABILITIES

Approximately 47% of children with specific learning disabilities have regular classroom placements.

The IDEA definition of a specific learning disability (SLD) will not provide much assistance when attempting to determine whether a child has a SLD. The problems associated with specific learning disabilities are many but a major change is underway in the determination of a specific learning disability from a discrepancy model (a discrepancy between mental ability and achievement) to a response-to-intervention. But exactly what is a specific learning disability? A specific learning disability entails four areas: (1) meaning, (2) manifestation, (3) conditions, and (4) exclusions.

A. **Meaning:** specific learning disability means a disorder in one or more of the basic psychological processes involved in understanding or in using language, spoken or written,

B. **Manifestation:** that may manifest itself in the imperfect ability to
   - listen
   - think
   - speak
   - read
   - write
   - spell
   - do mathematical calculations

C. **Conditions:** including conditions such as
   - perceptual disabilities
   - brain injury
   - minimal brain dysfunction
   - dyslexia
   - and developmental aphasia

D. **Exclusions:** Specific learning disability does not include learning problems that are primarily the result of
   - Visual impairments
   - Hearing impairments
   - motor disabilities
   - mental retardation
   - emotional disturbance
   - environmental disadvantage
   - cultural disadvantage
   - or economic disadvantage

To this list can be added limited English proficiency and lack of instruction. In addition to the many factors that can preclude the definition SLD, other disabilities are not always easily differentiated from SLD. For example, SLD is often difficult to differentiate from emotional disturbance or ADD/ADHD. In the case of emotional disturbance the question is whether the specific learning disability causes the emotional disturbance or vice versa. Although ADD/ADHD can be reported under the Other Health Impairment category, ADD/ADHD is a frequently reported as a characteristic of SLD. In the 25th annual report to congress 41 percent of parents reported ADD/ADHD a characteristic of SLD.[170]

Specific Learning Disability Checklist
☐ Below average performance
☐ Research-based instruction prior to referral
☐ Repeated measurements
☐ Below average in one of the eight designated areas
☐ A pattern of strengths and weaknesses
☐ Failure to meet State standards
☐ Not the result of MR, ED, cultural, environmental or instruction
☐ Mental ability/Achievement discrepancy

The IDEA-2004 has made extensive modifications to the conceptualization of a specific learning disability. Prior to IDEA-2004 the essence of a specific learning disability was a discrepancy between mental ability (viz., IQ) and achievement. The regulations for IDEA-2004 deemphasize the discrepancy model so that the evaluation of a specific learning disability "must permit the use of a process that determines if the child responds to scientific, research-based intervention" or "the use of other alternative research-based procedures for determining whether a child has a specific learning disability.[171] States are no longer required to use a discrepancy model and may actually prohibit using a discrepancy between mental ability and achievement when determining a specific learning disability.[172]

What to Do?

Below average performance: A specific learning disability involves below average performance, commensurate with the child's age or State-approved grade level standards after having been provided with appropriate learning experiences in listening comprehension, oral expression, basic reading skills, etc.[173] The prevailing concept in SLD is the emphasis on appropriate instruction and learning experiences before referral and before disability determination. The classroom teacher is actually at the forefront of reducing the number of children with SLD by providing appropriate instruction and learning experiences.

RTI: Critical to the new conceptualization of a specific learning disability is the provision of appropriate high-quality, research-based instruction in regular education settings.[174] The response-to-intervention (RTI) model requires data-based documentation of repeated assessments of achievement at reasonable intervals, reflecting formal assessment of student progress during instruction.[175] Obviously, the classroom teacher is key to the RTI approach to SLD in that this data-based, systematic and high-quality instruction is within the province of regular and not special education. Thus, a child cannot have a SLD due to lack of appropriate instruction in reading, if child was not provided appropriate instruction in regular education settings, or for lack of data-based documentation of student progress.[176]

Disabilities: The areas in which a child can have a specific learning disability has increased from seven to eight by the addition of **reading fluency skills** and includes oral expression, listening comprehension. written expression, basic reading skill, reading fluency skills, reading comprehension, mathematics calculation, and mathematics problem solving.

Area	Ability (1 = poor...5 = good)				
Listening Comprehension	1	2	3	4	5
Oral Expression					
Basic Reading Skills					
Reading Fluency Skills					
Reading Comprehension					
Written Expression					
Mathematics Calculation					
Mathematics Problem Solving					

Standard: The primary standard for assessment is a failure to make progress "to meet State-approved results...when assessed with a response to scientific, research-based intervention process."[177]

Pattern: One of the deficiencies of specific learning disabilities has always been the lack of "specificity." Many IEPs indicate that a child has specific learning disabilities in all areas but no attempt is made to specify the disability or to denote strengths and weakness. As per IDEA-2004 a child must exhibit a pattern of strengths and weaknesses in performance, achievement or both, relative to age, State standards, or intellectual ability.

Exclusions: As with prior versions of IDEA a child cannot have a specific learning disability as a result of (1) visual, hearing, or motor disability; (2) mental retardation; (3) emotional disturbance; (4) cultural factors; (5) environmental or economic disadvantage; or (6) if the determinant factor identification is a lack of appropriate instruction in reading, lack if instruction in mathematics, or Limited English proficiency.[178]

Determining a Specific Learning Disability

First, remember to focus on the "specific" of a specific learning disability. There is no such thing as a "general" learning disability to explain away any and all problems. A specific learning disability occurs when a child's educational achievement is not commensurate with the child's age in one or more of the following areas when provided with high quality instruction:

1. **Oral expression**

2. **Listening comprehension**

3. **Written expression**

4. **Basic reading skill**

5. **Reading fluency skills**

6. **Reading comprehension**

7. **Mathematics calculation**

8. **Mathematics problem solving**[179]

To have a specific learning disability a child has a disability in one of the eight areas defined in the regulations (and shown immediately above). Thus, a child has a specific learning disability in _____ (oral expression, listening comprehension, etc.). A child does not simply have a specific learning disability.

> ## New SLD Category: Reading Fluency
>
> **Reading fluency is defined by the NCLB act as one of the essential components of reading instruction and has therefore been added to the list of IDEA specific learning disability categories. Reading fluency allows a reader to read text smoothly so that the task is not focused on individual word recognition/identification but to read and comprehend connected text.**

Second, high quality instruction by qualified personnel is part of the referral process and must be provided prior to a determination of a SLD. As was said, the classroom teacher plays an important role not only in determining the existence of a SLD, but reducing the overuse of this category by providing high-quality, systematic, and data-based instruction.

Third, the collection of actual data that shows progress (or lack thereof) "reflecting formal assessment of progress during instruction through repeated assessments of achievement at reasonable intervals is provided to the parents."[180]

Fourth, The determination of a specific learning disability requires "a finding that the child failed to make sufficient progress in meeting State approved results when using a response to scientific, research-based intervention process, or the child exhibits a pattern of strengths and weaknesses that the team determines is relevant to the identification of an SLD. The pattern of strengths and weaknesses may be in performance, achievement, or both or may be in performance, achievement, or both relative to intellectual development."[181]

Fifth, focus on the fundamental problem. If a child has difficulty with basic reading skills, of course the child will likely have difficulty writing. But writing is not the basic problem and not the "specific" learning disability. Writing could be a problem, but until the child develops adequate reading skill the child will obviously have difficulty writing. Likewise, if a child lacks reading fluency, reading comprehension will likely be affected. If the child exhibits normal comprehension skills in other areas, poor reading comprehension might be an artifact of poor reading fluency.

Sixth, sensory factors, poor overall cognitive skill, emotional problems, cultural factors, environmental or economic disadvantage, and lack of instruction can preclude the determination of a specific learning disability.

By the Numbers

How do you determine a discrepancy between mental ability and achievement? Here is how it is done but if there is one section in this book that can be skipped, this it is! Prior to IDEA-2004 a key component of specific learning disabilities was a difference between mental ability and achievement. In other words, to have a specific learning disability a child's IQ score was required to be higher than achievement. For example, if a child's IQ is 100 and the child is below average in reading, this would be a discrepancy. There is even a formula to determine a 50 percent discrepancy which is

$$CA\left(\frac{IQ}{300} + .17\right) - 2.5$$

Example: If a child's age is 10 (CA=10) and the child's IQ is 70, the discrepancy would be

$$10.0\left(\frac{70}{300} + .17\right) - 2.5$$

For a child with a CA of 10, an IQ of 70, the expected achievement (based on that nasty IQ index) is 3.0, or, based on a CA of 10 and an IQ of 70, you would **expect** an achievement level of 3.0. So, 50 percent of this expected achievement is 1.5 which means that the discrepancy between the actual achievement of a child with a CA of 10 and an IQ of 70, would need to be greater than 1.5 years to be a significant discrepancy. For a child with a CA of 10, an IQ of 70 and a grade achievement of 2.0? No discrepancy. For a child with a CA of 10, an IQ of 70 and a grade achievement of 1.4? A significant discrepancy (using the above formula).

With a heavy heart I suggest you not use this formula . . . or any formula! Confession: I have dabbled in many a statistical analysis relating to discrepancy formulas and the fact is that all formulas are flawed for the simple reason that all are based on IQ. In that IQ measures learning, prior instruction, economic advantage (or disadvantage), cultural factors, probably (to some degree) basic intelligence, and everything else, including the kitchen sink, using IQ as an index of potential is wrong from the beginning.

▼ **For the classroom teacher: don't use IQ to determine a discrepancy. If you think a child can achieve, can grow, can learn, you are saying that there is a discrepancy between what the child does and what the child can do. For determining a discrepancy this is not only simple but more sensitive and productive than comparing several standardized scores.**

An important reinterpretation of specific learning disabilities is the belief that the IQ discrepancy model places too much emphasis on standardized scores and little or no consideration is given to intervention. The current RTI approach to SLD, based on systematic assessment of high quality, research-based general education instruction, places emphasis on evaluation that promotes instruction.

---

34 CFR 300.8(b)(6) SPECIFIC LEARNING DISABILITIES. –

(A) IN GENERAL. – Notwithstanding section 607(b), when determining whether a child has a specific learning disability as defined in section 602, a local educational agency shall not be required to take into consideration whether a child has a severe discrepancy between achievement and intellectual ability in oral expression, listening comprehension, written expression, basic reading skill, reading comprehension, mathematical calculation, or mathematical reasoning.

(B) ADDITIONAL AUTHORITY. – In determining whether a child has a specific learning disability, a local educational agency may use a process that determines if the child responds to scientific, research-based intervention as a part of the evaluation procedures described in paragraphs (2) and (3).

53. THE SAD STORY OF IQ

There are not many good things that you can say about IQ tests, IQ scores, or the use of IQ . . . for anything. To make matters even worse an IQ is not really an IQ. Anyway, here is the sad story. At one time IQ meant an Intelligence Quotient that was determined by first finding a child's mental age using a standardized test. For example, a child is able to copy a diamond. The child is given several months credit in the mental ability category. After a whole bunch of tasks are given, Voilà, you have a mental age or MA. This is how it was done in the good old days . . . or at least the old days.

After a mental age had been determined a quotient between mental ability (MA) and chronological age (CA) was found by the famous (infamous) formula MA/CA(100). Books still mention this formula (this book!) but the formula is rarely used because IQ is actually not a quotient but a standard deviation. In other words an IQ of 85 indicates that the score is one standard deviation below the mean. Virtually all reputable IQ tests (this might be a misnomer) report scores as standard scores so that an IQ is not a quotient but a score that indicates the number of standard deviations a score is above or below the mean.

Do you need to know any of this? Not at all. The only thing to keep in mind is that IQ is not an Intelligence Quotient but a score on a test comprised of a lot of idiosyncratic tasks that often has little bearing on the complexity of human intelligence . . . and often even less on what you do in the regular classroom.

Unfortunately, and contrary to the law and regulations, many decisions are made on the basis of IQ. The IQ is really a nasty little index and no matter how clear the guidelines are for not using IQ, children are classified as disabled (especially mentally retarded) and removed from classrooms based on little more than an IQ score. Ok, the score business is a bit irksome but the real problem with IQ is that it measures all sorts of things besides intelligence including culture, learning experiences, education, social-economic factors . . . the list is endless.

Classroom Teacher Tips

IQ is not "the" answer. The test will tell you nothing of use. If a child has difficulty reading, listen to the child read and not have someone discuss the meaning of child's ability to repeat a series of digits backward. Oh, it means you can (or cannot) read a series of digits backwards . . . good life skill!

The "gut feeling test." If your "gut feeling" is that a child has intellectual potential, go with that feeling.

Classroom assessments. Believe in classroom assessments and classroom behavior as the best index of classroom performance (and this is sort of obvious)...but you must believe in what you do as actually being more precise and more accurate, and more everything than the alleged precision of an IQ score.

Don't be hoodwinked. If you need an IQ test to determine whether a child has cognitive needs that require special education, you have not done a very good job of evaluating the child's needs. If a child has extensive self-help, language, and social needs, you hardly need an IQ test to tell you that the child needs to learn to dress, use a glass, etc.

Get real. Often mental retardation requires a score below 70. If one child is classified as retarded because of a score of 69 and another not because of a score one point higher, even by IQ standards this is a pathetic interpretation of IQ scores.

Mental retardation. This is simply a nasty term. Why not use a child with cognitive or developmental needs? Better yet, simply state specific areas of need such as self-help, social, language, physical needs, etc.

IQ is not a good index of potential. We can estimate and guestimate all we want, but gauging a child's potential is risky. Remember the story of the self-fulfilling prophecy: If a teacher is told a child has a certain potential, there is a tendency to behave (and teach) that will fulfill the prophecy. Maybe we should call IQ the IQP or IQ-prophecy score?

Have high expectations. Congress included in IDEA a finding that after "almost 30 years of research and experience has demonstrated that the education of children with disabilities can be made more effective by having high expectations for such children and ensuring their access to the general education curriculum in the regular classroom, to the maximum extent possible."[182]

54. SPEECH/LANGUAGE IMPAIRMENT

Over 86% of children identified as having speech or language impairments have regular classroom placements.

A speech or language impairment is defined in the regulations as a communication disorder, such as stuttering, impaired articulation, a language impairment, or a voice impairment, that adversely affects a child's educational performance.[183] Speech or language impairment constitutes the second largest disability category (1,112,119 or 18.66%) of children receiving IDEA services. Based on data for the 2000–01 school year over 85 percent of children receiving speech or language services under IDEA receive these services in the regular classroom.[184]

A speech or language impairment can require either special education services or a related service. The difference is this: A speech or language disability requires specially designed instruction which focuses on speech or language; when speech or language is a related service, the service is provided to enable a child with a disability other than speech or language to benefit from special education. A child can also receive speech or language services under Section 504 if the impairment limits a major life activity (speech or language) but does not require specially designed instruction.

▼ **For the classroom teacher: help the child with a disability to generalize speech/language skills acquired in a one-to-one remedial setting to nonremedial classroom situations.**

Assessment

All children will exhibit some degree of nonfluency or irregular speech and/or language on occasion. This is normal. Not every nonfluency event rises to the level of disorder or impairment. If a child does have a speech or language impairment, the child may need specially designed instruction or a specific service/accommodation. Obviously age is an important factor and many nonfluent speech patterns will simply cease without intervention. Remember there is a concept referred to as "normal dysfluency." Here are several speech intelligibility benchmarks:

18 months: speech is 25% intelligible

24 months: speech is 50–75% intelligible

36 months: speech is 75–100% intelligible

There is an important distinction between speech and language disorders. Speech disorders can range from dysfluency problems (stuttering) to specific articulation problems which include omission errors (**ar** for **car**, **ensa** for **pencil**), substitution errors (**wun** for **run**, **pen** for **ben**, **thaw** for **saw**) and distortions. Language disorders can be a far greater problem than speech disorders. Language disorders can involve understanding or expressing ideas, limited vocabulary, the ability to formulate syntax (e.g., *I home go* rather than *I go home*), and verbal recall.

Classroom Teacher Tips

☞ **Speech and language requires real-life practice and the regular classroom is a great "real-life place."**

☞ **The essence of speech therapy is to generalize to real-life situations. Meet with the speech therapist to discuss how skills can be generalized.**

☞ **The curriculum can be an important part of the material used for therapy.**

☞ **The speech specialists and classroom teacher should collaborate to develop successful communication experiences.**

☞ **Consider speech or language as a related service for every child with a disability. A common area of noncompliance is to not consider speech or language for all disability categories.**

☞ **Help identify specific speech or language goals in a child's IEP to better enable classroom success.**

Behavior, Language and Sensory Impairment

Children with hearing impairments will most likely have speech and language difficulties. According to the IDEA regulations a *hearing impairment* means an impairment in hearing, whether permanent or fluctuating, that adversely affects a child's educational performance but that is not included under the definition of deafness. Deafness means a hearing impairment that is so severe that the child is impaired in processing linguistic information through hearing, with or without amplification, that adversely affects a child's educational performance.[185]

For a child who is deaf the need for evaluation/services is often indicated before school because of a lack of language development, limited or poor speech development, good social development and good cognitive skills. For a child with a hearing loss, the clues might be less than obvious. For the classroom teacher consider the behaviors listed below, especially in conjunction with speech/language difficulties.

Hearing Checklist	
☐	Does not turn head when spoken to
☐	Does not respond when spoken to
☐	Is startled or aware of noises/sounds
☐	Articulation errors
☐	Language disorders (e.g., voice, syntax, vocabulary)
☐	Nasality
☐	Very loud speaking voice
☐	Very soft speaking voice
☐	Does not follow directions
☐	Difficulty following conversation
☐	Problems involving language arts
☐	Difficulty understanding speech or language

Teacher Tips

For the classroom teacher an essential task is to include children with hearing impairments in language activities; talk and listen to children with hearing impairments. For a child with a hearing impairment, communication is a primary need. A child might be difficult to understand or not; no matter, communicate. Communication is what a child with a hearing impairment needs, so communicate. Also, be sure that all necessary devices are being used and are working (e.g., hearing aids).

- Make sure that amplification devices are used.
- Ensure task comprehension.
- Read the child's IEP for permissible test accommodations.
- Always consider preferential seating (near the teacher).
- Don't exaggerate speech when speaking.
- Make sure that there is eye contact when speaking.
- If there is an interpreter, speak to the child.
- Write all assignments on the board (which is good for all).
- Use captioned films.
- More, not less, communication experiences are needed.
- If a child signs, learn a sign or two (it's fun).
- No, you don't sign a reading test.
- Rule: No special treatment.

55. MEASURING READING FLUENCY

Reading fluency: the latest addition to the Specific Learning Disabilities categories.

The following is not intended to be a definitive guide for assessing reading fluency but rather to provide the classroom teacher with several easy-to-use and effective strategies for measuring reading fluency. These techniques can be used with all children but for a child with a suspected disability, or a child who is already receiving services, information concerning reading fluency can be used at IEP meetings, for reporting progress to parents, and for selecting appropriate measurable annual goals and accommodations.

▼ Repeated Oral Reading: "The best strategy for developing reading fluency is to provide your students with many opportunities to read the same passage orally several times."[186]

Oral Reading

Have two copies of a reading passage, one for the student and one for the teacher. Have the child read the passage and note errors such as word substitutions, word deletions, unknown words, pronunciation. Indicate pauses between words by a /. To score count the number of errors (word errors), and the number of pauses (slash marks). This basic information will provide a benchmark for evaluating future performance and for determining measurable annual goals.

Basic oral reading data can yield several reading fluency scores: Divide the number of errors by the number of words in the reading passage and multiply by 100. Do the same for the number of pauses. If either percentage is greater than 10 percent, the child is likely experiencing difficulty when reading. If the second percentage (pauses) is greater than 20 percent, or there is a 10 percent discrepancy between the error and pause percentage, reading dysfluency is a likely problem.

Reading Rate

There are a variety of estimates as to how many words a student should read per minute at different grade levels. No matter what estimate is used factors such as content, vocabulary, grade level material and general interest will all affect the number of words read per minute. If a child's reading at a rate significantly low (see chart below), reading fluency might be a matter for concern. The following provides a general guideline for grade level reading rates.

Grade level	WPM
1	50
2	85
3	110
4	135
5	160
6	185

Assessment: Determine the amount of time in seconds a student reads a passage. This is a good activity for the entire class and not just for a child with a disability. Determine the number of words in the passage, divide by the number of seconds, and multiply by 60. Words read per minute is determined by

WPM = Words / Seconds x 60

If students read a 560 word passage in 5 minutes and 10 seconds, WPM would be determined by 560/310 x 60 or 108 words per minute. A second index is the number of words correctly read per minute (WCPM). If a child correctly reads 500 of 560 words in 5 minutes and 10 seconds, WCPM would be 500/310 x 60 or 96 words read correctly per minute.

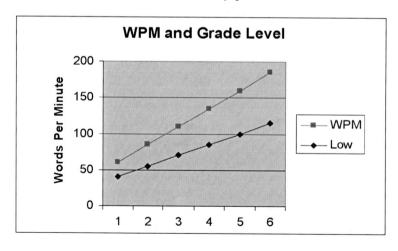

Reading rate is contingent on many factors such as motivation, content, readability, etc. There is no ideal reading rate, but if a child's rate is extremely slow, the lack of connectedness between words for the nonfluent reader, will detract from reading comprehension. A simple reading rate for classroom material is also a nice index to bring to the IEP meeting. Reading rate might help understand a child's reading needs, and serve as a benchmark for gauging progress via a measurable annual goal.

Tips for Improving Reading Fluency

More: the more we read, the better we get.

Prereading: Before reading a passage have the students preread the material and then discuss important details, characters, plot, etc.

Highlighting: Provide the class (student) with a list of new or difficult words.

Word attack: Develop word attack skills such as structural analysis, context clues. Less time decoding specific words will result in greater fluency.

Dictionary: Develop dictionary skills. Help the student become an independent reader, able to independently determine word meanings.

Model: Read to the class to model reading skills.

Importance: Focus on important or critical vocabulary words.

Repeated reading: Let the child experience fluency with repeated readings of short passages or even sentences.

Tape-assisted reading: With so much available on tape many tape-assisted exercises can be designed to improve reading fluency.

Choral reading: Great for improving reading fluency.

Partner reading: Have two students read alternate passages or sentences.

Rereading: The teacher reads a sentence and the students repeats the sentence.

56. MEASURING READING VOCABULARY

No single standard of vocabulary assessment emerged from the studies reviewed. However, the panel concluded that appropriate conclusions about instruction are derived when the assessments match the instruction. This will provide better information about the specific learning of the students related directly to that instruction.[187]

Measuring content vocabulary is relatively simple, and content vocabulary data is extremely useful for assessing levels of performance and progress. For the classroom teacher measuring reading in the content area can be useful for all children, and can provide classroom-based data that can be used as part of an individual evaluation and to develop appropriate IEP goals.

Content area vocabulary can be measured by developing a bank of content area words. Select content words prior to a lesson and determine which words are recognized and which are not. The key words can be used as a study guide and also as a source for content vocabulary assessment.

The consultant teacher or special education teacher can easily create a content vocabulary word bank using 3 x 5 cards (one word per card) or a Microsoft Word file. Words can be periodically reviewed, or used to assess content vocabulary as part of the periodic progress reports. Adding several words to the word bank (e.g., conduction, optimization, topography, etc.), or having the student add words, is not time-consuming and a very efficient way to focus on specific vocabulary needs.

57. MEASURING READING COMPREHENSION

An effective assessment system should provide not only important information about a child's relative standing in appropriate normative populations (school, state, and national norms groups), but also important information about the child's relative strengths and weaknesses for purposes of educational planning.[188]

You attend an IEP meeting and learn that a goal for a student is to comprehend what is read at the 85 percent level as determined by teacher observation. Ok. You are the teacher so exactly how were you able to make this observation of reading, and then translate what you observed into a percentage?

▼ **For the classroom teacher: If an IEP goal is to comprehend grade-level content at the 85% level as determined by teacher observation, be able to specify the beginning level of performance.**

Before the IEP meeting take a few minutes to reflect on the child's reading. This is not a question of grades, standardized tests and so on, but rather what you think about a child's reading in the classroom. The simplest method for doing this would be to give a holistic rating much like you would give a grade to a student project. For example, your estimation might be that the child comprehends 65 percent of what is read based on your observations. Not exactly a data-based index, and probably not all that precise, but at least a percentage is generated.

You can be a little more exact by an informal evaluation of the child's various reading skills by means of a checklist (and add or delete checklist categories as deem appropriate.

☐	**Reads fluently**
☐	**Self-corrects**
☐	**Reads for understanding**
☐	**Comprehends main idea**
☐	**Understands and setting**

☐	**Identifies characters and sequence**
☐	**Knows basic vocabulary**
☐	**Knows technical words**
☐	**Can summarize material**
☐	**Can evaluate text**

A rating scale could also be used to rate various components of reading comprehension. The above checklist could be converted to a rating scale as follows:

Skill	Developing	Satisfactory	Excellent
Reads fluently	1	2	3
Self-corrects	1	2	3
Reads for understanding	1	2	3
Comprehends main idea	1	2	3
Understands and setting	1	2	3
Identifies characters and sequence	1	2	3
Knows basic vocabulary	1	2	3
Knows technical words	1	2	3
Can summarize material	1	2	3
Can evaluate text	1	2	3

Decide what information will best discern a child's classroom performance. You might want to focus on reading comprehension, and then create a reading comprehension rating for different content areas. The scale shown below is comprised of 15 items and each item is rated via a 5-point scale. If the sum of a student's rating is 24, and the maximum overall rating is 75, the percentage is 24/75 x 100 or 32 percent. Is this better than a single holistic rating? Probable in that more items make for a more reliable rating scale.

Ability to comprehend	Low		OK		Good
Understands plot/theme	1	2	3	4	5
Fiction	1	2	3	4	5
Grade level material	1	2	3	4	5
Math content	1	2	3	4	5
Sequence of events/ideas	1	2	3	4	5
Science content	1	2	3	4	5
Social studies content	1	2	3	4	5
Knows main characters	1	2	3	4	5
Summarizes	1	2	3	4	5
Draws inferences	1	2	3	4	5
Remembers detail	1	2	3	4	5
Understands basic concepts	1	2	3	4	5
Makes connections	1	2	3	4	5
Understands vocabulary	1	2	3	4	5
Evaluates material	1	2	3	4	5

Question/Answer

A question/answer assessment of reading comprehension can be either informal or quasi-formal. Following the reading of a passage ask questions relating to detail (e.g., names, location, dates, etc.), plot, characters, and sequence. The goal is not to evaluate every bit of information in the passage but to focus on basic reading comprehension and understanding. Questions should be clear and straightforward. Reason: the more time spent on individual questions (and answers), the less focus will be on explicit reading comprehension. Record the number of questions asked and correctly answered. You might have asked 10 questions and the child answered two correctly for a percentage of 2/10 x 100 = 20%. Over a period of time this data will provide useful benchmark information for developing goals and measuring progress.

Cloze Technique

The cloze technique entails deleting words from a passage and then having the child read the passage and insert the missing words. The cloze procedure is useful because it is an easy task to construct (simply delete words from a reading section) and can be used with a variety of content. When selecting words to delete, one recommended approach is to delete words using a specific word count such as deleting every fifth or seventh word. I would not do this. The idea is to measure comprehension and not the ability to succeed on an esoteric cloze task. For children with reading comprehension needs, a traditional cloze task can result in an incomprehensible passage of missing words. Use a modified cloze technique in which specific content area words are deleted. The resulting task can be used by the entire class, and specific vocabulary words are highlighted.

Before giving a cloze task be sure that the child understands the task by beginning with a passage that can be read but where only a few words are deleted. For some children with limited comprehension skills, you might need to reduce the task to sentence level.

After selecting the content and deleting words, keep two copies of the passage (one with and one without deletions). If 20 words have been deleted and the student is able to correctly identify 12, the resulting percentage is $12/20 \times 100 = 60\%$. Another feature of the cloze technique, especially when given to the entire class, is that you will have useful data for evaluating reading comprehension with respect to the entire class.

Simplified Retelling

First, quickly review the passage for content, detail, characters, plot, to approximate a score.

Second, have the student read the material and then retell what was read.

#	Detail (topic, character, sequence, etc.)

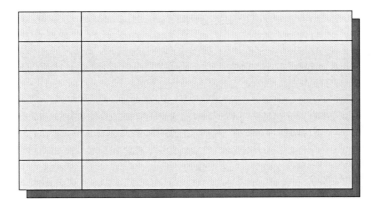

Third, score the retelling by counting the number of items (detail, plot, sequence), or use a rubric such as

4. **Mastery:** Excellent detail for topic, plot, sequence.

3. **Very Good:** Understands main idea and provides supporting detail.

2. **Satisfactory:** General topic understood and some detail.

1. **Developing:** Vague idea of topic and little detail.

The Bottom Line

The bottom line is that you want a relatively easy method for making a simple statement concerning a child's reading comprehension. At the IEP meeting you want to be able to say that when a student reads a passage from a textbook or other classroom material the student was able to understand very little, some of what was read, or the child was able to comprehend most of the material. The IEP Team doesn't need more standardized scores from the classroom teacher but basic information relating to what the student does in the classroom with respect to reading. You don't need to develop a 50-item multiple choice task to accomplish this but simply ask a few questions, one-to-one, to get a real idea of what the student comprehends.

58. THE FULL AND INDIVIDUAL EVALUATION

A State educational agency shall conduct a full and individual initial evaluation before the initial provision of special education and related services to a child with a disability under this part.[189]

To provide that often elusive "appropriate" education requires a free education (at public expense) that follows State standards, and an education at the appropriate level (preschool, elementary or secondary) that conforms with the child's individual education program. The evaluation process plays an essential role in providing FAPE. First, the evaluation determines whether a child has a disability under IDEA. If a child does not have a disability, FAPE under IDEA is not required. Second, the evaluation considers the need for special education. If special education is not required, services or accommodations are not provided under IDEA. Third, the evaluation determines the child's special educational needs. This is necessary to identify the services, accommodations and supports that a child might need. Fourth, the evaluation helps determine the content of a child's IEP.

As a teacher you might be part of the team that determines a child's eligibility for services. The classroom teacher certainly could be (should be) one of the important "qualified professionals" that can make essential contributions to the individual evaluation. When the evaluation is completed by the group of qualified professionals and the parents, a determination is made as to whether the child has a disability and whether the child needs special education.[190]

Psychological assessment and other evaluation is **not** precise science. Certain disabilities have fairly straightforward criteria such as visual impairments, hearing impairments, orthopedic impairments, traumatic brain injury, and so forth. But many disabilities are not at all easily defined, and not always easily differentiated from other disabilities such as specific learning disabilities (despite the "specific"), emotional disturbance, mental retardation, and ADHD.

The evaluation must be comprehensive, must use a variety of data sources, and must include all areas affected by a child's disability. The regular classroom is central to the determination of an IDEA disability in that for each disability a child must meet the **IDEA disability criteria** and the disability must **affect academic performance**. To this end data relating to classroom performance is an absolute necessary component of the individual evaluation. Data, work samples, reports, quizzes, grades, observations, etc. should be considered (1) during the prereferral process to ensure that quality instruction was provided before referral, (2) during the evaluation to supplement standardized assessments, and (3) during the development of the IEP. Specific information relating to classroom performance can include

- **Checklists**
- **Classroom grades**
- **Classroom observations**
- **Classroom work**
- **Districtwide tests**
- **Homework samples**
- **Informal inventories**
- **Observations**

- **Quizzes**
- **Rating scales**
- **Reports**
- **Reports to parents**
- **Standardized tests**
- **State tests**
- **Classroom quizzes**
- **Wide-range tests**

59. MENTAL RETARDATION

Nothing in the Act requires that children be classified by their disability so long as each child who has a disability that is listed in § 300.8 and who, by reason of that disability, needs special education and related services.[191]

The regulations define mental retardation as meaning significantly subaverage general intellectual functioning, existing concurrently with deficits in adaptive behavior and manifested during the developmental period, that adversely affects a child's educational performance.[192] The American Association on Mental Retardation's definition of adaptive behavior includes "significant limitations in adaptive behavior impact a person's daily life and affect the ability to respond to a particular situation or to the environment."[193]

The euphemism "subaverage intellectual functioning" really mean IQ as in IQ test (really standard deviation-type) score. A typical criterion for IQ score to fall into that "subaverage intellectual functioning" range is a score of 70 or an IQ two standard deviations below the mean. In addition to low IQ (Oh, right "subaverage intellectual functioning") a child must have an impairment in adaptive behavior. The psychologist at the meeting might go bonkers over the score but you should focus on the more important of the two criteria: **adaptive behavior**. Does a child need help with basic communication, self-help skills, socialization, toileting, dressing, and independent living? These are the areas (see the rating scale below) that should guide a determination of mental retardation rather than a score on a standardized test.

Adaptive Behavior Rating Scale					
Area	**low**		**average**		**high**
Physical Development	1	2	3	4	5
Cognitive Development	1	2	3	4	5
Communication Development	1	2	3	4	5
Adaptive skill	1	2	3	4	5
Language Ability	1	2	3	4	5

Social Development	1	2	3	4	5
Emotional Development	1	2	3	4	5
Regular Classroom Participation	1	2	3	4	5
Self-help Skills	1	2	3	4	5
Daily-Living Skills	1	2	3	4	5

If a child's adaptive behavior is average or near average, consider disabilities other than mental retardation. No doubt someone will state that a child is not able to adapt to the regular classroom curriculum. This is nonsense and not at all what adaptive behavior means. Not being able to adapt to the regular classroom curriculum is a part of "subaverage intellectual functioning." Let's face it. IQ measures, in addition to performance on a variety of esoteric tasks, environment, language background, socioeconomic status, emotional factors, and certainly academic achievement skills. The IQ score is a trap that snares teachers repeatedly. The environment, poor instruction, cultural factors all converge in the form of a low IQ score; these same factors result in low grades; but low IQ and low grades (which both have the same underlying basis) are said to provide two independent criteria for the determination of mental retardation. This is ridiculous. The IEP meeting and the school psychologist might focus on IQ, you must focus on adaptive behavior.

Alternatives to Mental Retardation

If a child has extensive language, communication and self-help needs, is not able to function independently, and there is a reason to suspect an impairment in cognitive functioning, a classification of mental retardation might provide the services and accommodations necessary for a child to function as independently as possible. If a child is not doing well in school and IQ is below 70, but has developed language skills and is able to achieve basic self-help tasks, consider options other than a classification of mental retardation.

Developmental Delay: For children aged three to nine the term **developmental delay** can be used to determine eligibility for special education (if permitted by the State and the school district) for children experiencing developmental delays in physical development, cognitive development, communication development, social or emotional development, or adaptive development.[194]

Specific learning disability (listening comprehension): This type of disability explains why a child would score below average on an IQ test, and also have difficulty with most educational tasks. If a child is not able to process or comprehend verbal input, all other language tasks including auditory expression (speaking), reading and written communication will be affected. More discrepancy silliness: a child has low IQ and low achievement because of environmental factors but there is no discrepancy between IQ and achievement scores, and thus no specific learning disability. This argument ignores the fact that we don't really know what the child's intelligence is, other than a silly score derived of picayune tasks and affected by a whole bunch of factors; and until we provide that systematic, high-quality, data-based instruction, we are not sure what the child's educational potential is.

No disability: You think that a specific learning disability designation for a child with low IQ and low achievement scores is inappropriate. I tend to agree. Don't classify the child. Most of these children simply do not have disabilities, and a disability determination is not educationally advantageous. Use school-wide services and school remedial programs, aides, and in-service workshops to better individual instruction.

Other Health Impairment: The IDEA definition for OHI includes having limited strength, vitality or alertness, including a heightened alertness to environmental stimuli, that results in limited alertness with respect to the educational environment. If "environmental stimuli" have not been all that good for a child, especially because of socioeconomic deprivation, one could well imagine "limited alertness with respect to the educational environment."

Severe language impairment: Excellent category in that most children in the 50 to 70 IQ range are classified because of deficient language skills. Language, after all, is the primary criterion for determining mental retardation.

What if you are told that a child is mentally retarded and that using another classification would be wrong? Not true. We create the category of mental retardation. We decide who will be called mentally retarded and who will not. "We" being the evaluation team and the parents. There is no imprimatur that somehow identifies children as mentally retarded, a sign or test score that indicates a child's cognitive functioning or how socioeconomic factors affect academic and cognitive performance.

Suppose you are told that mental retardation is an "appropriate" classification? This is often a self-serving interpretation of the law and nothing more than an excuse to exclude a child from the regular classroom.

LD, MR and the Regular Classroom

There has been a gradual increase in regular classroom placements (see the Chart below[195]) for children in the mental retardation and specific learning disabilities category. However, this increase has been leveling out to about 44 percent for specific learning disabilities and 13.5 percent for mental retardation as shown in the chart below.

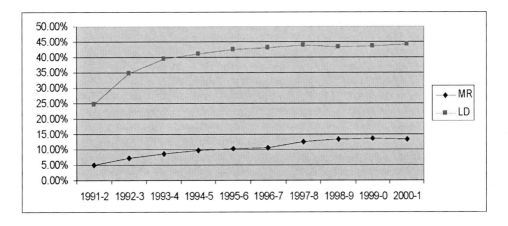

A "To-do List" for the Classroom Teacher

1. Focus on the child and not the label.

2. Familiarize yourself with the child's IEP.

3. Help the child participate in the general curriculum.

4. Help relate general curriculum goals to alternate performance indicators.

5. Have "high expectations." Believe that children can succeed without being called mentally retarded.

6. Determine what the child "can do" academically.

7. Include the child in classroom activities.

8. Focus on the gap between what the child can and cannot do (e.g., if the child has 10 sight words, set a goal of 20).

60. DISABILITY AND RACE

African-American children are identified as having
mental retardation and emotional disturbance at rates
greater than their White counterparts.

The use of IQ to remove a child from the mainstream applies to every child, but parents of black children, parents affected by socioeconomic factors, must be particularly vigilant. The big lie of testing: "Well, the IQ score speaks for itself. If you really want to help the child, you would do what is best in terms of providing special education services." The only thing IQ speaks for is a tendency toward racism and a rationale for excluding children from the regular classroom. For example, the rate of black children classified in South Carolina per 1000 children is 35.36 but the corresponding rate for white children is 8.60. Do you really think these rates reflect a deep concern to identify children with mental retardation and to better meet individual learning needs; or a concern to roundup children with low IQs, many of whom are black, and then exclude these children from regular classes under the guise of help?

Are black children more likely to have mental retardation than whites? The answer to this question is not based on the idiocy of IQ testing but on fact. The Center of Disease Control reports that Down syndrome is the most common cause of mental retardation and that approximately one in 800 children (or a prevalence rate of 1.25 per 1,000 children).[196] Most importantly, the rate is approximately equal for different racial groups. Curious: More black children are retarded when IQ is the measure, but not when an empirical measure (Down syndrome) of actual retardation is available.

But the story gets more interesting. The survival rate for white children with Down syndrome has improved from less than 50 percent in the 1940s to 91 percent in a 1980–1996 comparison group. The median age at death for whites increased from two years in 1968 to 50 years in 1997, while the median age for blacks increased from 0 in 1968 to 25 years in 1997. Why the dissimilar survival rates for white and blacks? The CDD suggest that "differences in the frequency of life-threatening malformations and differences in social factors and care provided to persons with DS." Ah, bad care, people die; bad social stuff, people die. What we learn from this study of Down syndrome is that there is no innate inclination for mental retardation among blacks, and that the lower IQ scores of black children is a manifestation of socioeconomic and environmental factors and not mental retardation.

Table 8 shows the breakdown of disability by race.[197] Three areas are noteworthy: First, the higher percentage of blacks than whites for the mental retardation and emotional disturbance categories; second, the higher percentage of white than blacks for the speech or language impairments and for the other health-impaired category as a result of ADD/ADHD; and third, the comparability between whites and blacks for categories that require relatively objective criteria (deafness, blindness, deaf-blindness).

Table 8. Disability and Race

Disability	American Indian/ Alaskan	Asian/ Pacific Islander	Black	Hispanic	White
Specific Learn. Dis.	55.24%	41.04%	45.40%	59.17%	48.09%
Speech or Lang. Imp.	17.04%	25.74%	14.65%	17.96%	20.04%
Mental Retardation	8.40%	9.52%	17.35%	7.25%	8.62%
Emotional Dist.	7.74%	5.09%	11.34%	5.28%	7.98%
Multiple Dis.	2.19%	2.67%	2.14%	1.97%	2.25%
Hearing	1.14%	3.02%	0.98%	1.59%	1.15%
Orthopedic Imp.	0.85%	1.87%	0.90%	1.32%	1.36%
Other Health Imp.	4.69%	4.43%	4.25%	3.20%	7.00%
Vision	0.39%	0.86%	0.38%	0.45%	0.44%
Autism	0.81%	4.25%	1.42%	1.09%	1.85%
Deaf-Blindness	0.04%	0.05%	0.02%	0.03%	0.03%
Traumatic Brain Inj.	0.33%	0.43%	0.32%	0.27%	0.39%
Developmental Delay	1.14%	1.04%	0.86%	0.43%	0.81%
All	100.00%	100.00%	100.00%	100.00%	100.00%

Over 100,000 black children are misidentified as mentally retarded, and this category of disability is most likely to be placed outside of the regular education classroom. This is costly and segregative. In the introduction to IDEA, Congress[198] identified several specific problems associated with misclassification:

> (1) **More minority children continue to be served in special education than would be expected from the percentage of minority students in the general school population; (2) In the 1998–1999 school year, African-American children represented just 14.8 percent of the population aged 6 through 21, but comprised 20.2 percent of all children with disabilities; (3) Studies have found that schools with predominately White students and teachers have placed disproportionately high numbers of their minority students into special education; (4) and African-American children are identified as having mental retardation and emotional disturbance at rates greater than their White counterparts.**

The classroom teacher can do much to prevent misclassification by actively participating in the prereferral process. The classroom teacher should actively seek help to enable a child to achieve in the classroom without special education. For children identified as having specific learning disabilities, emotional disturbance (which also has a larger number of minority students) and mental retardation, prereferral interventions and school-wide interventions should be used to reduce the number of children who actually require special education. What is important to understand is that special education is not for every learning or behavioral problem, and that special education does not mean removal from the regular classroom. Finally, before making a referral, consider obvious environmental, socioeconomic, learning opportunity and cultural factors.

Part V
IEP Essentials

If the child is being educated in regular classrooms, as here, the IEP should be reasonably calculated to enable the child to achieve passing marks and advance from grade to grade.[199]

61. THE IEP TEAM

A regular education teacher of the child, as a member of the IEP Team, must participate in the review and revision of the IEP of the child.[200]

The regular education teacher is not merely a guest at the IEP meeting to fulfill a bureaucratic requirement. The regular education teacher is an integral team member who provides input regarding classroom performance, who is an important part of the decision-making process, who helps formulate the IEP, and who actively participates in the determination of the least restrictive placement.

The requirement for the regular classroom teacher regarding IEP membership is not less than one regular classroom teacher of the child if the child is or may be participating in the regular classroom. For children who are participating in the regular classroom the classroom teacher provides insights and observations to enable success, and helps to identify strengths and weaknesses and curriculum needs. For children who might participate in the regular classroom the classroom teacher provides expertise concerning the curriculum and skills needed to participate in the general curriculum.

The IDEA IEP Team participants are as follows:

1. The parents of the child.

2. **Not less than one regular education teacher of the child (if the child is, or may be, participating in the regular education environment).**

3. Not less than one special education teacher of the child, or where appropriate, not less then one special education provider of the child.

4. A representative of the public agency who (i) Is qualified to provide, or supervise the provision of, specially designed instruction to meet the unique needs of children with disabilities; (ii) **Is knowledgeable about the general education curriculum**; and (iii) Is knowledgeable about the availability of resources of the public agency.

5. An individual who can interpret the instructional implications of evaluation results, who may be a member of the team described in paragraphs (a)(2) through (a)(6) of this section.

6. At the discretion of the parent or the agency, other individuals who have knowledge or special expertise regarding the child, including related services personnel as appropriate.

7. Whenever appropriate, the child with a disability.[201]

Do children attend IEP meetings? Yes, but for younger children IEP Team participation may not be appropriate, or may not be appropriate for the entire meeting. For older students, especially when transition services are being considered, the school must invite the student to attend "if a purpose of the meeting will be the consideration of the postsecondary goals for the child and the transition services needed to assist the child in reaching those goals."[202] If a student does not attend the meeting, a classroom teacher might have useful information concerning the students academic and nonacademic interests (which must be taken into account if a student does not attend the meeting).

> ▼ **"A member of the IEP Team shall not be required to attend an IEP meeting, in whole or in part, if the parent of a child with a disability and the local educational agency agree that the attendance of such member is not necessary because the member's area of the curriculum or related services is not being modified or discussed in the meeting."[203]**

IEP Team Responsibilities

The IEP Team is responsible for developing a reasonably calculated plan to enable a child to "to be involved in and make progress in the general education curriculum, and to meet each of the child's other educational needs that result from the child's disability." For most children with disabilities the frame of reference for developing goals is the regular classroom, and a corollary to this is that the regular classroom teacher must play an active role to enable participation in the classroom and progress in the general education curriculum in order to achieve these goals. The classroom teacher makes this important contribution by evaluating the extent of classroom participation with and without special education, and helping to determine effective classroom accommodations and interventions. An important goal for the classroom teacher is to assist every child to successfully participate in State- and school-wide evaluations. The ability to participate in these assessments is predicated, to a large degree, on the child's ability to participate in the general curriculum. The input the classroom teacher provides at the IEP meeting regarding the extent of general curriculum participation provides the foundation for determining necessary assessment accommodations. How the child successfully participates in the general curriculum should be a guide for successful participation in assessments.

Basic IEP Team meeting responsibilities for the classroom teacher include IEP meeting attendance when classroom performance is being considered, providing specific examples of classroom performance and/or behavior, and contributing to the overall team discussion regarding goals, supports, services and accommodations, strategies and interventions that will result in successful classroom participation.

What if there is no discussion regarding classroom success? Attend the meeting, make sure that you discuss classroom success, and then you will have done your job. There is a limit as to what you can do, so try and do the right thing, and that is about all you can do.

Cooperation

The committee is discouraged to hear that many parents, teachers, and school officials find that some current IDEA provisions encourage an adversarial, rather than a cooperative, atmosphere, in regards to special education. In response, the committee has made changes to promote better cooperation and understanding between parents and schools, leading to better educational programs and related services for children with disabilities.[204]

62. IEP DEVELOPMENT

The centerpiece of the Act is the individualized education program or IEP.[205]

The IEP is developed by the IEP Team and the parents. The reason why the classroom teacher of the child being provided services attends the IEP meeting, and not just "a classroom teacher," is to provide expertise concerning necessary accommodations, effective classroom interventions, relevant classroom goals, and supports to enable classroom participation. This does not mean that the classroom teacher is responsible for determining necessary serves, supports and accommodations, but that the classroom teacher may have insights or even data that should be considered.

IEP Team Considerations

Every child with a disability must be provided with assistive technology (AT) services. However, AT does not mean that the concept of "least restrictive" and maximizing independence is abandoned. Text readers are readily available, but this does not mean that a child should not acquire literacy skills. The classroom teacher should be aware of what AT services are specified in a child's IEP, and what AT accommodations may or may not be appropriate. If a classroom spelling test is being given, using spell check would not be appropriate; if computational skill is being measured, a calculator should not be used. The use of a calculator might be specified in a child's IEP, but use common sense. If an assessment is designed to measure primary fact skills, the use of a calculator could actually prevent not only the determination of what a child has learned but also opportunities to learn this particular skill in the future. Likewise, a student might require a reader for assessments, but a reader would obviously be inappropriate for a reading test. I don't know what reading a "reading test" to a student would measure, maybe some type of oral understanding; but I do know that this would not measure reading. If you come across a student who is reading at grade level as measured by a standardized test, but the student is demonstrably below grade level, check to see if the so-called reading test was read to the student.

The regular classroom teacher must understand that a child cannot be identified as a child with a disability if the determinant factor is limited English proficiency. Limited English proficiency, in and of itself, is not a disability;

limited English proficiency without a corresponding disability does not qualify for services under IDEA or Section 504. If a child does have a disability, the IEP Team must consider the language needs of the child within the context of the IEP. If a child is identified as having emotional disturbance and the child's primary language is not English, ESL instruction/guidance and other language needs would be specified in the child's IEP.

Classroom behavior is often the one factor that prevents participation in the regular classroom. If behavior is either a direct manifestation of the child's disability or impacted by the child's disability, the regular classroom teacher should participate in the development of the functional behavioral assessment (FBA) that determines what causes the behavior and what strategies and interventions are effective for addressing the behavior. Likewise, the classroom teacher should be part of the team that develops the Behavioral Intervention Plan (BIP) to address the behavior. If a behavior affects classroom participation, the classroom teacher can help specify these behaviors and identify strategies and interventions that might be successful (or not) for dealing with the behavior within the context of the regular classroom.

What to do if classroom behavior is a problem yet the difficulty is not addressed in the IEP? Request the development of a FBA and BIP. If this is not possible, request a goal or accommodation. For example, if the child abruptly leaves the classroom on a average of 10 times a day, request an IEP goal to decrease this behavior, or an accommodation might be appropriate such as designated out-of-classroom breaks.

Requirement with Respect to Regular Education Teacher[206]

A regular education teacher of the child, as a member of the IEP Team, must, consistent with paragraph (a)(3) of this section, participate in the review and revision of the IEP of the child to identify needs, select goals, services, program modifications, interventions, strategies, supplemental aids, and appropriate classroom support.

63. SECTION 504 SERVICES

Section 504 of the Rehabilitation Act of 1973 is designed to eliminate discrimination on the basis of disability in any program or activity receiving Federal financial assistance.[207]

The definition of an IDEA disability is important because if a child does not meet the disability requirements as defined in the regulations, services cannot be provided under IDEA. The regulations for IDEA (Section 34 CFR 300.8) require that a child has one of the 13 abilities defined in the regulations, and that the child needs special education. Lack of instruction or economic disadvantage are not disabilities under IDEA or Section 504 and therefore cannot result in services under either. However, asymptomatic HIV positive is not a disability under IDEA but it is a disability under Section 504.[208] This means that a HIV positive student might not need either services or accommodations, but the student cannot be discriminated against because of the HIV (e.g., excluding the student from school). On the other hand, for a student with symptomatic HIV or full-blown AIDS, a range of services and accommodations might be necessary such as accommodations for fatigue during classes, missing classes or even homebound instruction. If a child with AIDS requires special education, services can be provide via Other Health Impairment under IDEA; if a child requires only an accommodation (being late for class, classroom breaks), Section 504 can be used. Other situations where Section 504 might apply but not IDEA include ADD/ADHD, cosmetic disfigurement, heart disease, HIV/AIDS, IDEA declassification, skin and endocrine disorders, social maladjustment, and substance abuse.

What exactly is Section 504? Unlike most laws, Section 504 is brief and to the point.

▼ **No otherwise qualified individual with a disability in the United States, as defined in section 706(8) of this title, shall, solely by reason of her or his disability, be excluded from the participation in, be denied the benefits of, or be subjected to discrimination under any program or activity receiving Federal financial assistance or under any program or activity conducted by any Executive agency or by the United States Postal Service.[209]**

Not only must a child have a disability defined by IDEA to receive IDEA services, but the child must need special education. If a child needs only an accommodation (e.g., large print) but not special education, the accommodation (without special education) cannot be provided under IDEA. However, an accommodation without special education is permissible under Section 504. If a child needs only a related service such as speech or physical therapy, the related service (without special education) cannot be provided under IDEA but the related service could be provided under Section 504. If the related service entails special education (as can be the case with speech and language development), IDEA can be used to provide the service.

> ## Equal Opportunity
>
> **For purposes of this part, aids, benefits, and services, to be equally effective, are not required to produce the identical result or level of achievement for handicapped and nonhandicapped persons, but must afford handicapped persons equal opportunity to obtain the same result, to gain the same benefit, or to reach the same level of achievement, in the most integrated setting appropriate to the person's needs.[210]**

Why is this Section 504 important for the classroom teacher? Before you recommend a child for evaluation you should have some idea what the problem is and to whom the recommendation is being made. If a lack of instruction or socioeconomic factors seem to affect a child's classroom performance, this should be considered in the referral or this knowledge might even prevent a referral for an IDEA disability determination. If a child simply needs an accommodation or a specific related service, but otherwise has no special education needs, the request for the accommodation should be made to the individual responsible for Section 504.

Section 504 Responsibilities

➢ **Read the Section 504 plan.**

➢ **Determine what services and accommodations are detailed in the plan.**

➢ **Determine your role for providing the service or accommodation.**

➤ Request support for providing accommodations when necessary.

➤ Request special assistance (e.g., scribe, reader, translator) when necessary.

➤ Know that the regular education teacher must implement Section 504 plans.

➤ The intent of 504 is not to provide special education (although this can be provided under Section 504) but to provide necessary services and accommodations so as not to discriminate.

➤ Failure to implement a Section 504 plan can result in a determination of noncompliance.

➤ The Office of Civil Rights can seek voluntary compliance via a corrective action agreement; initiate action to terminate Department of Education financial assistance; seek judicial action through the Department of Justice.

Otherwise Qualified

"Otherwise qualified" is an important Section 504 phrase. The term means that an individual is qualified as disability for a job, in spite of a disability, if the individual can meet the basic job requirements with reasonable accommodations (that does not pose an undue hardship on the employer). For example, an HIV-infected surgical technician might be ruled not otherwise qualified because of the risk of transmission. For school-age children all children who have disabilities are "otherwise qualified" to receive a free appropriate public education.

▼ The Section 504 standard is to meet the needs of children with disabilities as "adequately" as the needs of nondisabled children.

64. WHAT ARE SECTION 504 SERVICES?

Because Section 504 often results in specific accommodations designed to meet specific disability needs in the regular classroom, and thus prevent discrimination based on disability, these accommodations are extremely important for the classroom teacher. Historically, Section 504 is used to provide accommodations for students who do not need special education. For example, a child requires frequent breaks or rest periods because of an illness or disability. If the child's physical or mental impairment substantially limits one or more of the major life activities of an individual, a reasonable accommodation must be provided to mitigate the effects of the disability. If a child has a hearing impairment but does not need special education, accommodations might be provided in the form of preferential seating; for a child with a visual impairment large print material might be required; and for a child with an orthopedic impairment adaptive furniture and an accessible classroom might be more than sufficient to ensure participation in classroom activities and the curriculum.

Although Section 504 is frequently used to provide specific accommodations for a child who has a disability but does not need special education, Section 504 can be used to provide any and all services. If a child has been declassified, then a determination is made that special education is appropriate in some form, the specially designed instruction can be provided under Section 504.

There are three prongs to a Section 504 disability: (1) a physical or mental impairment that substantially limits one or more of the major life activities of an individual, (2) a record of such an impairment, or (3) being regarded as having such an impairment.

1. *Major life activities* means functions such as caring for one's self, performing manual tasks, walking, seeing, hearing, speaking, breathing, learning, and working.

2. *Has a record of such an impairment* means has a history of, or has been misclassified as having, a mental or physical impairment that substantially limits one or more major life activities.

3. *Is regarded as having an impairment* means
   a. has a physical or mental impairment that does not substantially limit major life activities but that is treated by a recipient as constituting such a limitation;

175

b. has a physical or mental impairment that substantially limits major life activities only as a result of the attitudes of others toward such impairment; or

c. has none of the impairments but is treated by a recipient as having such an impairment.[211]

Section 504 Essentials

Who to contact: If you have a Section 504 question there is one individual who must be designated to coordinate Section 504 efforts. As a practical matter the IEP Team (the IEP Team chairperson) might be responsible for Section 504, the Child Study team (CST), the Student Study Team (SST), or there might be a specific Section 504 Team.

Major life activity: If a child is not eligible for IDEA because the child does not have a disability, has been declassified, or does not need special education, but a specific accommodation is necessary, consider Section 504. Not all disabilities affect a major life activity. However, if a child had a temporary disability that did not affect a major life activity (a right-handed child with a broken left-arm), this would not meet the Section 504 criteria for disability.

Misclassified students: If a child does not have a disability, and has been misclassified and treated as disabled, the child meets the Section 504 definition of a disability. If a child is mistakenly removed from the classroom, this might adversely affect academic development and thereby require, not special education, but appropriate remedial services under Section 504 to rectify this mistake.

Plan: Many schools require a Section 504 plan which can be an IEP or a specific Section 504 plan. If a child is receiving Section 504 services, ask to see the plan, read the plan, become familiar with what accommodations or services are required by the plan.

Classroom: Determine what your role is in the implementation of a Section 504 plan. Remember that a child receiving Section 504 is not receiving special education under IDEA so your role might actually be expanded in terms of implementation and accommodation supervision.

Enforcement: Section 504 complaints and monitoring responsibilities are the responsibility of The United States Department of Education, Office of Civil Rights (OCR).

Complaints: Anyone can file a complaint relating to discrimination because of disability for yourself or on behalf of another. The OCR

Discrimination Complaint form can be found at

http://www.hhs.gov/ocr/discrimhowtofile.doc.

The complaint requires a response to each of the following:

Who do you think discriminated against you (or someone else)?

When do you believe that the discrimination took place?

Describe briefly what happened. How and why do you believe you (or someone else) were discriminated against? Please be as specific as possible.

IDEA and Section 504 Disabilities

The following table shows various situations when IDEA and Section 504 qualify a child for services under IDEA or Section 504. The distinction between an IDEA disability and Section 504 disability is that an IDEA disability refers to the specific criteria cited in the regulations. A Section 504 disability refers to a child who does not meet the IDEA disability requirements but does meet the generally more broad Section 504 requirements that a disability affects a major life activity, has a record of an impairment, or is regarded as having an impairment.

Table 9. Services and Accommodations for IDEA and Section 504 Disabilities

Disability and Needs	Services
IDEA Disability and special education needed	All IDEA services
IDEA disability, special education and accommodations needed	All IDEA services
IDEA disability but special education services not needed	No IDEA services
IDEA disability but only a related service needed	No IDEA services but Section 504 services possible
IDEA disability and parents refuse services	No IDEA services
Section 504 disability and special education services needed	Section 504 services

Section 504 disability and only a related service needed	Section 504 services
Section 504 Disability and only an accommodation needed	Section 504 services
No IDEA disability but Section 504 disability	Section 504 services or accommodations
No IDEA disability	No IDEA services
No IDEA or Section 504 disability	No services or accommodations

Section 504 for Teachers

Section 504 can also apply to teachers. Consider the case of this teacher (Gene Arline) with a record of an impairment in which, at one time, the disease was definitely contagious.[212] After suffering a third relapse because of tuberculosis the teacher was dismissed by the school board. She was not dismissed because of performance but because of her disability. The district court reversed this decision and found that Arline fell "neatly within the statutory and regulatory framework" of a Section 504 disability.

In upholding Arline's status as "otherwise qualified," the appellate court remanded the case to determine the risk of infection and whether any reasonable accommodations were possible.

The Supreme Court agreed with the appellate court and stated that in order to determine whether a contagious disease is "otherwise qualified" under Section 504, the district court must conduct an individualized inquiry, based on reasonable medical judgments, about

1. the nature of the risk (e. g., how the disease is transmitted),

2. the duration of the risk (how long is the carrier infectious),

3. the severity of the risk (what is the potential harm to third parties), and

4. the probabilities the disease will be transmitted and will cause varying degrees of harm.

Upon deferring to the reasonable medical judgments of public health officials, the district court reconsidered the matter, as outlined by the Supreme Court, and found as follows:[213]

Nature of the risk: Medication culture tests were negative.

Duration of the risk: Smear test indicated that transmission would be rare.

Severity of the risk: Treatment resulted in little risk or harm.

Probability of transmission and harm: The court concluded that there was no threat of transmission based on "reasonable medical judgments."

What the court ordered:

> **The Court finds that Plaintiff is entitled to full back pay, plus benefits, for the four school years commencing with the year 1979–1980, less any time for which she would not have been compensated because of her pregnancy. Due to the lack of evidence, the Court is unable to determine the amount of such damages. Plaintiff's failure to mitigate her damages precludes any award after the four-year period above-mentioned.**

and

> **Based upon the medical testimony and the conclusions of this Court, Plaintiff poses no risk to the students at present as she is cured of tuberculosis. Therefore, Plaintiff is entitled to reinstatement to her position as a third grade teacher in the Nassau County School System. The Defendants are afforded the choice of either reinstating Plaintiff, or paying her front pay in lieu of reinstatement. Based upon the expert testimony, which was undisputed, the present value of what Plaintiff would earn from the 1988-89 school year until her retirement at age 65 is $768,724.00.**

65. IEP MEETINGS

"If one teacher could be excused from five percent of these meetings, the final regulation could result in savings of $40 million."[214]

The cost and benefits section of the regulations for IDEA-2004 estimates that the average IEP meeting is 1.5 hours and that each child will have approximately 1.2 meetings. To save money and time one of the changes in IDEA allows the school and parents to excuse members from meetings when that member's attendance is deemed unnecessary. One of the problems with this cost savings effort is the pie in the sky fantasy that 1.5 hours will be devoted to every child. Indeed, the amount of time spent on each child might be more in the range of 15 minutes (or 5 or 10) rather than 1.5 hours. Precious little time is often devoted to each child which underscores the importance of IEP meeting participation, especially on the part of the regular classroom teacher.

In a case involving the Federal Way School District (FWSD) a regular classroom teacher did not attend the IEP meeting or help evaluate the facts to determine whether the IEP was reasonably calculated to provide a child with autism FAPE.[215] The regular classroom teacher did write a letter which stated that the child had "made good progress" and recommended that the child remain in a general education kindergarten classroom with the support of a one-on-one aide. The IEP Team (sans parents or regular education teacher) recommended a self-contained setting where the child would do the proverbially "better."

An eight-day hearing (and this is not cheap) determined that the IEP Team was reasonably constituted. The parents then went to District court (for the Western District of Washington). The District court found that because the child was not participating in regular education classes at the time of the meeting, regular teacher participation at the IEP meeting was not necessary. The appellate court (United States Court of Appeals for the Ninth Circuit) decided that the school's failure to include the participation of a regular education teacher on the IEP Team, when there was a possibility the child would be placed in an integrated classroom, was a significant violation of the structural requirements of the IDEA. Upon remand, the district court was instructed to enter an order directing the school district to select an IEP Team that fully complies with the procedural requirements of the IDEA.

IEP Meeting Attendance and Congress

The committee has heard from many individuals that the amount of time spent preparing for and attending IEP meetings, and the number of individuals required to attend such meetings, reduces the amount of time that personnel spend with students. Scheduling IEP meetings involves coordinating the schedules of a number of individuals, including parents, who are balancing work and family demands. At the same time, a certain member of the IEP Team may not be needed at an IEP meeting if the topics of discussion do not involve that member. Or, an IEP meeting may be scheduled, but an IEP member later learns that they have an unavoidable scheduling conflict, which could force the cancellation of the IEP meeting. [216]

The Moral: Attend IEP Meetings When Necessary

And if it is not necessary as the regular education teacher to attend the IEP meeting, be sure that the school and parents agree to your nonattendance. Prior to IDEA-2004, IEP meeting attendance was required by all. The IDEA-2004 has been modified so that an attendance by a member is not required if the member's area of curriculum or related service expertise is not being discussed at the meeting or is otherwise not necessary. This must be an agreement in writing between the school and the parent. For example, if reading goals are being considered, a speech pathologist who is a team member might be excused from the meeting. If reading goals are being discussed, must a social studies teacher (who is a team member) attend? Probably, especially if reading in the content area is an area of consideration. If the meeting concerns placement, the regular classroom teacher would certainly have important input concerning the regular classroom placement. If the meeting concerns transportation to and from school, there might be no need to convene the entire team.

▼ EXCUSAL. – A member of the IEP Team may be excused from attending an IEP meeting, in whole or in part, when the meeting involves a modification to or discussion of the member's area of the curriculum or related services, if –
   a. the parent and the local educational agency consent to the excusal; and

    **b. the member submits, in writing to the parent
and the IEP Team, input into the development
of the IEP prior to the meeting.**[217]

Even if a teacher's area of expertise is being discussed, the member might be excused, in whole or in part, if the school and parent consent in writing and the excused committee member submits in writing pertinent information relating to the IEP. The rationale for IEP meeting excusals was that

> **Congress did not envision regular education teacher participating in all aspects of IEP-related activities. In the final regulations we recommend strongly that you provide a wide range of examples about how regular education teacher expertise, knowledge and concerns may shape IEP development and revision. The final regulations should also clarify that compliance . . . is not limited to the physical presence of the regular education teachers in meetings to develop or revise IEPs.**[218]

When Not to Have an IEP Meeting?

In the past changes to the IEP required the consideration by the entire IEP Team. When minor or common sense changes are needed to an IEP, this often results in delay, implementation without IEP Team participation, and often a difference between what is being done and what is included in the IEP. The IDEA has attempted to streamline the review process by the following:[219]

- ☛ **In making changes to a child's IEP after the annual IEP meeting for a school year, the parent of a child with a disability and the school may agree not to convene an IEP meeting for the purposes of making such changes, and instead may develop a written document to amend or modify the child's current IEP.**

- ☛ **To the extent possible, the local educational agency shall encourage the consolidation of reevaluation meetings for the child and other IEP Team meetings for the child.**

- ☛ **Changes to the IEP may be made either by the entire IEP Team or by amending the IEP rather than by redrafting the entire IEP. Upon request, a parent shall be provided with a revised copy of the IEP with the amendments incorporated.**

What to Do at the IEP Meeting?

What do you do if one member of the IEP Team dominates the meeting and you are not asked, nor expected, to provide input. Provide input anyway. This is your opportunity to identify important concerns that you have regarding classroom performance and success. If time is short, or even if the IEP has already been written (yes, this is done), be specific and to the point and, at the very least, state what you think the child needs for classroom success and the necessary classroom support.

The child's performance in the classroom is valued information (or should be). Identify classroom strengths and weaknesses, and provide information concerning what accommodations have been effective and those that have not. If behavior is a concern, identify specific behaviors (e.g., hitting, kicking, loud noises, animal noises, etc.) rather than "doesn't follow classroom rules." Most importantly, consider what classroom supports in the way of aides, consultant teacher services, resource room services, or related services might help promote successful classroom performance. You are more likely to get appropriate classroom support if you can identify what that support is. Most members attending the IEP meeting won't know what you need, and what the child with a disability needs, to succeed in the classroom. Provide input from your perspective as the classroom teacher and increase the likelihood that IEP-designated supports and services will be appropriate and effective and not a matter of IEP Team whim.

66. IEP CONTENT AND THE CLASSROOM TEACHER

The term 'individualized education program' or 'IEP' means a written statement for each child with a disability that is developed, reviewed, and revised in accordance with section 614(d).

Who Would Have Thought?

IDEA 108-446 eliminated the need for benchmarks as a way to reduce unnecessary paperwork (except for children taking alternate assessments). The cost saving for this is estimated to be as follows:[220]

> **Based on average compensation for teachers of $46.25 per hour, a reduction in time as modest as 15 minutes could save approximately $11.56 per IEP or $74.5 million total in opportunity costs for teachers related to the development of IEPs during the 2005–2006 school year for the 6.445 million children with disabilities who do not take alternate assessments aligned to alternate achievement standards.**

And by eliminating benchmarks and short-term objectives Congress estimates that

> **If half of these meetings concerned amendments or modifications to an IEP and parents and agenccy representatives agreed to forego a meeting and develop a written document in half of these cases...the combined opportunity costs for personnel participating in a typical IEP meeting are estimated at $297. If drafting a written document to amend or modify an IEP is assumed to cost half as much as a meeting, then this change could result in savings of $51.4 million.**

The IEP, considered by many to be the cornerstone of special education, is a written statement developed by the IEP Team and the parents to document accommodations and services that will provide a child with a free and

184

appropriate public education. Prior to Public Law 108-446 (the 2004 version of IDEA) many IEPs were a nightmare of bureaucratic paperwork. A major thrust of the new special education law is to limit excessive paperwork, reduce redundancy within the IEP, and to focus every IEP on the eight basic requirements cited in the law. Although the IEP is used as a compliance document, the primary purpose of every IEP is not to document the good deeds of the school system but the reasonably calculated individualized program for each child with a disability.

> **The Cost of Mainstreaming**
> **School Cost v. Real Cost**
>
> **The District contended that it would cost $109,000 to educate Rachel full-time in a regular classroom. This figure was based on the cost of providing a full-time aide for Rachel plus an estimated $80,000 for schoolwide sensitivity training. The court found that the District did not establish that such training was necessary. Further, the court noted that even if such training were necessary, there was evidence from the California Department of Education that the training could be had at no cost. Moreover, the court found that it would be inappropriate to assign the total cost of the training to Rachel when other children with disabilities would benefit. In addition, the court concluded that the evidence did not suggest that Rachel required a full-time aide.**[221]

For the classroom teacher the ability of a child to achieve satisfactorily in the classroom is an essential component of the IEP. The IEP is not based on a series of specialized tests that may or may not be related to classroom performance, but rather on how a child's disability affects "involvement and progress in the general curriculum." For the majority of children receiving IDEA services in the regular classroom, the classroom teacher obviously has the important task of describing classroom performance. If behavior is an issue, exactly what behavior affects classroom performance should be cited. If participation in the curriculum is affected, how a child participates (or does not) should be shown. If reading is a cause of concern, how the child reads should be documented by work samples, grades, quizzes, test scores and performance on specific reading assessments.

The individual evaluation will contain a variety of standardized scores, often ad nauseam, but nothing is more important than actual classroom performance. One of the best ways to understand regular classroom participation is to provide samples of a child's classroom work. Whether the problem is in reading, writing or mathematics, a sample of the student's classroom work often provides the best evidence of curriculum participation. Samples of work might include homework, classroom quiz, an essay, etc. Don't overwhelm the committee with boxes of student work but select several items that best characterizes a child's classroom performance. What you do in the regular classroom, what the child does, is the essence of a meaningful IEP to enable successful classroom performance.

IEP Basics

The classroom teacher should consider the child's strengths and academic needs before IEP the meeting. At the IEP meeting, the classroom teacher must be able to address each of the following (which, of course, does not happen if the IEP has been written before the meeting):

- **Classroom-based evaluations**
- **A child's strengths**
- **The child's weaknesses**
- **Specific academic needs**
- **Behavior concerns (if any)**
- **Effective interventions**
- **Effective accommodations**
- **Needed classroom supports**

Be a real member of the IEP Team. Attend the meeting; be able to identify specific classroom needs; identify what you think are necessary supplementary aids and services (e.g., services, supports, and accommodations). Remember that the IEP is developed by the IEP Team. If a completed IEP appears at the meeting, developed by the special education teacher, do not consider this a finished product (even if the chairperson does). Remember that the IEP is "developed" by the IEP Team. What you offer might be ignored, but do the right thing and consider the child's real classroom needs and how these needs should best be met from the vantage point of the regular classroom teacher.

What to do when presented with a completed IEP at the meeting? Unhappily, not much. You will be told that the IEP is not a completed IEP and that changes can be made. If you know how IEPs are developed by the special education teacher (or whoever), talk to the teacher before the meeting and provide input concerning classroom interventions, services and accommodations. If you are familiar with parent concerns, say a word or two on behalf of the parents. Contrary to the expectation and law that parents are essential in the development of the IEP, parents are all too frequently disenfranchised from the IEP process.

As a member of the IEP Team you should contribute to the development of the IEP. You will have firsthand knowledge as to what accommodations are and are not effective in the classroom. You will be able to help the Team understand a child's strengths and weaknesses, and identify goals that will help a child be involved in the regular classroom and the general curriculum.

If you have a child with a disability in your classroom, request to see the IEP. How can you meet a child's educational and disability needs without seeing the plan that addressed these needs (in theory) and was designed to enable participation in the curriculum? Before a child receives services the child must have an IEP, and if a child with a disability is in your classroom, see this IEP. If you are told that the IEP is confidential, remind the confidentially-concerned individual that "each public agency must ensure that the child's IEP is accessible to each regular education teacher, special education teacher, related service provider, and other service provider who is responsible for its implementation."[222]

67. IEP DEVELOPMENT AND THE CLASSROOM TEACHER

Goal: to be involved in and make progress in the general education curriculum.

The role of the classroom teacher is to provide an environment in which a child with a disability can participate with nondisabled children successfully. The regular classroom teacher is not expected to modify the curriculum beyond recognition or to neglect nondisabled students because of the needs of a child with a disability. However, the regular classroom teacher is part of a team and contributes to this team effort by identifying necessary supplementary aids and services (i.e., what is needed for classroom success), and encouraging participation in the curriculum. The following describes the essential components of every IEP required by IDEA, and the role of the classroom teacher to develop a truly individualized and effective IEP.[223]

The foundation for every IEP can be found in the statement of present levels of academic achievement and functional performance which includes how the child's disability affects involvement and progress in the general education curriculum. For the classroom teacher focus on "progress" in the curriculum in the form of work samples, tests, quizzes, observational data, and so on. The classroom teacher is the curriculum expert, and what the child does or does not do is essential to the full and individual evaluation. Present levels of academic performance is not solely determined by a standardized test but how the child actually performs academically.

If present levels of performance have been identified, a statement of measurable annual goals to enable involvement and progress in the general education curriculum (and meet each of the child's other educational needs) can be developed. Help identify goals which enable participation in the curriculum and to "pass from grade to grade." Simple question: what specifically does the child need to do to participate in the classroom? Talk more? Talk less? Read content material? Do homework? The evaluation process need not be overcomplicated. Identify practical skills and behaviors that will enable classroom success. Common sense would suggest that if a child is not able to participate in the classroom or classroom participation is affected, goals should be developed to increase this participation. The primary concern for the classroom teacher should be input concerning realistic goals to enable classroom success.

▼ **Teacher tip: be practical; think in terms of what can be accomplished. Don't always focus on standardized test score results but identify what skills need to be achieved.**

Meet with the special education teacher to identify important goals. The IEP must identify how the child's progress toward meeting the annual goals will be measured and when periodic reports on the progress toward meeting these (concurrent with report cards) will be provided. Help evaluate the effectiveness of goals that enable classroom participation. If you have a child with a disability in the classroom, take five minutes to summarize and evaluate classroom participation. For example, on a scale from 1 (poor) to 10 (excellent) weekly progress is evaluated as follows:

Classroom	Week							
	1	2	3	4	5	6	7	8
Behavior	2	1	3	3	4	4	4	5
Curriculum	5	4	5	4	6	5	7	6

The above data is easily graphed to show progress, lack of success, or specific areas of need in relation the classroom:

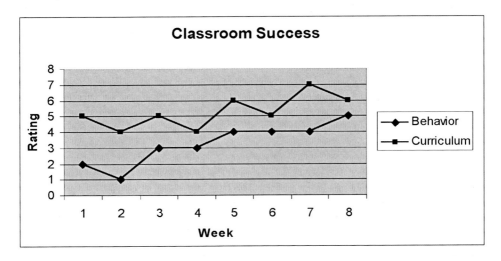

Use a scale from 1 to 4, 1 to 5, or 7 to 1, etc. What really matters is to take a few moments each week to evaluate what you consider progress in relevant areas. This simple data will give you a frame of reference for discussing class-room needs, and for evaluating successful classroom participation. Over a period of weeks this easy-to-do data summary will provide a useful picture of classroom participation.

Present levels of performance help identify goals, and goals help determine services. The IEP includes a statement of the special education, related services and supplementary aids and services, program modifications or supports for school personnel needed for the child to be involved in and make progress in the general education curriculum and to participate in extracurricular and other nonacademic activities. Based on classroom performance, help select supports and accommodations. Is more direct consultant teacher time necessary? Is the child receiving all necessary support to enable participation in the curriculum? Does the child need an aide? Or less time with an aide? You might not be a special education expert but you are the classroom expert, especially regarding academic success...and this should be the real focus of special education. One of the reasons a school lost in court *(Greer v. Rome City School District)* is that the school district offered no proof that the child could not be educated in a regular classroom with aids and supplementary services.[224] No need to think in terms of "proof," but definitely focus on what the child needs to be educated in the regular classroom.

The IEP requires an explanation of the extent, if any, a child will not participate with nondisabled children in the regular class and in the activities. Input into this area is a must for the classroom teacher. Provide first-hand experience why participation in the classroom or curriculum is possible or not. Remember that the standard is not "best" but adequate. What activities are possible? How can the curriculum be modified to enable participation? What works? What does not? These are the important questions that should be considered at a child's IEP meeting.

The important role of the classroom is never more apparent than when determining individual appropriate accommodations that are necessary to measure the academic achievement and functional performance of the child on State and district-wide assessments, or a statement of why the child cannot participate in these assessments. Accommodations used in the classroom should provide the basis for Statewide and district-wide test accommodations. Based on classroom experience, help select appropriate and effective accommodations. Provide input concerning what accommodations enable participation in the curriculum and what accommodations do not. Help make the IEP practical; help make the IEP a truly reasonable calculated plan to meet each child's learning needs. Think of the classroom as the standard for most accommodations; that is, if an accommodation is required in the classroom, it is likely necessary for high-stake tests.

The IEP specifies the projected date for services, and the anticipated frequency, location, and duration of those services and modifications. The classroom teacher must be prepared to collaborate with other personnel when selecting the location, frequency and duration of services. Of particular importance is classroom scheduling that might remove a child from the classroom during important instructional periods (e.g., test preparation, reading). If a child needs help in reading, don't remove the child from regular classroom reading activities. In this case the goal is to promote participation in reading, and not solve the reading "problem" by removing the child from the regular classroom reading curriculum.

Oh, here is a related irksome situation that should be dealt with quickly. A special education teacher or related services comes to the classroom to pull a child for a service at a convenient time for the service provider. This is not good. Children should be pulled from the classroom at specific times as a result of specific planning, and not at the whim or convenience of the service provider.

For older students transition services to enable the transition from school to work and post-school activities is essential. Beginning not later than when the child is 16 the IEP must include appropriate measurable postsecondary goals based upon age-appropriate transition assessments related to training, education, employment, and, if necessary, independent living skills. Often the classroom teacher can provide insight into a student's post-school ambitions. What does the student want? What does the student talk about? What does the student like to do? Does the student discuss work or vocational interests? The classroom should be the starting point for the development of a successful transition plan.

68. INDIVIDUALIZED FAMILY SERVICE PLAN (IFSP)

The Individualized Family Service Plan or IFSP is similar to an IEP but designed for children aged 3 through 5 or, at the discretion of the State educational agency, a 2-year-old child with a disability who will turn age 3 during the school year).[225] An IFSP emphasizes developmental needs more so than academic concerns. As a result IFSP content is often useful to consider for all children having serious developmental needs:

CONTENT OF PLAN. – The individualized family service plan shall be in writing and contain –[226]

1. a statement of the infant's or toddler's present levels of physical development, cognitive development, communication development, social or emotional development, and adaptive development, based on objective criteria;

2. a statement of the family's resources, priorities, and concerns relating to enhancing the development of the family's infant or toddler with a disability;

3. a statement of the measurable results or outcomes expected to be achieved for the infant or toddler and the family, including pre-literacy and language skills, as developmentally appropriate for the child, and the criteria, procedures, and timelines used to determine the degree to which progress toward achieving the results or outcomes is being made and whether modifications or revisions of the results or outcomes or services are necessary;

4. a statement of specific early intervention services based on peer-reviewed research, to the extent practicable, necessary to meet the unique needs of the infant or toddler and the family, including the frequency, intensity, and method of delivering services;

5. a statement of the natural environments in which early intervention services will appropriately be provided, including a justification of the extent, if any, to which the services will not be provided in a natural environment;

6. the projected dates for initiation of services and the anticipated length, duration, and frequency of the services;

7. the identification of the service coordinator from the profession most immediately relevant to the infant's or toddler's or family's needs (or who is otherwise qualified to carry out all applicable responsibilities under this part) who will be responsible for the implementation of the plan and coordination with other agencies and persons, including transition services; and

8. the steps to be taken to support the transition of the toddler with a disability to preschool or other appropriate services.

69. WHAT TO DO AS AN IEP MEMBER?

The task of the IEP Team is not to chit-chat about a child, offer a platitude or two, and then sign-off on an IEP written by the special education teacher. As a member of the IEP Team the classroom teacher should keep two words in mind: **discuss** and **identify**.

Discuss:

- the child's current involvement in the classroom
- the child strengths and weakness
- needed supplementary aids and services
- effective strategies and interventions
- what supports you will need

Identify:

- present levels of academic achievement and functional performance
- specific academic or learning needs (e.g., the percent of reading material comprehended at grade level)
- the least restrictive special education services
- related services (e.g., speech, occupational therapy, physical therapy, etc.)
- all reasonable accommodations needed to participate in assessments
- Annual measurable goals

The IEP Litmus Test: Measurable Annual Goals

70. MEASURABLE ANNUAL GOALS

Goals to improve classroom performance that do not take into consideration classroom performance are doomed to failure.

This is where most IEPs break down and become nothing more than a written statement to show that the school has complied with the regulations but not necessarily provided an appropriate education. As the classroom teacher, a quick review of IEP goals will indicate whether the IEP is a legitimate attempt to provide a reasonably calculated individualized program, or simply a document to show that the school has complied with IDEA.

Select meaningful goals, select goals that are based on beginning or measured levels of performance. For example, if you are shown a goal that a child "will read and write a narrative with less than 10 errors per 100 words," ask what the beginning level of performance is. How many errors does a child make now? If the answer is 10, the goal might be too easy; if the answer is 100, the goal might be too difficult. In all likelihood there is no answer because no one has measured this ability... and no one will measure this at the end of the year. Maybe, just maybe, a teacher might make a totally subjective judgment that a child did (or often did not) achieve this goal. Discuss measurement! How goals were first assessed, and how goals will be measured at the end of the year.

If the problem is basic reading skills, take five minutes to determine the child's ability to identify basic sight words. If the problem is reading comprehension, have the child read a passage from a text and then ask a series of 10 questions. If the problem entails basic computational skills, give the child an assessment involving basic primary facts. In other words, determine what the child can do, what the child does, and then determine a logical goal based on this data.

How simple is it to collect curriculum-based data? Very simple. For example, copy the 60 words from the following list, ask the child to read each word, and the result will be a ton of data that will tell you much about a child's basic reading skills.

Primer	First	Second	Third
all	ask	always	better
ate	every	around	cut
brown	every	because	done
eat	give	don't	grow
good	give	found	hot
good	how	gave	kind
he	how	gave	laugh
new	know	green	light
no	live	read	much
please	may	sing	never
ride	old	sleep	seven
she	some	which	small
soon	stop	work	start
what	take	write	together
white	thank	write	warm

As a classroom teacher you do not have a vast amount of time to scrutinize IEPs in detail (many of which would try the patience of Job). However, a quick reading of the measurable annual goals will reveal whether the IEP is reasonably calculated to provide an appropriate education, or whether the IEP is a collection of frivolous information compiled to give the appearance of IDEA compliance. For the less than reasonably calculated IEP, goals are rarely measured, were never intended to be measured, and were written to meet a bureaucratic requirement.

> ▼ Telltale sign of a bad IEP: every IEP goal (no matter how inappropriate) incants that 85% level of performance (and, of course, "as determined by teacher observation").

The following are several examples of the all too often unreasonably calculated IEP goals:

Improve reading comprehension as determined by teacher observation to the 80% level.
Say what? No mention of what the teacher will observe or how that ubiquitous "80%" is calculated.

Improve reading comprehension to grade level as determined by teacher observation.
A nice sentiment but estimating grade level reading comprehension is hardly a realistic measurement...but the thought is nice or at least sounds nice.

Improve self-concept as determined by teacher observation to the 80% level.
Can an 80% level of self-concept have meaning to someone, somewhere, somehow?

To be able to use short-vowels three out of four times.
If this is someone's idea of an annual goal, this IEP probably has two hundred goals. This is called "IEP-by-thickness." How could anyone criticize an IEP that contains 100, 200 or whatever number of goals? After all, someone (maybe a secretary) spent 15 minutes computer-generating goals that are overly specific, will never be measured, and may or may not be appropriate.

Meaningful Goals and IDEA

The following is what is required in IDEA-2004 (Public Law 108-446):

Goals and IDEA

A statement of measurable annual goals, including academic and functional goals, designed to –

1. **meet the child's needs that result from the child's disability to enable the child to be involved in and make progress in the general education curriculum; and**

2. **meet each of the child's other educational needs that result from the child's disability.**

Measurable annual goals should represent a serious effort to meet that elusive Rowley standard which mandates that the individualized educational program (IEP) developed by following IDEA procedures is "reasonably calculated to enable the child to receive educational benefits."[227] Nothing is a better indication of a reasonably calculated IEP than measurable annual goals.

▼ **A measurable annual goal should contain these elements:**
  1. **Measurable behavior, skill or ability**
  2. **Beginning level of performance**
  3. **Annual level of performance**

You have seen a variation of this in the form of behavioral objectives. Robert Mager's *Preparing Instructional Objectives* (Fearon, Palo Alto, CA, 1962) described three important elements of a behavioral objective: (1) a **behavior** (i.e., a visible activity), (2) **terminal behavior** (the behavior to be acquired), and (3) the **criterion** (the standard or test). Measurable annual goals are similar to behavioral objectives but with several important differences. Measurable annual goals provide an estimation of what a child can accomplish over the course of the year. Measurable annual goals are not intended to outline daily teaching activities but are designed to offer a yearly plan for meeting a child's needs and monitoring progress over the course of a year.

The **beginning level of performance** solves many measurable annual goal problems. If there is a beginning level of performance, there is no need to create pretend assessments ("as determined by teacher observation"). If a child has been determined to comprehend 20 percent of a grade level basal reader, a measurement of some sort must have been used to determine this 20 percent. Maybe the child was asked to read a section of material, 20 questions were asked, and the child was able to answer 2; or a cloze procedure (missing words) was used and the child was able to complete 4 of 20 items.

With a beginning level of performance not only can an end-of-the-year criterion be thoughtfully estimated, but an assessment actually exists to measure the projected annual level of performance or achievement.

Reading is the most cited need for children with disabilities but reading goals are often anything but measurable. For example, a generic nonmeasurable reading goal would be "To improve reading as determined by teacher observation to the 80 percent level." This sounds a bit like a measurable annual goal, and the 80 percent adds a bit of quantitative legitimacy to the goal. But what does "improve" mean? Improve word attack skills, comprehension, oral reading, vocabulary? The goal offers no guidance as to what will be improved and no direction is given as to the needed specially designed education that meet the child's reading needs.

If "teacher observation" is actually used to measure a beginning level of performance, this observation must result in some form of measurement. For example, at the beginning of the year a teacher uses a rating scale to measure **classroom skills** on a scale from 1 (Developing) to 5 (proficient). The scale consists of 10 items and a child receives an average rating of 2 or 40 percent. Based on this beginning level the measurable annual goal might be to increase the classroom skills rating to 80 percent.

There is a distinction between measurable annual goals (which are intended to be measured) and compliance statements listed under the goals section of an IEP (which are never intended to be measured). A teacher could actually observe a child's reading and use a rating scale or simply give a holistic value to observed reading performance. But for the vast majority of goals which cite "as determined by teacher observation," teacher observation or otherwise is never considered, determined or done.

> ▼ **IEPs and Incantations: "Although the IEP repeatedly incants these phrases – "teacher observation," "80% success" – because there is little indication of what Frank's level of success was when the IEP was written, it fails to specify strategies for adequately evaluating Frank's academic progress and determining which teaching methods are effective and which need to be revised."[228]**

Don't be fooled by the 80 percent or 85 percent level that is attached to many goals. If there is no beginning level of performance, rest assured that the cited 85 percent of performance is not even guess work but a blatant attempt to give credibility to a meaningless goal. Whenever you see the 85 percent criterion, ask what the beginning level of performance is. Common sense indicates that before you state a criterion you must have some idea of the beginning level of performance. If the beginning level of performance is zero percent, then 80 percent might be a tad too high; of if the beginning level is 75 percent, 80 percent might be too low. In any case, no beginning level of performance generally means that there was no initial measurement; and if there is no initial measurement, an end-of-the-year measurement is unlikely.

Every goal must have four elements: (1) need for the goal, (2) goal specificity, (3) a beginning level of performance, and (4) an annual level of performance. For most goals the annual level of anticipated performance will vary. The goal for reading comprehension might be to raise performance from 10 percent to 65 percent as determined by a curriculum-based assessment; or the annual goal might be to reduce inappropriate classroom remarks from 15 a day to zero; or the goal might be to improve completed assignments form zero percent to 100 percent.

71. HOW TO SELECT GOALS

Select meaningful goals and not simply goals to include in an IEP that does not provide a blueprint for specially designed instruction.

Every IEP should be a unique collection of goals and services to reflect the individual needs of the child. If the content of every IEP is eerily similar, the IEPs are probably boiler plate contrivances. There is no requirement that every child's IEP must include 10, 20, or 100 goals. As a matter of fact, if every IEP has a suspiciously similar number of goals, there is a good chance that IEPs are not reasonably calculated to provide an appropriate education, but are cookie-cutter produced to *appear* to comply with the law. For the classroom teacher the task is clear: Help identify goals that meet the child's needs that result from the child's disability, and select goals to enable the child to be involved in and make progress in the general education curriculum.[229] If a child's disability entails motor needs, an assistive technology service or device might be appropriate; for a child with hearing needs the ability to use residual hearing, or the need to develop communication skills must be considered; for a child with emotional needs, the child's behavior must be considered; and for a child with a specific learning disability in reading comprehension, there should be a measurable and measured reading comprehension goal.

Goals are not selected to meet every educational contingency; goals are not selected without considering need; goals are selected by focusing on how the disability affects education performance. If a child does not need a goal, the goal should not be in the IEP. Not only is an unnecessary goal restrictive (time might be devoted to achieve an unnecessary goal), but real needs might be ignored.

Selecting meaningful goals is not rocket science. The process should be simple and straightforward: identify an important need based on data, and develop a goal that will address that need. Unfortunately, there is often a void between classroom performance and what is recorded in the IEP. The reason for this is that special education is viewed as the solution. Goals are listed in the IEP but are not really considered vital and are not really used. Whereas the ultimate goal should be satisfactory performance in the regular classroom, many cling to the antiquated view that special education, in and of itself, is all that we should aspire. The "goal" is special education, and not the development of goals to enable progress in the general education curriculum and to meet a child's other needs.

What to Do?

For the classroom teacher, help focus attention to needs resulting from the child's disability that affect academic performance in the classroom. If behavior affects performance, there should be a goal. If the disability is reading fluency (as in a specific learning disability), there should be a goal to improve reading fluency. Help identify when goals are not needed. If a child is doing fine in mathematics, a mathematics goal is not needed.

Goal Guidelines

Thus, a public agency is not required to include in an IEP annual goals that relate to areas of the general curriculum in which the child's disability does not affect the child's ability to be involved in and progress in the general curriculum. If a child with a disability needs only modifications or accommodations in order to progress in an area of the general curriculum, the IEP does not need to include a goal for that area; however, the IEP would need to specify those modifications or accommodations.[230]

Goals should not be developed as an afterthought at the IEP meeting but should address important "academic and functional" needs that enable progress in the general education curriculum. The task is not to create needs at the IEP meeting, or to theorize about possible needs; the task is to develop goals based on data and academic performance.

If the goal addresses a need, is considerate of the general curriculum, and has a measured beginning level of performance and a realistic annual level of performance, there is a strong probability that the goal is a "good goal" and a well-intentioned effort that contributes to the development of a reasonably calculated IEP. For "bad goals" see the beginning of this chapter. Remember that goals require specificity so that "improving reading" or "reading at grade level" might be commendable in concept but lacking in specificity.

The one attribute that is a sign of a meaningful goal is the measured beginning level of performance. This one element, beginning level of performance, is often the key to an appropriate educational plan. If performance has not been measured at the beginning of the year, there is not much likelihood that performance will be measured at the end of the year. Even more important, if a goal has not been measured initially, there is no way to logically estimate the projected annual level of progress. If the goal is to improve basic reading skills to 85 percent, the beginning level of performance provides the benchmark for projecting the annual degree of progress. Is the beginning level zero percent, 50 percent, 75 percent? Obviously, the beginning level of performance is an important factor in the determination of a logical and reasonably calculated annual level of performance.

Measurable annual goals are not short-term instructional objectives. The selection of an annual level of progress is based on the measured level of progress at the beginning of the year, and an estimation of the child's projected level of progress at the end of the year. What can a child reasonably accomplish over the course of a year? If every goal is "85 percent," there is little likelihood that the annual level of performance represents a considered estimation of possible annual progress. Give some thought to where a child is, and actually consider what a child might achieve over the course of the year. If a goal can be achieved in a very short period of time (e.g., decreasing classroom outbursts, being late, not completing homework assignments), not to worry. Some goals will be achieved in less than a year and some will be a work in progress. But if goals are always carried over (computerized IEPs delight in "cloning" goals from one year to the next), and the annual level of performance always remains the same, you probably are dealing with bogus goals.

Goals and Classroom

If measurable annual goals are developed apart from the regular classroom, developing effective goals to enable the child to be involved in and make progress in the general education curriculum is unlikely. The question to be asked is simple: What does the child do or not do that requires change? Every child who has a disability under IDEA requires specialized instruction. For the classroom teacher, focus on enabling a child with a disability to participate in the curriculum. What services does a child need to participate in the general curriculum? What classroom supports are necessary? What accommodations does a child need to participate in classroom activities and testing? The following are several areas of regular classroom performance that might affect regular classroom participation and thus might require a measurable annual goal:

Attendance	Homework
Attention	Independent seat work
Basic reading skills	Mathematics oral reading
Classroom behavior	Off-task behavior
Classroom quizzes	Planning/organization
Classroom tests	Reading comprehension
Completing assignments	Reading fluency
Districtwide tests	Silent reading
Expressive language	Statewide tests
Following classroom rules	Teacher ratings
Grades	Teacher reports
Group projects	Work book assignments
Group reading	Writing activities

You don't need a standardized test to determine important classroom needs. Actually, goals should not be based on standardized test performance. The law is not intended to enable successful standardized test performance, but to enable successful classroom performance. A standardized test can be useful for determining the extent of a need, but what is really important is knowing what affects a child's academic performance, and what can be done to enable a child to be educated with nondisabled children. Listen to a child read. The child might be a word reader, has difficulty decoding many words, or the child cannot recall what has been read. This information, what a child actually does in the classroom, is the key to enabling regular classroom participation. And this is the stuff that makes for appropriate IEP goals.

72. THE BOTTOM LINE: GRADUATION

Over 45% of students with disabilities graduated with a standard high school diploma.

There are a variety of reasons why a child with a disability will exit special education including graduation with a regular high school diploma, receiving a certificate of completion, reaching the maximum age for services, and dropping out of school among others. One goal of special education, an important performance indicator for improving the educational progress of students with disabilities, is **graduation with a regular high school diploma**. The IDEA provides every child with a Free Appropriate Public Education, but FAPE does not guarantee a high school diploma. As stated by the Michigan Department of Education

> **"The federal Individuals with Disabilities Act (IDEA) is very clear that all students with disabilities have a right to access, participate and perform in the general education curriculum. While IDEA guarantees FAPE, it does not provide a guarantee that a student with disabilities is entitled to a diploma. Diploma granting is a local board decision, but school boards now have specific graduation requirements they must address, and these are spelled out in state law."**[231]

A shown in Table 10 the average dropout rate in special education is 43 percent. Although the extremely high dropout rate in emotional disturbance (66.2%) is a concern, from 1994 to 2001 there has been a gradual decline in the overall dropout rate from 45.1 percent to 37.6 percent. The largest decrease in dropout rate has been for speech or language impairments, autism specific learning disabilities, visual impairments, and emotional disturbance.

Table 10. Percentage of Students Age 14 and Older with Disabilities Who Dropped Out of School: 1992 through 2000[232]

Disability	1993–4	1995–6	1997–8	1999–0	2001–2	Average
Deaf-blindness	24.5	12.8	11.8	27	27.3	20.6
Visual impairments	24.5	22.3	21.7	20.3	17.8	21.3
Autism	25.9	23.8	19.2	23.7	17.6	22.0
Hearing impairments	24.3	28.3	23.5	23.7	21	24.1
Multiple disabilities	24.6	27.4	26.3	25.8	25.9	26
Orthopedic impair.	25.1	28.9	24.3	30.4	24.3	26.6
Traumatic brain inj.	28.2	30.7	26.1	28.8	24.6	27.6
Mental retardation	35.4	38	36.3	35.7	31.2	35.3
Other health impair.	37.4	36.8	34.9	35.1	32.7	35.3
Specific learning dis.	43.1	44.4	41.3	39.9	35.4	40.8
Speech/language	49.3	50.4	44.5	39.4	35.8	43.8
Emotional dist.	67.8	69.9	67.2	65.2	61.2	66.2
All disabilities	45.1	46.8	43.7	42.1	37.6	43.0

Race and Graduation

All this brings us to race. The graduation rate for white students with disabilities is 56.8 percent and the graduation rate for blacks is 36.5 percent.[233] Inversely, the dropout rate for white students with disabilities is 33.9 percent and the dropout rate for blacks is 44.5 percent. A 44.5 percent dropout rate and a 33 percent graduation rate for black students with disabilities is a disgrace. We could do better than this; we should do better than this. But the highest dropout race is not for black students but for American Indian/Alaska Natives (52.2%), while the dropout rate for Hispanics is 43.5 percent (with a corresponding graduation rate of 47.5%).

Why such disparate percentages for white and black students? Racism, socioeconomic factors, differential treatment, de jure segregation, de factor segregation? Who cares? We need to do more, to do something, to help all children with disabilities not dropout, and then to graduate. This is not just about special education, but about schools and regular classroom teachers, and helping all students to achieve the ultimate purpose of a school: graduation with a diploma.

Special education is important but don't lose sight of the game and especially the ball. Help all students not to dropout of school; help all students graduate.

Table 11 shows the percentage of students 14 and older who graduated with a high school diploma from 1994 to 2001. Visual impairments has the highest graduation rate (66.1%), followed by hearing impairments (62.2%), and then traumatic brain injury (57.6%). The lowest graduation rates are for emotional disturbance (28%), mental retardation (34.1%), multiple disabilities (39.5%) and autism (40.1%). These data indicate that the severity of the disability, and the impact on educational performance and graduation, must be considered in relation to behavior. A school or classroom teacher might well accommodate a child with a severe impairment in the regular classroom if the child's behavior does not affect other students or the teacher. On the other hand, there are many students identified as having emotional disturbance who are more than capable of achieving in school but are removed from the regular education because of behavior.

Table 11. Percentage of Students Age 14 and Older with Disabilities Who Graduated with a Standard Diploma: 1994–95 through 2000–01[234]

Disability	1993–4	1995–6	1997–8	1999–0	2001–2	Average
Visual impairments	63.5	65	65.1	66.4	70.8	66.1
Hearing impairments	61.9	58.8	62.3	61.4	66.9	62.2
Traumatic brain inj.	54.6	54	58.2	56.8	64.4	57.6
Other health impair.	54.6	53	56.8	56.5	59.2	56.0
Specific learning dis.	49.1	48.2	51	51.6	56.9	51.3
Orthopedic impair.	56.7	53.6	57.9	51.5	56.4	55.2
Speech/language impair.	42.9	42.2	48.1	53.2	55.7	48.4
Autism	33.7	36.4	38.7	40.8	51.1	40.1
Deaf-blindness	34.7	39.5	67.7	37.4	49.1	45.6
Multiple disabilities	36.1	35.3	39	42.3	45.2	39.5
Mental retardation	35	34	34.3	34.4	37.8	35.1
Emotional dist.	27	25.1	27.4	28.6	32.1	28.0
All disabilities	43.5	42.4	45.3	46.1	51.1	45.6

These are the real-life special education choices (in order of use): graduate with a diploma, dropout, declassification, or receive what is often referred to as an IEP certificate. If at all possible, the goal should be to receive a high school diploma. The currency of the education world is a high school diploma.[235] One of the greatest achievements for a classroom teacher is for students with disabilities to graduate.

For the majority of children with disabilities a high school diploma should be a primary goal. For the 2001–2002 year over 190,000 students with disabilities received high school diplomas (see Table 12). That a child needs to receive a high school diploma should be given consideration at every IEP meeting. This includes a progress report by a regular classroom teacher concerning progress in the curriculum, needed reasonable accommodation to pass statewide assessments, and other services and supports. Most importantly, for students capable of receiving a high school diploma, courses should be selected that will result in graduation.

Table 12. Students Exiting Special Education[236]

Age	Diploma	Certificate	Dropped
14	–	131	2,695
15	–	123	5,944
16	1,506	370	16,193
17	52,906	6,109	22,472
18	87,936	14,376	20,197
19	36,059	8,225	8,758
20	7,579	3,050	2,562
21	4,965	3,226	923
All	**190,951**	**35,610**	**79,744**

How to prevent dropouts? Develop meaningful programs; give the student a reason to stay in school. Develop programs that are student-centered; programs that meet student-perceived needs and programs that prepare the student for the transition from school to work or postsecondary independent living. Consider each of the following:

Meaningfulness: A 15, 16-year-old is well aware if he or she is wasting time. Make programs meaningful; make IEPs meaningful; give the student a reason not to dropout.

Parents: Not easy; not always possible or productive, but remember that special education is a partnership between school and parents.

Individualization: A small amount of individual attention does not take a vast amount of time and gives the student a sense of belonging.

Progress: Small progress or big progress, no matter. Students must know that they are making progress toward graduation, toward passing courses, toward learning basic skills.

Graduation: Not every student with a disability will graduate but this should be a goal for every student, and this is an important goal for focusing on participation in the general curriculum.

Transition: At least by the time a student is 16 (or earlier) the focus of the IEP should be transition activities from school to work and other post-school activities. Effective transition activities enable students to realize that school can prepare them for post-school work and activities.

Student-centered: Student-center plans provide the essence of the Rehabilitation Act's Individualized Plan for Employment (IPE) for adults. The IPE "affords eligible individuals the opportunity to exercise informed choice in selecting an employment outcome."[237]

Post-school: Prepare students for life after special education because special education does end when the student reaches the age of 21.

Risk: Closely track dropout rates and corresponding risk factors at the school level. Risk factors include excessive absences, significant discipline problems, one or more suspensions from school, juvenile justice involvement, previously retained in grade, limited English proficiency, older than norm for grade, family or economic problems.[238]

73. DECLASSIFICATION

"Overall, about 8 in 10 students with disabilities who leave special education do so, according to their parents, because they no longer need services, including students who have met their IEP goals; about one-quarter specifically mention the school as the source of this declassification."[239]

Is it possible for a child to have a disability one day and not the next? This can occur but certainly not on a regular basis. Consider this case described by Brady and Lind in which an adult patient who became totally blind (for two years) while on a shopping trip.[240] Using successive approximations (small steps toward seeing such as first recognizing brightness) and both social and tangible rewards, the patient regained his sight. Sometimes disabilities do abate; sometimes students outgrow the disability (which often happens with speech impairments); and sometimes the disability no longer requires special education.

▼ **An important goal for the regular classroom teacher: help identify students who no longer need services.**

For the majority of children with IDEA disabilities declassification occurs because IDEA services are no longer needed, specially designed instruction is no longer needed, or the child no longer meets the criteria for an IDEA disability. Speech or language impairments has the largest number of children declassified. As shown below for children ages 6–11: 35 percent of children have speech or language impairments, compared to five percent for students ages 12–17, and 1.8 percent for students ages 18–21. This is in contrast to the percent of students with specific learning disabilities that peaks at ages 12–17, while over 23 percent of students with disabilities are identified as having mental retardation for ages 18–21.[241] Speech or language is one of the few categories which might have a specific guideline for the termination of services (e.g., improvement has plateaued for a specific period of time).

Students Served under IDEA			
Ages	SLD	Speech	MR
6-11	35.7	35.0	7.4
12-17	60.0	5.0	10.8
18-21	48.5	1.8	23.2

There are also situations, especially for older students, when declassification is used in preparation for the cessation of services because of age (21) or as part of a school to post-school transition program. For every reevaluation declassification is always a possibility in that a decision must be made "whether the child continues to have such a disability."[242]

Before determining that a child no longer has a disability, an evaluation must be conducted. This evaluation is not required if the termination of services is a result of age (21) or graduation with a high school diploma.[243] If services are terminated because of age or graduation, the school must provide the student with a summary of academic/function performance, and recommendations for achieving postsecondary goals.[244]

Even though a declassified child is no longer eligible for IDEA services, the child must be provided with all necessary services under Section 504 in that the declassified student has a "record" or a "history" of an impairment (which is part of the definition of a disability under Section 504).

Steps Toward Declassification

The classroom teacher should not think of a magic leap from disability to declassification, but rather envision a progression from unsuccessful academic performance to success in the classroom. The first step is participation. Before performance can be changed there must be performance. Whenever possible, engage every child in the general curriculum. The child might not succeed, but deprive the child of this and failure is assured. Promote more classroom participation and not less.

Encourage and reward independent behavior, and expect aides and other classroom personnel to develop independent skills. The easy solution, the nice solution, is to avoid academic failure. The best way to do this is to avoid academics altogether. Special education is a response to academic failure and is intended to result in academic success. Identify current levels of performance, and then reach beyond this point.

Help plan programs that focus on the regular classroom rather than specialized instruction. Work with special education and related service personnel to generalize specialized instruction to the regular classroom. Help students with disabilities succeed in the classroom, and this success is measured by passing grades. When all this is accomplished, when the child can succeed in the classroom independently, consider declassification. Declassification does not end the school's obligation to provide reasonable accommodations to meet a child's disability, but declassification does signal that specially designed instruction is no longer necessary. A nice goal; a good thing to do when special education is no longer necessary.

Declassification and Reevaluation

IDEA regulations also include provisions for declassification.

For example, a school district is required to reevaluate a student with a disability if there is a question whether the student continues to need special education services. If a school determines that a student is no longer eligible for or no longer needs special education services, a declassification status is documented on the student's individualized education program (IEP), with recommendations for any services the student might continue to need, such as testing accommodation or other support services.[245]

Part VI
Individual Accommodations

A statement of any individual appropriate accommodations that are necessary to measure the academic achievement and functional performance of the child on State and districtwide assessments.[246]

74. REASONABLE ACCOMMODATIONS

Reasonable accommodations should enable classroom participation and not low expectations.

The IEP requirement for IDEA is to include "any individual appropriate accommodations" to measure achievement or functional performance. The concept of an **appropriate** or **reasonable accommodation** must be given more than passing consideration. If an accommodation is excessive, or if an accommodation is not provided, a child's ability to receive an appropriate education could be impacted.

Not every conceivable accommodation must be provided. As was already said, providing unnecessary accommodations might limit a child's ability to participate in the general curriculum, and accommodations should not be an "undue hardship on the operation of its program or activity."[247] Examples of reasonable accommodations include Braille for a blind student, an interpreter for a student with a severe hearing loss, an assistive technology device for a child with cerebral palsy, adaptive furniture for a child with physical needs, or providing a reader for a child unable to read a content-based test (e.g., social studies, biology, etc.).

> ## Section 504
> ## §104.12 Reasonable accommodation.
>
> a. A recipient shall make reasonable accommodation to the known physical or mental limitations of an otherwise qualified handicapped applicant or employee unless the recipient can demonstrate that the accommodation would impose an undue hardship on the operation of its program or activity.
>
> b. Reasonable accommodation may include:
>   1. Making facilities used by employees readily accessible to and usable by handicapped persons, and (2) Job restructuring, part-time or modified work schedules, acquisition or modification of equipment or devices, the provision of readers or interpreters, and other similar actions.

c. In determining pursuant to paragraph (a) of this section whether an accommodation would impose an undue hardship on the operation of a recipient's program or activity, factors to be considered include:
   1. The overall size of the recipient's program or activity with respect to number of employees, number and type of facilities, and size of budget;
   2. The type of the recipient's operation, including the composition and structure of the recipient's workforce; and
   3. The nature and cost of the accommodation needed.

d. A recipient may not deny any employment opportunity to a qualified handicapped employee or applicant if the basis for the denial is the need to make reasonable accommodation to the physical or mental limitations of the employee or applicant.

Unreasonable Accommodations?

What is not a reasonable accommodation? Well, having a scribe write on behalf of a child (and not just recording what the child says) would more likely deny rather than enable participation in the curriculum. The most famous "unreasonable" (my word) accommodation is the landmark *Hudson v. Rowley Supreme Court* decision where the Court concluded that evidence showed that Amy, a deaf child, did not require a sign language interpreter because she was receiving an **adequate education**. Here "adequate" was defined as meaning Amy was performing better than average and was advancing from grade to grade.

Other accommodations might not be permissible under State law such as helping a child formulate an answer, providing punctuation and vocabulary assistance when measuring writing, or not requiring a child to read (e.g., a reader) when measuring reading.

Of course, whenever an accommodation is not needed, but included in a child's IEP, the accommodation is unreasonable and restrictive. Providing extra time is unreasonable and restrictive if a child does not need extra time in that the extra time might provide an advantage, which is not the intent of an accommodation; or extra time might result in an erroneous belief that the child is not able to participate in an assessment without extra time. Of course, the greatest problem is that an unnecessary accommodation might actually exacerbate the problem. If a child is ADHD, and needs shorter work periods, extra time might do more harm than good.

75. ACCOMMODATIONS IN THE CLASSROOM

Classroom accommodations are often the basis for overall testing accommodations.

Generally speaking, there are usually fewer accommodations made in the regular classroom than in special education classrooms. The following table from the 26th Annual report to Congress shows that **additional time for tests** is the most frequently used accommodation in both regular (61.9%) and special education classrooms (79.9%). The one discrepancy between the two settings concerns "slower-paced instructions" which is used 30.4 percent of the time in regular classes but 79 percent in special education classes.

Table 13. Accommodations Use in Regular and Special Education Classrooms[248]

Accommodation	Classroom	
	Regular	Special
IEP support	85.3	98.9
More time for tests	61.9	79.9
More time for assignments	57.5	79.6
Shorter/different assignments	36.8	64.0
Tests read to student	35.3	67.4
Modified tests	33.4	60.0
Frequent feedback	33.3	66.2
Slower-paced instructions	30.4	79.0
Modified grading standards	29.3	51.3
Physical adaptations	22.7	23.8
Alternative tests/assessments	19.7	46.5

Classroom Teacher Tips

- Slow down a bit. It is probably good for everyone in the class.
- Provide more time for assignments if necessary.
- Provide clear directions.
- Provide sequential (step-by-step) directions.
- Monitor student progress.
- Make sure that the task is understood.
- Use a sample task to ensure task comprehension.
- Provide frequent feedback (I know I say this a lot).
- Provide encouragement (I should say this more).

Grading Standards

For a small percentage of children with disabilities major changes to the curriculum might be required. Note, however, that the goal is to provide children with disabilities the same education curriculum that is provided to nondisabled children, and major curriculum changes should be a last resort. This is especially true for grading standards in that modifying how a child is graded could impact eligibility for other courses, programs or even graduation.

76. HOW TO SELECT ACCOMMODATIONS

A child with a disability is not removed from education in age appropriate regular classrooms solely because of needed modifications in the general education curriculum.[249]

Schools must ensure that children with disabilities are included in all general State and district-wide assessment programs **with appropriate accommodations that are included in each child's IEP**, and district/school accommodation guidelines must be developed to ensure this participation.[250]

Begin selecting accommodations by first considering what is needed to mitigate the effects of the disability. Accommodations are not included in the IEP to provide extra help, to give an advantage, or simply because an accommodation seems like a "good idea." Every accommodation should be based on need and to mitigate the effects of a disability. With respect to classroom accommodations, the classroom teacher can provide help relating to four important areas: (1) Help determine what, when and where a classroom accommodation might be necessary; (2) Help evaluate the effectiveness of accommodations; (3) Help implement, or support the implementation, of classroom accommodations; (4) Help ensure the appropriate use of accommodations (especially by aides).

Ensuring that IEP accommodations are implemented does not mean that the classroom teacher must sign tests, learn Braille, or otherwise develop instant expertise in assistive technology. However, the classroom teacher can provide material to a specialist to convert to a different mode of communication, and monitor general curriculum content in the development of accommodations. The IEP might indicate that a child requires periodic breaks during activities and tests because of a health impairment. Unless the test prohibits this type of accommodation, the classroom teacher's role might be to simply allow this accommodation to occur (e.g., in a separate location), to help determine an appropriate time for testing in a separate location that does not interfere with important classroom instruction, and to ensure that necessary materials are available.

Common Sense Accommodations

If an IEP includes a lengthy list of accommodations, and the IEP Team selects accommodations haphazardly, there is a good likelihood that no one will ever look at the list of accommodations much less attempt to systematically implement the accommodations specified. An IEP might indicate the following accommodations (among a list of many): prorate test items, eliminate biased items, highlight text, increase item spacing, place items on a single line, simplify item layout. This is not to say that any accommodation can be discounted because the needs of each child are truly unique, but if an accommodation is important enough to be included in the IEP, some thought should be given to implementation. Who will, after all, decide to eliminate items? Who will be rewriting tests so that the item layout is simplified? Who will decide exactly what "simplified" means? This is certainly not the responsibility of the classroom teacher. Also, if an aide or special educator is assigned the task to modify tests, there must be planning time for the classroom teacher to provide input concerning the test, test protocol, test administration, and test content.

Rather than listing every conceivable accommodations, focus on specific accommodations that are necessary to mitigate the effects of the disability. Common-sense test techniques such as providing extra examples, developing rapport, and giving enhanced instructions are strategies that will be useful to children with and without disabilities.

Disability-Based Accommodations

Often the disability will indicate the type of accommodations required. When an interpreter, reader, scribe, translator, assistive technology specialist, Braille specialist, etc. is needed, appropriate support must be included in the IEP. If the IEP Team decides that all tests should be in large print, a child needs a reader for content-area tests or an American sign language (ASL) interpreter, the IEP should indicate the appropriate personnel who will implement these accommodations. The classroom teacher, as a member of the IEP Team, should not be disinclined to ask who will be responsible for an IEP-designated accommodation and what exactly his or her role will be.

Permissible Accommodations

The classroom teacher should be aware of impermissible accommodations, especially those forbidden by the State Department of Education. Reading a reading test would be inappropriate as would the use of a calculator for a test which measures computational skills. If a State permits an accommodation, the State rather than common sense will prevail. In Massachusetts, a reading test can be read to a student if the child's impairment greatly limits the ability to decode text. Of course, if a reading test is read to a student, the test no longer measures reading and reading for this student is relegated to the lost-cause category.[251]

Classroom-based Accommodations

Several States incorporate classroom and instruction accommodations as the basis for IEP test accommodations. One of New York's quality indicators for test accommodations is that they "are consistent with the instructional accommodations currently used during classroom instruction."[252] Alabama requires that "when determining appropriate accommodations for an assessment, the IEP Team must look at accommodations regularly being made on the student's classroom tests over time in that particular subject area."[253] Using classroom-based accommodations as one element for determining the permissibility of IEP accommodations emphasizes the importance of classroom teacher input for evaluating what accommodations are currently being used in the classroom, what accommodations are effective, and what additional accommodations might be needed.

The Virginia State Assessment Program Guideline

Accommodations should be chosen based on what the student generally uses during classroom instruction and assessment as identified on the student's IEP or management tool. These accommodations are those which the student uses on a daily basis and are not just used for participating in the VSAP. The use of an unfamiliar accommodation during testing may have a negative impact on the student's performance. Finally, an accommodation based solely on potential to enhance performance beyond providing equal opportunity to perform is inappropriate.[254]

Selecting IEP Accommodations

The following are just a few of the almost endless list of test accommodations.

What not to do? Don't go through an IEP checking this or that without an indication of real need.

What to do? Select accommodations based on demonstrated need, and determine need from classroom evaluations, classroom performance, and all other assessments, observations and reports. Always remember that limiting a child's access to high-stakes tests can be restrictive with respect to academic success (e.g., a high school diploma) and future educational performance. With these provisos in mind below the following gives a sample of the types of accommodations that can be cited in a child's IEP:

Abacus	Exemptions (test or subtest)	Recorded responses
Acoustics		Recorded tests
Adaptive furniture	Extended time	Reduced text per page
Adaptive response	Facilitated communication	
Additional test examples		Reduced time
Alternative scores	Foreign language	Respond in any manner
Amanuensis[255]	Guessing strategies	
Amplification aids	Highlight text	Response simplification
Arithmetic tables	Increased spacing	Revised scoring
Assistive technology	Individualized testing	Scribe
Auditory amplification	Item layout	Scripted tests
Augmentative communication	Item pacing	Separate test location
	Item placement	Signing instructions
Between-test breaks	Large print bubble sheet	Signing items
Braille materials	Large print test	Simplified format
Bubble format	LEP format	Simplified instructions
Calculators	LEP instructions	Single switch technology
Cassette	Magnification devices	
Color coding	Manipulatives	Small group testing
Communication device	Markers for answering	Special location
Computational aids	Masks for reading items	Special marker/pen
Computer aids	Modified grading	Special seating
Credit prorated	Multi-day testing	Special tables
Critical-range testing	Multiple-choice modifications	Spell check
Developing rapport		Student-determined time
Developing test strategies	Nonverbal responses	
	Note-taker	Test breaks
Diagnostic interpretation	Oral responses	Time cues
	Practice tests	Time management
Different test location	Preferential seating	Transcriber
Eliminating biased items	Problem-solving aids	Translator
	Questions omitted	Using local norms
Eliminating subtests	Reading aids	Using special norms
End-of-test strategies	Reading content questions	Visual aids
Enhanced instructions	Reading instructions	Waive time
Examiner feedback	Reading stands	Within-test breaks
Examiner rapport	Record answers in test booklet	Writing aids
Examiner training		Writing on test

77. SECTION 504 ACCOMMODATIONS

If a child has a disability but does not need special education, needed accommodations are provided under Section 504.

Section 504 is extremely important for the regular education teacher in that many children do not require specially designed instruction but only an accommodation to participate in the classroom. If a child has a disability, needs an accommodation but not special education, the accommodation must be provided under Section 504 and not IDEA. A child might be identified as ADHD, but the child is able to do well in school, pass tests, and otherwise not have a need for specially designed instruction. A diagnosis of ADHD by a physician/psychologist might indicate the need for breaks during sustained work sessions, organizational help, periodic on-task prompting, preferential seating and other accommodations that do not require specially designed instruction. For this child the accommodation is provided under Section 504: the child has a disability, needs an accommodation, but does not need special education.

How is a Section 504 accommodation made? A Section 504 can be made via a Section 504 plan, using an IEP-like document, or a statement of accommodation. Although accommodations can vary from a very simple and easily provided accommodation (preferential seating, using the school elevator, rest periods to accommodate fatigue) to complex accommodation plans, Section 504 accommodations tend to be more focused than IEP accommodations in that a child might only need an accommodation and not an IEP as required by IDEA. For example, the American Diabetes Association has provided an excellent sample of a detailed Section 504 plan and accompanying Diabetes Medical Management Plan (DMMP) for a child with diabetes.[256] In addition to straightforward and relevant classroom guidelines (e.g., recognizing hypoglycemia, unrestricted use of bathroom, storage of student's insulin pump), specific information is provided for school personnel for a variety of contingencies as exemplified by the following:

> **4.3 All school personnel will permit the student to eat a snack in the classroom or wherever the child is (including, but not limited to classrooms, gym, auditorium, playground, field trips, and school bus) at times designated in the Diabetes Medical Management Plan and whenever needed to treat**

hypoglycemia or in response to a change in the student's regular schedule. A source of glucose will be immediately available wherever the student is.[257]

Section 504 Plans

The Council for Administrators of Special Education (CASE)[258] have developed a four-step planning sequence for Section 504. The plan should describe

> ➢ **The nature of the concern.**

> ➢ **The basis for the determination of handicap (if any).**

> ➢ **How the handicap affects a major life activity.**

> ➢ **The reasonable accommodations that are necessary.**

There are no requirements for a Section 504 plan but a document entitled Section 504 plan indicates that the accommodation or services are being provided under Section 504. The basic components of the plan should indicate the disability (that meets the Section 504 definition of a disability), the specific need, and the reasonable accommodation that will address this need.

Section 504 Plans and IEPs

The basic requirement of Section 504 is the provision of an appropriate education that is designed to meet individual educational needs of children with disabilities as adequately as the needs of children who do not have disabilities. The only documentation requirement cited in Section 504 regulations is that the school must "establish procedures to ensure that information obtained from all such sources is documented and carefully considered."[259] This could be interpreted to mean minutes from a meeting, documentation from a physician, a Section 504 agreement, plan, summary, or statement of needs. The "implementation of an Individualized Education Program" is one means of meeting the vague documentation requirement,[260] but most Section 504 accommodations do not need all the requisite elements of an IEP.

Are Section 504 accommodations different than IEP accommodations? No, the difference is that an IEP accommodation under IDEA is part of a special education plan to provide an appropriate education; Section 504 accommodations more often than not are intended to meet a relatively specific need (e.g., a child with asthma requires an air purifier, or a child requires multiple day testing because o chronic fatigue). Typical Section 504 accommodations include:

- Adaptive/special furniture/tools
- Air purifier
- Assistance with note-taking
- Assistive technology
- Audiocassettes
- Auditory amplification
- Blood tests for blood sugar levels
- Calculator
- Classroom aide
- Colored overlays
- Colored paper
- Computer accommodations
- Counseling
- Eliminating classroom allergens
- Enlarged print Extended time
- Frequent breaks
- Highlighted textbooks/material
- Homebound accommodations
- Humidifier
- Individualized testing
- Large block answer sheet
- Modified classroom schedule
- Modify assignments
- Modify PE
- Modify recess
- Multiple day testing
- Oral responses
- Oral testing
- Peer tutor
- Plastic covered pages
- Preferential seating
- Private room
- Reader
- Rearranging class schedules
- Record answers in test booklet
- School nurse services
- Scribe
- Signed responses
- Small group setting
- Special acoustics
- Special lighting
- Study guides
- Tape recorder
- Taping lectures
- Testing location
- Textbooks for home
- Time of testing
- Transportation
- Use of a highlighter
- Use of a nebulizer
- Use of the school elevator
- Visual magnification device

78. EASY CLASSROOM ACCOMMODATIONS

True, the classroom teacher is not the special education teacher (even if the classroom teacher is certified in special education), but there are a variety of strategies that can be used in the classroom to address classroom needs, before and after referral, that are easy to implement and can benefit all children in the classroom. Preferential seating is a simple accommodation that may or may not be specified in a child's IEP. If a child has a visual impairment, shows signs of not being able to see the blackboard/screen/overhead (e.g., squints), or a child has a hearing impairment or simply does not hear well, having the child sit at the front of the room to better see should not require a mandate from Congress. Preferential seating might be used to separate children, to provide a child with natural light (near a window), or to allow a child to be near an exit (to better meet a child's wheelchair needs).

A child might require a dehumidifier but an appropriate classroom climate will likely benefit all. If you have a child with a disability, consider the following list of accommodations, and check those that will especially benefit the child. In all likelihood, each item checked will also benefit many children who are not disabled, and all that is necessary to implement the accommodation is a bit of conscious effort:

	Ask questions to ensure comprehension
	Be supportive
	Check on classroom work periodically
	Clarify classroom rules
	Collaborate with the special education teacher
	Communicate with the child
	Develop participatory lessons
	Encourage classroom participation
	Generalize from special to regular education
	Give frequent quizzes rather than long tests
	Give step-by-step directions

Model appropriate responses
Outline or highlight key concepts
Preferential seating
Provide a wide range of task difficulty for all students
Provide classroom structure
Provide encouragement no matter what
Provide feedback
Provide frequent clarification during lessons
Provide lots of positive reinforcement
Provide pre-lesson/quiz practice
Simplify tasks
Slow-down the pace
Supervise aides
Use shorter lessons

Focusing on what a child with a disability might need in the classroom will also help the classroom teacher focus on techniques and strategies that will benefit all children. Providing more individual feedback will certainly benefit all children, as will the creation of study guides, outlines, and visual aids. Likewise, highlighting questions on a classroom test, large print or providing enhanced instructions and additional sample might be beneficial to the entire class.

79. CLASSROOM TEST ACCOMMODATIONS

Classroom test accommodations are often a perquisite and/or basis for IEP-mandated test accommodations.

How are test accommodations selected? Certainly a child's disability can play an important role in determining needed test accommodations. If a child is blind and uses Braille, there is no question that all tests involving literacy skills should be in Braille. To provide these accommodations the regular education teacher will require indirect support (e.g., transcribing or selecting materials) and direct support (test administration, Braille training) to effectively provide Braille formatted materials and tests.

If there is one guideline that should guide the use of accommodations, it is the goal of providing children with disabilities an even playing field. The goal is not to give a child with a disability an advantage, to make a test easier, or because it is a nice thing to do. What we want to do, what the law requires us to do, is to be fair and provide reasonable accommodations that best mitigate the effects of the disability.

Classroom accommodations require preparation, and preparation consists of training and supervision. Training entails practice for the student and personnel providing the accommodation. If a test is being read to a child, the first time that a child actually does this task (has a test read) should not be in the form of a high-stakes test. Accommodations require practice for both the person providing the accommodation and the student. Reading a test to a student requires training (especially for aides) and/or practice (for either the regular or special education teacher).

The classroom teacher will often make day-to-day IEP accommodations to accommodate a child's needs for children with and without disabilities. Extra time might be required to complete a task or to understand what the task is. For a child with a visual impairment preferential seating might be given, and for a child with asthma an air purifier is **available and working**. If a child has a health impairment that prevents sustained work efforts, common sense would indicate that some accommodation should be made to the modify length of the assignment or the time to complete the assignment. If a test is read to a student, having a test read orally will often require more time than a traditional testing format. Extra time is not provided to give an advantage, or "because a child has a disability," but to provide a fair and equitable format. Regarding the same accommodation for all children with disabilities, this is inherently discriminatory in that all children will not need the accommodation. If all children receive an accommodation, whether necessary or not, the accommodation is being provided because the child has a disability and not because the child needs the accommodation.

▼ **Remember: An accommodation is intended to mitigate the effects of the disability and not to give preferential treatment or to make a test easier.**

Many test accommodations will be similar to those used in the classroom but all accommodations that are necessary to fairly assess a child must be documented in the IEP. The following are several common IEP accommodations that, before inclusion in an IEP, should be considered and evaluated in the regular classroom:

Which of the following accommodations have been effective for classroom use?	
Assistive technology	Oral responses
Braille	Provide breaks
Calculator	Preteaching
Classroom seating	Problem solving guides
Computer aids	Reader
Dictate responses	Remove distractions
Enhanced instructions	Reducing test time
Extra sample items	Repeating material
Extended time	Scribe
Flexible scheduling	Signing
Highlighting	Shortened assignments
Individualized testing	Simplified test format
Interpreter	Small group testing
Large print	Study guides
Multiple-choice format	Writing in test booklet

Yes, the regular classroom should be where test accommodations have been tried and evaluated by means of using and evaluating classroom accommodations. This trial and evaluation process of accommodations could occur as part of a response-to-intervention, or during the full and individual evaluation. Individualized testing and extended time are frequent accommodations, but the classroom teacher might report (and have collaborating test data from quizzes) that individualized testing or extended time are not beneficial. If this were the case, the argument that these would be reasonable test accommodations would be weak.

Accommodations Provide Access

The IEP for Virginia stipulates that "accommodations/modifications provided as part of the instructional and testing/assessment process will allow the student equal opportunity to access the curriculum and demonstrate achievement. Accommodations and modifications also provide access to nonacademic and extracurricular activities and educationally related settings. Accommodations/modification based solely on the potential to enhance performance beyond providing equal access are inappropriate."[261]

Planning

If a Child Study Team, Child Assistance Team, and so forth is available to consider prereferral needs, the regular classroom teacher will be the primary source for identifying specific needs and possible accommodations that might be used in the classroom. Prereferral interventions are an important consideration in the determination of a specific learning disability where response-to-intervention model requires data-based documentation of repeated assessments of achievement at reasonable intervals, reflecting formal assessment of student progress during instruction.[262] The classroom teacher often has important classroom data regarding academic performance in the form of grades, test scores, quizzes, and, most importantly, samples of work. Often a sample of writing performance or classroom work will provide insights as to appropriate accommodations (e.g., lined paper, using a computer, reducing the amount of written material, reducing the complexity of the written task). Because of the availability of high technology devices, IEP writing accommodations require careful consideration before the meeting. The need for using computer software, voice recognition software, single switch or augmentative communication technology, word prediction, spell check, computer grammar, a thesaurus, online dictionary must be tried and evaluated before the IEP meeting.

Supervision

Certain accommodations such as a scribe, reader, or translator often require a specialized skill, in addition to conducting the assessment in a separate location. The classroom teacher should be aware of what is permitted in terms of these accommodations, and how classroom-based assessments are formatted and presented. If an aide is modifying or giving a classroom test, the aide must be both trained and supervised. If the test involves the general curriculum, the classroom teacher should provide the last word concerning the validity of the modified test.

80. TIME ACCOMMODATIONS

A fairly consistent finding was that the accommodation of extended time improved the performance of students with disabilities more than it improved the performance of students without disabilities.[263]

Extended time is one of the most frequently used IEP accommodations. Before listing extended time as an IEP accommodation the IEP Team should carefully examine what the child needs, what has been used in the regular classroom, and what has been shown to be effective. For some children extended time might exacerbate the problem rather than providing a solution. Instead of extended time, a child with a short attention span might require activities or tests in short blocks of time, multi-day testing, or frequent breaks. Common sense and a healthy dose of data (in the form of classroom performance) should guide the selection of time accommodations. Providing unlimited time might seem like a good idea, but what is the point of providing unlimited time if the child is off-task after two minutes. In this situation unlimited time might actually increase distractibility and off-task behavior, and result in a complete misinterpretation of a child's ability.

Certain disabilities, because of a primary disability-related accommodation, will require extended time accommodations. Braille might require as much as two to three times the time to read than normal print. Likewise, using a reader, an assistive technology device, audiocassette or even large print will require extended time. The need for extended time should be determined during the individual evaluation, based on reports from specialists (e.g., Braille, assistive technology, etc.), and also from performance in the classroom. The classroom teacher need not focus solely on one child during classroom testing but there are several questions that can be asked (and hopefully answered) based on classroom performance. These include:

Yes	No	Is a lack of time a problem?
Yes	No	Do many tests go unfinished because of lack of time?
Yes	No	Is too much time (long test or activities) a problem?
Yes	No	Is extended time needed in some areas but not in others?
Yes	No	Is the problem poor use of time (e.g., impulsivity)?

231

Yes	No	Does behavior affect the ability to complete tests?
Yes	No	Are there strategies that allow a child to remain on-task?
Yes	No	Is reduced time effective for optimizing performance?
Yes	No	Does individualized testing improve performance?
Yes	No	Does testing in a separate location improve performance?
Yes	No	Do test breaks improve performance?

The Continuum of Accommodations

The accommodation needs of a child with a disability can be complex. The most extreme "time" accommodation is simply to exempt a child from a test. This, of course, should be a last resort in that a test exemption restricts access to an important part of the general curriculum (viz., high-stakes testing), and access to all benefits which result from successful test performance. In short, as shown in the table below,[264] a time accommodation can be many things of which extended time is only one possibility.

Accommodation	Type	
Scheduling	Time of day Day of week Multi-day testing	Between-test breaks Within-test breaks Fixed time periods
Time Management	Time strategy Time cues Item pacing	Behavior management Response strategies End-of-test strategies
Extended Time	Extended time Student-determined time Examiner judgment	Waive time Disability-based time Comparable time
Reduced Time	Test Breaks Eliminate items Eliminate subtests	Critical-range testing Individualized testing Exemptions

81. ACCOMMODATIONS: READERS

The need for a reader to enable participation in statewide testing should not eliminate the need to develop literacy skills.

When test items are read to a child with a disability, the entire test must be read including reading passages, questions, multiple choice items, and so on. Unless, of course, the child is allowed to respond orally. Before a test is read to a student, several factors must be considered relating to individualized testing, testing in a separate location, reading pace, reader clarification (usually not allowed), rereading (usually allowed), reading style (don't give answers to questions), and reader expertise (know the vocabulary content).

▼ **New York allows test clarification to "tests and quizzes that are teacher developed and administered. In these instances, test questions and items may be clarified at the discretion of the teacher because the teacher, having developed the assessment, is best able to determine whether, and the extent to which, any clarification may be provided without compromising test validity."[265]**

Test content can usually be read either by state rule or in accordance with the individual student's IEP or 504 plan. To accommodate the extra time to read a test (and a child's listening skills), reading a test should be conducted individually and in a separate location. Readers must be appropriately trained, and know the vocabulary for what is being read. Content should be read in a neutral manner without drawing attention to key words or the answer. Passages and items should be read exactly as written. The reader must not clarify, add, delete, simplify or otherwise change the text. If an aide is the reader, the basic rules for reading a test should be in writing. The following are several guidelines for readers:

- **The use of a reader must be specified in the child's IEP.**

- **Reading a test is a valid accommodation if reading interferes with the assessment of the content area skill (e.g., the test measures poor reading skill rather than knowledge in social studies, biology, etc.).**

- Readers must not change test content or simplify content.

- A reading test cannot be read to the student (well, not in every State).

- Readers must be trained. Actually, everyone should be trained in reading a test and this is easy to do. At a meeting for teachers, teacher assistants and set aside 15 to 20 practice reading test items.

- The reader should be familiar with the test content and vocabulary. The reader should definitely preread the material and be aware of difficult or technical words.

- Readers must be trained to read clearly, with appropriate inflections and at an appropriate speed (which is usually a relatively slow pace).

- A child requiring a reader should be tested individually and in a separate location.

- Readers must be given instructions concerning the permissibility of rereading material, or how frequently material can be reread.

- Depending on test length two readers can be used to read test items. This is good for training and also for providing readers a rest fro longer tests.

- Readers should be told of any special IEP requirements prior to testing.

82. ACCOMMODATIONS: SCRIBES

"The guiding principle in scribing is only to assist the student in accessing the test and responding to it. The purpose of scribing is neither to penalize the student nor to enhance the student's constructed response."[266]

A scribe might be assigned to a student to record answers in a test booklet (e.g., motor problem), or to record what a child dictates. The purpose of a scribe is not to obviate writing needs so that using an aide to assume all writing tasks for a child in the classroom, because writing is not easy, would be inappropriate. This is the same as exempting a child from all reading tasks because reading is difficult. Certain tests are read to a student because reading interferes with content assessment; but reading is always an important part of the curriculum. Likewise, the goal for writing should be to **maximize student authorship, and not to maximize the scribe's authorship.**

A scribe is used when recording answers or writing interferes with what is being measured. If the task is to measure writing usage (e.g., a short paragraph) but lack of fine motor coordination detracts from the fluidity necessary for writing a coherent paragraph, a scribe might be necessary. If the task is to measure writing ability in order to assess appropriate classroom interventions, a child with a disability might be tested in the same manner as nondisabled children in order to determine writing needs.

What to do when using a scribe? The primary thing to do is to ensure that the student and not the scribe is the author of the resulting work, and to achieve this the classroom teacher should consider each of the following:

- **Record exactly what the child dictates.**
- **Do not guide the student in terms of content.**
- **The student, and not the scribe, is author.**
- **The scribe must take his or her role as a "scribe" (and only a scribe) literally.**
- **Do not insert vocabulary, spelling, punctuation or capitalization.**
- **The child may be required to spell difficult words.**
- **The child should be given an opportunity to insert capitalization and punctuation.**

- The child should be allowed to read the material to indicate needed changes.

- By having a clearly defined role as a scribe the student is able to demonstrate proficiency or areas of need. Neither can be determined if the scribe is responsible for all or part of the student's response.

83. INTERPRETERS IN THE CLASSROOM

Accurately, Faithfully, Impartially

One of the guidelines for the **Federal Court Interpreter Ethics and Protocol**[267] is that primary function of an interpreter is "to interpret accurately and faithfully, and with complete impartiality." The interpreter in the classroom is not the gatekeeper for communication, for answering all questions on behalf of a child, or "helping" a child respond in all matters...needed or not.

The role of the interpreter must be known to the classroom teacher, and this role should be as least restrictive as possible. If the IEP states that an interpreter can be used to translate test directions form spoken English to ASL, an interpreter should not go beyond this accommodation. For a reading test the directions can be signed but not the test content. The interpreter should be aware of basic guidelines for signing tests (e.g., know content vocabulary signs; don't prompt or indicate mistakes; don't clarify). Although tempting, especially when a child signs "I don't understand," don't teach signs/vocabulary. Be aware of special instructions concerning repeating material, breaking material down into small blocks, or allowing the student to take notes.

According to the Registry of Interpreters for the Deaf the interpreter's supervisor is not necessarily an interpreter, but the supervisor should understand the role of the interpreter, including the interpreter as part of the educational team, and when interpreting is appropriate. "If the supervisor is not qualified to evaluate interpreting skills or performance, an outside consultant knowledgable in interpreter assessment and skill development should be hired."[268]

Tips for the Classroom Teacher

- **You can and should communicate directly to the student. Every word and every utterance need not be routed through the interpreter. Students in the classroom will communicate directly to the student, and so too can the classroom teacher.**

- **Learn essential signs. It is easy and fun (e.g., "yes," "no,"; Begin, "stop," "Do you understand?"**

- **The interpreter might need help with technical words or concepts.**

- The classroom interpreter is part of a team effort.

- The interpreter is not the classroom teacher.

- The interpreter does not define the curriculum, not a test, and not how a test is administered.

- The classroom teacher should make available test material that will be used by the interpreter beforehand whenever possible.

- The interpreter's role is not to help in all matters, not to respond on behalf of the child, but to interpret.

- Consideration should be given for assessment in a separate location when appropriate.

- If an interpreter is needed as part of an assessment, additional time will be needed.

- Interpreters should be trained before an assessment is given.

- For state assessments understand what is permitted by the interpreter and what is not.

84. LARGE PRINT

The American Printing House for the Blind takes the position that large print for use by the low vision population is print that is eighteen points in size or larger.[269]

   Large print is a simple and relatively straightforward accommodation that, if needed, should be specified in the child's IEP. The difficulty with large print accommodations is the possibility that not all standardized tests will have this format. For classroom tests and materials, the primary consideration is who will provide this accommodation if specified in the IEP. In limited cases large print might be a format used by all children in which case the classroom teacher or classroom aide can provide the large print format. For children with disabilities requiring a large print format for all written material, the classroom teacher will need support. The classroom teacher decides the curriculum or test content and an aide, assistant teacher, volunteer, consultant teacher, or other school personnel should make the necessary changes to the test or quiz format.

Large Print Guidelines

☛ Specify the need for large print in the IEP.

☛ Indicate the support that will be used to implement the accommodation.

☛ Use a simple or sans serif font (this line is Futura) *and avoid stylistic font (and this is Sanvito.)*

☛ Point size should be at least 18 point as is this line, which is 18 point Futura.

Part VII
Classroom Behavior

The committee wants to emphasize that schools must be safe harbors for all children and classrooms must be conducive to learning. S. 1248 adds provisions to assist teachers and other educational personnel by supporting training to address behavioral issues, and clarifying rules for implementing disciplinary decisions. These provisions will help schools keep classrooms safer, while balancing the child's right to receive appropriate educational and related services under IDEA.[270]

85. BEHAVIOR AND THE CLASSROOM TEACHER

Conduct a functional behavioral assessment, unless the LEA had conducted a functional behavioral assessment before the behavior that resulted in the change of placement occurred, and implement a behavioral intervention plan for the child.[271]

Do not assume that all children in special education will have behavioral needs. The behavior of a child with a disability will often be excellent. Most children with specific learning disabilities will be much like other children, save the specific learning disability (in reading, math, etc.). As the classroom teacher you should be aware if a child does have behavioral needs, what supports you will be provided for dealing with these behavioral needs, and appropriate classroom interventions. When dealing with possible behavior problems consider each of the following areas:

Understanding: If a child with a disability is in your classroom and behavior is a concern, understand the disability and why the disability impacts behavior.

Specificity: You must be able to specify behavior problems. To say that a child is emotionally disturbed is not a specific behavior but a disability category. Jumping out of his/her seat, on the average of 23 times a day is specific; calling the classroom teacher, other students, and anyone else who ventures into a classroom a "dumb idiot," or worse is also specific (and not so nice). Specificity helps determine what to do. If a child jumps out of her seat repeatedly over the course of the school day, you do not need to be John Dewey to know that a good goal would be to reduce or eliminate this behavior.

School-wide solutions: The first step when dealing with behavioral needs is to seek school-wide solutions through Child Study Team assistance, regular education intervention planning, and school-wide resources such as counseling, school psychologists, and social workers. Before you ever consider a referral for special education, be sure that the parents are well-informed and that classroom interventions have been tried prior to the referral.

IEP meeting: If behavior is an issue, attend the IEP meeting and contribute. One role of the classroom teacher is to help determine appropriate "behavioral interventions and supports, and other strategies" that can be used in the classroom."[272]

244 The Essential Special Education Guide for the Regular Education Teacher

Data: If a child with a disability exhibits problems in the classroom, collect data or otherwise document the behavior. As said above, be specific as possible. Saying that a child "acts out," is "disruptive" or "emotionally disturbed" often results in nothing being done because the problem has not been specified. Record/observe exactly what a child does or does not do that is a concern, and then report this data to the IEP Team.

What Causes What?

Does the disability cause the behavior? Or is the behavior the disability? If a child has a specific learning disability in reading comprehension, the child might act out as a result of frustration, failure, avoidance, and so forth. If the problem is emotional disturbance, reading comprehension and other areas of learning might be affected because of an underlying emotional need. The simple truth, more often than not, is that we frequently don't know what causes what. There are some children who are classified as having a specific learning disability when the real disability is emotional disturbance, and vice versa. The classroom teacher must focus on observable classroom needs. If behavior interferes or prevents classroom participation, this need must be met; when a child's behavior permits classroom participation, academic needs can be met. We might not know what causes a problem in reading comprehension but we can develop strategies to improve reading comprehension. Very often we will not know what causes a serious emotional problem so we must address the outward manifestation of the underlying problem as best we can. If a child screams in class, the reason for this behavior may never be known. Indeed, determining the underlying cause by a qualified professional might be deemed an important task. However, the regular classroom teacher does not practice clinical psychology in the classroom; but the classroom teacher is certainly interested in changing the child's specific and immediate behavior.

Stay-put Provision

A common misconception among regular education teachers is a belief that once a child has been identified as having an IDEA disability, the child is beyond the pale of school discipline. One essential element of the famous *Honig v. Doe* Supreme Court decision regarding the suspension of students with disabilities is the "stay-put" provision that "prohibits state or local school authorities from unilaterally excluding disabled children from the classroom for dangerous or disruptive conduct growing out of their disabilities during the pendency of review proceedings."[273]

Honig v. Doe (484 U. S. 305)

The problem: On November 6, 1980, Doe responded to the taunts of a fellow student in precisely the explosive manner anticipated by his IEP. He choked the student with sufficient force to leave abrasions on the child's neck, and kicked out a school window while being escorted to the principal's office afterwards. By any standard this is neither good nor acceptable school behavior

The court: Today we must decide whether, in the face of this statutory proscription, state or local school authorities may nevertheless unilaterally exclude disabled children from the classroom for dangerous or disruptive conduct growing out of their disabilities. The present dispute grows out of the efforts of certain officials of the San Francisco Unified School District (SFUSD) to expel two emotionally disturbed children from school indefinitely for violent and disruptive conduct related to their disabilities. Thereafter, his principal referred the matter to the Student Placement Committee with the recommendation that Doe be expelled.

The result: The result of *Honig v. Doe* is an affirmation of IDEA which requires that schools:
- **Actively involve parents when a problem occurs.**
- **If the disability causes a behavior, change the IEP and develop an appropriate plan.**
- **Don't unilaterally exclude students with disabilities without considering all required procedural safeguards.**

Manifestation Determination

The essence of the *Honig v. Doe* decision is to ensure that the disability is not the cause of the behavior. If a behavior warrants school discipline, whether or not a child can be disciplined like other children depends on whether the behavior is caused by the disability. This is called a **manifestation determination**. If the determination is that the disability caused the behavior, the IEP Team must modify the IEP and develop a behavioral intervention plan. If the behavior was not caused by the disability, the child can be disciplined like other children.

Manifestation Determination

Within 10 school days of any decision to change the placement of a child with a disability because of a violation of a code of student conduct, the LEA, the parent, and relevant members of the child's IEP Team (as determined by the parent and the LEA) must review all relevant information in the student's file, including the child's IEP, any teacher observations, and any relevant information provided by the parents to determine if the conduct in question was caused by, or had a direct and substantial relationship to, the child's disability; or if the conduct in question was the direct result of the local educational agency's failure to implement the IEP.[274]

If the behavior is the result of the disability, basic civil rights (viz., Section 504) requires that the child not be discriminated against because of the child's disability. *Honig v. Doe* does not mean that a child with a disability cannot be disciplined or removed from the regular classroom as is sometimes thought. What Honig does mean is that the disability is not ignored when considering an appropriate course of action or discipline.

If, because of a violation of a code of student conduct, the school intends to place the child in a different setting, within 10 days the school, parent, and relevant members of the IEP Team are required to review all relevant information in the student's file. This includes the child's IEP, **any teacher observations**, and any relevant information provided by the parents to determine if the behavior was caused by the disability or because a failure to implement the IEP. The 10-day period can be increased to 45 days for possessing an illegal weapon, for inflicting bodily injury on another, for selling, and/or using an illegal substance.

If the behavior is a manifestation of the child's disability, the IDEA requires that the IEP Team must

1. **conduct a functional behavioral assessment, and implement a behavioral intervention plan for such child, provided that the local educational agency had not conducted such assessment prior to such determination before the behavior that resulted in a change in placement described in subparagraph (C) or (G);**

2. in the situation where a behavioral intervention plan has been developed, review the behavioral intervention plan if the child already has such a behavioral intervention plan, and modify it, as necessary, to address the behavior; and

3. return the child to the placement from which the child was removed, unless the parent and the local educational agency agree to a change of placement as part of the modification of the behavioral intervention plan.

If the parent disagrees with the manifestation determination, or if the school believes that maintaining the current placement of the child is substantially likely to result in injury to the child or to others, a hearing can be requested. The hearing officer may (1) return a child with a disability to the placement from which the child was removed; or (2) order a change in placement of a child with a disability to an appropriate interim alternative educational setting for not more than 45 school days if the hearing officer determines that maintaining the current placement of such child is substantially likely to result in injury to the child or to others.

> ▼ "While a placement may not be changed during a complaint proceeding, a school can use normal procedures for dealing with children who are endangering themselves or others. "Such procedures may include the use of study carrels, time-outs, detention, or the restriction of privileges. More drastically, where a student poses an immediate threat to the safety of others, officials may temporarily suspend him or her for up to 10 school days."[275]

If a child has engaged in behavior that violates a code of student conduct, but the child is not disabled, the child might be entitled to IDEA protections if the school had knowledge that the child was a child with a disability before the behavior occurred. The existence of a disability is assumed if the parents expressed a concern in writing for the need of services, an individual evaluation has been requested, or a teacher or other school personnel have expressed a concern. This does not apply if the parents have refused an evaluation or services.

86. SUSPENSION AND DISABILITIES

School personnel may consider any unique circumstances on a case-by-case basis when determining whether a change in placement is appropriate for a child with a disability who violates a code of student conduct.[276]

Inappropriate classroom behavior is one of the primary factors that will prevent a child from being educated with nondisabled children. A child without severe cognitive needs might be included in the regular classroom for part or even all of the day, but a child who is disruptive and prevents other children from learning will very likely be assigned to an alternative placement. For the classroom teacher there are several questions that frequently arise concerning children with disabilities and discipline.

Can a child with a disability be disciplined? Absolutely. Over 146,000 disciplinary actions were taken regarding children with disabilities. These serious actions included removal to an Interim Alternative Educational Setting (IAES) because of drugs/weapons (13,424), by a hearing officer (1,527), and long (76,591) and short-term (55,033) suspensions and expulsions.

Are there racial disparities in school suspensions? Yes. Race is definitely a factor. According to the data from 26th Annual Report to Congress,[277] the rate of suspensions/expulsions per 1000 for black children is 5.7, for Hispanic students 2.2, and for white students 1.4.

Most children with emotional disturbance have been disciplined? Not so. Although the percentage of children with emotional disturbance receiving one of the four disciplinary actions cited in the 26th Annual Report to Congress[278] is quite high in comparison to other disabilities of the 481,069 children in the ED category, 58,997 were disciplined (8.1%). These data indicate that emotional disturbance is not synonymous with behavior that warrants disciplinary action, and that the majority of children with emotional disturbance are readily able to participate in the regular classroom.

What is Pendency? If the parents of school initiate a due process action, the child remains in the then-current educational placement of the child as specified in the child's IEP. Pendency does not mean a regular classroom placement but remaining in the current placement required by the IEP at the time of the due process action.

Do the procedures for suspending a child with a disability take into consideration individual need? Yes, school personnel may consider unique circumstances on a case-by-case basis when determining whether to order a change in placement for a child with a disability who violates a code of student conduct.

How long can school personnel suspend a child with a disability? Ten days.

Can a child with a disability ever be suspended for more than 10 days? Yes, if the behavior is not a manifestation of the child's disability "the relevant disciplinary procedures applicable to children without disabilities may be applied to the child in the same manner and for the same duration in which the procedures would be applied to children without disabilities."

Is discipline related to age? According to parents' reports over 8.7 percent of children 6–9 have been suspended compared to almost 18.9 percent for 10–12-year-olds.[279] The number of suspensions increases with age so that for 13–14-year-olds 27.3 percent have been suspended or expelled, 34.1 percent for 15-year-olds, 35.5 percent for 16-year-olds, and 35.7 percent for 17-year-olds.

Does special education end when a child is suspended? No, a child must be provided with services to enable participation in the general education curriculum, and to meet IEP goals.

Is the suspension of a child with a disability the "intervention"? Not exactly, a functional behavioral assessment and behavioral intervention services and modifications must be provided to address the reoccurrence of the behavior.

Is discipline related to type of disability? Yes, the following table shows the number of the types of disciplinary procedures by disability. What is surprising is the relatively high number of children in the specific learning disability category being disciplined (although only about two percent of all children in the SLD category are disciplined).[280]

Table 14. Disciplinary Procedures by Selected Disability

Disability	Removal by School Personnel	Removal by Hearing Officer	Suspension > 10 Days	Short Term Suspension	Total
All Disabilities	13,424	1,527	76,591	55,033	146,575
Specific Learn. Dis.	8,119	706	40,153	26,455	75,433
Speech or Language	284	6	1,909	1,486	3,685
MR	1,008	124	7,261	6,097	14,490

ED	2,673	574	19,928	15,822	38,997
Multiple Disabilities	116	15	607	468	1,206
Hearing	99	1	323	213	636
OHI	967	80	5,573	3,880	10,500

Reducing School Suspensions

Before a behavior rises to the level of suspension, attempt to identify and implement prereferral interventions. This requires a team effort (e.g., Child Study Team Student Assistance Team, and input from, guidance counselors, special education and related service personnel, school psychologist, etc.), or an actual plan involving the classroom teacher (or all of a student's classroom teachers), administration support, parent involvement, and school-linked services (social work, juvenile justice), and school-wide expertise (e.g., a consultant teacher might have useful ideas concerning prereferral strategies). If possible, conduct a functional behavioral assessment, implement a behavioral intervention plan, and provide positive behavioral interventions before a behavior has escalated to the point of suspension. Focus on why certain behaviors occur, and provide client-centered services.

87. BEHAVIOR: CLASSROOM STRATEGIES

Antecedent behavioral strategies are intended to accommodate potential problems before they occur.

Rapport: This can be difficult and often requires considerable focus on the part of the classroom teacher. Develop rapport with a student and life may not be hunky dory, but life in the classroom will be better.

Business: Everything that a child does is not directed at you. The same behavior probably occurs in other classes and at home. By and large much of a child's behavior that occurs in your classroom is just part of the child's business and not about you. Don't take things too personal. Of course, if the behavior only occurs in your classroom, then maybe there is a reason.

Positive: The task is to find something positive to say. This might be difficult, and might take some searching, but positive you must be.

Believe: Believe that the plan, classroom support and services will actually work and make a difference. You must believe.

Plan: Have a plan for dealing with behaviors; have a plan for classroom success. If there is no plan, there is no plan to succeed.

Planning: "Planning" is the basis for the "plan" (see above). Remember that a Behavioral Intervention Plan is a necessity when a child's disability is the cause of the behavior. Plan and then plan some more!

Parents: A great source for identifying useful strategies. Make parents part of the plan, and part of the planning.

Structure: Structure and routine can promote purposeful and productive behavior.

Talk: Talk to parents; talk to teachers; talk to specialists (e.g., the consultant teacher), but do constructive talking. Don't "at"; talk "to." Complaining about a child to anyone who will listen will not be very helpful and will annoy (especially others) more than help. Talk to find out what to do, what works, and what not to do. Talk to get ideas, to develop a plan. Talk is good; even good therapy. Talketh not too much . . . and complain even less!

Clarity: Be clear about assignments, direction, and so on.

Individualization: For example, eye contact is sometimes important to ensure that a child is attending to what is being said; and sometimes a child (with Asperger's) might be less than tolerant of eye contact. Parents can often provide good information as to the most appropriate approach. All said and done, each child is different and make an attempt to adjust to these individual differences.

School Threats and Violence

At least 85 percent of manifestation reviews resulted in disciplinary actions.[281]

Consider: Consider the behavior and your response. If a seven-year-old child is having a screaming tantrum and accidentally hits you with a flailing arm, the behavior is probably not intentional and your response should not be that it is. If a fifteen-year-old pushes you with clear malice, the behavior is intentional and you must treat it as such.

Data: For every serious problem relating to threats, violence and serious misconduct, record the event and the time and date it occurred.

Deal with the problem: Don't ignore problems involving threats, violence, substance abuse, bullying, and so on. Recognize the problem and consider the various measures described below.

Contact the principal: This is why principals earn the bucks. Also, just for the record jot down the time, date, and a brief description of the problem for your own record of the meeting.

Conferences: Teacher-student, teacher-student-parents, principal-student, teacher-student-principal, teacher meetings, and so forth. For serious problems have serious conferences and meetings.

Know school policy: Read whatever policy statement is available concerning discipline and the discipline of children with disabilities.

Police intervention: Being in special education is not a license for aggravated assault, vandalism, theft, and so on by a student. Your school might have a written policy for what behaviors require police intervention/notification.

Alert other teachers: Sometimes threats are subtle but if you perceive a problem, alert other teachers, the principal and the parents.

Safety: If safety is an issue, ask that the child be removed from your classroom. The administration can remove a child receiving special education for up to 10 days. During that time a determination must be made concerning the cause of the behavior, interventions (IEP modifications), and placement. A safety issue must be based on behavior and not a subjective belief that safety might be a problem. Of course, a serious threat, in and of itself, is a problem...and the carrying out of that threat even a greater problem.

Parent involvement: Always, always, always involve parents.

IEP-redux: If a behavior is caused by the disability, the IEP must be modified to address the problem. The classroom teacher on the IEP team provides data and possible solutions/suggestions for classroom interventions.

Counseling: A school psychologist, guidance counselor, social worker, and other specialist could be specified in the IEP.

Behavior manifestation determination: This is required to determine whether the behavior is a result of the disability. If it is not, the student can be disciplined like all other students.

FBA: Functional Behavioral Assessment is a must for all instances of school misconduct.

BIP: The Behavioral Intervention Plan might include behavior modification, behavior modification strategies, self-monitoring strategies, development of measurable annual goals, classroom accommodations, increased supervision, the use of aides, and so on.

Suspension: Yes, a student with a disability can be suspended, even expelled. However, the school must provide every child with a disability due process as defined in IDEA. The majority of manifestation determinations (approximately 85%) result in a determination that the behavior was not caused by the disability.

Alternative placement: Maybe the regular classroom is not the most appropriate placement...and the parents might agree to a change in placement. Discuss the problem with the parents and seek a solution that is best for the student, the school and the parents. **Think partnership.**

Referral to and Action by Law Enforcement and Judicial Authorities

Rule of Construction. – Nothing in this part shall be construed to prohibit an agency from reporting a crime committed by a child with a disability to appropriate authorities or to prevent State law enforcement and judicial authorities from exercising their responsibilities with regard to the application of Federal and State law to crimes committed by a child with a disability.[282]

88. OBSERVATIONAL DATA

The public agency must ensure that the child is observed in the child's learning environment (including the regular classroom setting) to document the child's academic performance and behavior in the areas of difficulty.[283]

As a member of the IEP, Team the regular classroom teacher has an important responsibility in the determination of appropriate behavioral interventions, strategies, supports, supplementary aids and services, and program modifications. As part of the individual evaluation, observing a child in the regular classroom is always relevant. Classroom-based observations and "observations by teachers and related services providers"[284] are important in the initial evaluation, the evaluation of annual progress, and reevaluations.

When the behavior of a child might result in disciplinary action, teacher observations should be one of the factors during the "manifestation determination" to determine whether the behavior was caused by the child's disability. If the classroom teacher has observed or has "prior knowledge" that a specific pattern of behavior indicated a disability, and the child has not been identified as a child with a disability, the child could be eligible for all IDEA procedural safeguards.[285]

Observational data from several teachers, related services providers and other school personnel will provide a better perspective on the what, why and when of the behavior. What exactly is the behavior? When does the behavior occur? Why does the behavior occur? When a specific learning disability is suspected, a person other than the child's classroom teacher should observe the child in the classroom to document classroom performance and behavior.[286]

There are a variety of elaborate observational systems that can be used to record behavior in the classroom including anecdotal recording, interval recording, duration recording, behavior recording, rating scales, teacher interviews, and academic observational reports. Whatever observational approach a classroom teacher uses, the time and effort to record classroom information must be realistic and not result in excessive time or paperwork. For the classroom teacher the task is not to abandon the class, but to select a simple method that will result in data which can be considered by the evaluation and/or IEP Team.

What to Do?

Here are several basic guidelines for the classroom teacher: **First**, collect data. You do not need to sit in the back of the room with a clicker recording every behavior, but you can identify specific problems and the number of occurrences at the end of the day. Over time this will be more valuable than most other behavioral assessments. **Second**, using this data and input from a Child Study Team (or an equivalent group), develop and implement classroom strategies and interventions. Spend a few minutes briefly recording the effectiveness of these strategies and interventions. No, you don't need a dissertation on the child's behavior, just a brief statement, very factual, very descriptive. If these are ineffective, be sure to discuss these strategies and interventions, and the effectiveness of each, at the IEP meeting. **Third**, prior to the IEP meeting, during the individual evaluation, provide the evaluation team with a brief outline of what you did and the results. Not a long jargon-filled report (use the report discussed above), but bullet each strategy and intervention followed by a very short description of what happened. **Fourth**, if behavior is a primary concern, request a Functional Behavioral Assessment. At the very least this should result in a formal evaluation of the behavior and reason why the behavior occurs.

Fifth, attend the IEP meeting and contribute, especially when classroom behavior affects you, or affects the learning of nondisabled students. One of the primary reasons for a classroom teacher to attend the IEP meeting, in addition to the IDEA requirement, is to ensure that goals, supports, services and accommodations are provided to address the behavior. When goals are being considered, be sure that the IEP has measurable annual goals that focus on the specific behavior, and that each goal has a specific beginning level of performance (e.g., jumps out of seat 40 times per day). When the IEP Team considers supplementary aids and services or supports for school personnel, indicate what you think are necessary supports (e.g., aides, consultant teacher, and accommodations, scribe, reader, specific accommodations, etc.). Two questions to consider before the meeting: (1) What the child needs to be successful in your classroom? (2) What do you need for the child to be successful in your classroom?

If you have a child with a disability in the classroom, and behavior is an issue, ask if there is a Behavioral Intervention Plan (BIP). If there is, read it. If there is not a BIP, request one be developed at the IEP. If behavior continues to be a problem in the classroom, don't do this alone. The problem in the classroom is a problem for the IEP Team, a problem for the school, and a problem for the IEP Team and all service providers and school personnel. You must use a team approach when dealing with persistent behavior problems in the classroom. Sources of help: consultant teachers, special education teachers, school psychologists, guidance counselors, other teachers, social workers, parents, child study team, IEP Team, grade-level teams, and so on. A behavior problem in the classroom is a school-wide problem so use all available school-wide resources. Work with parents, sometimes you can and other times not, but try. Finally, don't give up. If one strategy doesn't work, try another. We can't always be effective; we don't always know "the answer"; but we can be persistent.

89. PRACTICAL BEHAVIOR ASSESSMENT

There are many sophisticated techniques for observing and recording behavior. However, most classroom teachers do not have an abundance of free time to focus on one student. What to do? The following is a simple easy-to-use technique for collecting and graphing data that will requires less than a minute a day to accomplish.

First: Specify as much as possible the behaviors that seem to affect classroom participation. If a child has a tendency to shout out answers or make comments in the classroom that are disruptive, at then end of the day record the number of times each category of behavior occurred. Recording data once a week is probably insufficient in that by the end of the week your memory will probably be a bit muddled (so it is on Fridays), but recalling behavior frequencies at the end of each day should be reasonably sufficient. You don't need mechanical engineering accuracy, but merely how many times a certain behavior occurred every day.

Second: At the end of the week record the data in an Excel worksheet as shown below. By quickly accessing the chart wizard, the data is easily graphed as shown. This basis provides a basis for discussing the behavior and developing effective intervention strategies.

	Mon.	Tue.	Wed	Thu.	Fri.
Classroom Outbursts	2	4	8	6	10
Leaving Seat	1	3	2	1	5

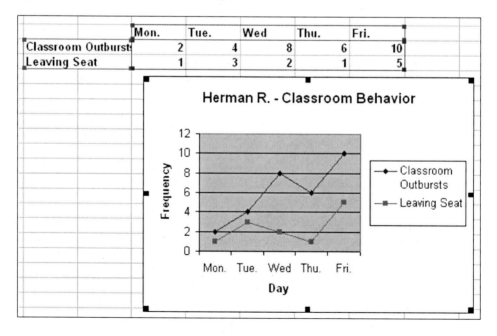

What to Do with Behavior Data

1. **Interventions:** Try a classroom intervention and see if the behavior changes. This is, after all, the heart and soul of response-to-intervention. If the intervention works, great job! You have done your job well. If the intervention doesn't work, you have data to better select the next intervention.

2. **Planning:** Show data to others, as part of a Child Study Team planning session, or planning with special education personnel. Team planning is more effective (more ideas, more perspectives) when the planning is based on data. Without data there is often no planning.

3. **Meetings:** Bring your data to the IEP meeting. Complaining about unspecified classroom behavior or inappropriate behavior at an IEP meeting might be ignored, but less so when the behavior is specific and visibly portrayed in a graph.

4. **Goals:** Develop a goal based on the data. This is how goals should be developed. If classroom outbursts occur 30 times a week on the average, maybe the first goal should be to reduce these outbursts to 15 times week.

5. **Accommodations:** A behavior might need an accommodation. If a child has chronic fatigue and engages in inappropriate classroom behavior when tired, shorter work periods would certainly seem to be a reasonable solution.

6. **Supports:** Classroom supports in the way of an individual aide might be necessary but this should be carefully planned. Providing an individual aide should not be used to ignore intervention efforts. If an aide is part of the solution, a plan must be develop to address the behavior, plan for the reduction of aide services, and evaluate classroom behavior when the aide is not present.

Behavior Problems and the General Curriculum

Removing a child from the regular classroom because of behavior is not a license to remove the child from the general curriculum. If a child with a disability is removed from the classroom for disciplinary reasons, irrespective of whether the behavior is determined to be a manifestation of the child's disability, the child "must be allowed to participate in the general education curriculum, although in another setting, and to progress toward meeting his or her IEP goals."[287]

90. CLASSROOM RATING SCALES

Rating scales provide a simple technique for quantifying classroom behavior, especially for use as an initial level of performance for goals. Easy-to-use rating scales can help focus a teacher's concerns on data that can be used to formulate goals, gauge progress and chart performance.

First, select the categories or areas to be rated. This is where the regular classroom teacher's expertise is important. General classroom areas might include organization, note-taking, and so forth as shown in the rating scale below. Rating scale categories could be developed for specific reading or writing tasks such as prosodic reading (inflection and expression), reading speed, reading accuracy, reading comprehension, work attack skills, reading vocabulary. Writing categories might include grammar, punctuation, spelling, syntax, ideation, and so on. The categories could just as easily be behavior concerns (e.g., paying attention, completing work, following rules), or behaviors that interfere with classroom performance (e.g., interrupting, physical aggression, inattention, etc.). When selecting rating scale categories, maintain polarity. In other words, don't combine reading comprehension with excessive talking so that each might be rated "high," but for far different reasons.

Instructions: rate each item from 1 (low) to high (5).					
Area	Low		Average		High
Organization	1	2	3	(4)	5
Notetaking	1	(2)	3	4	5
Studying	(1)	2	3	4	5
Concentration	1	2	(3)	4	5
Homework	1	(2)	3	4	5
Classroom work	1	2	(3)	4	5
Daily preparation	(1)	2	3	4	5
Read. Comp.	1	(2)	3	4	5
Oral Reading	1	2	(3)	4	5
Assignments	1	(2)	3	4	5

Second, select the scale for rating each category. This could be in the form of a numerical scale from 1 to 5 or 1 to 7. More than seven rating categories is generally not needed in that five or seven provide a reasonable basis for reliable ratings. A brief instruction should be included to remind others (and yourself) what you are rating. In the above rating scale, items are rated from 1 (low) to 5 (high). Obviously, you can use whatever descriptors that seem most appropriate but don't be too negative ("awful" isn't a nice description) or positive (rarely is something "perfect") but "outstanding" or "excellent" might do.

Third, try out the rating scale for one or more students.

Fourth, analyze the results. The summated rating is the total of all the ratings. For the above, the sum of the 10 ratings is 23 and the mean rating is 23 divided by 10 or 2.3. For a scale of 1 to 5 a 2.3 is somewhat below the hypothetical mean of 2.5. In terms of a percentage this is 46 percent or 23 divided by the maximum possible summated rating of 50 (10 x 5) and multiplied by 100.

Items =	10
Summated Score =	23
Mean Score (items/Score) =	2.3
Maximum Score =	50
Percent (Mean/Max)X100 =	46%

Fifth, graph the data. An easy way to record and graph rating scale data is to use Microsoft Excel. The following figure shows how the data is entered into an Excel worksheet, and then the chart wizard is used to quickly graph the results. This is also excellent for comparing a series of ratings over a period of time,

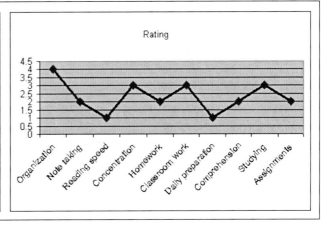

Area	Rating
Organization	4
Note taking	2
Reading speed	1
Concentration	3
Homework	2
Classroom work	3
Daily preparation	1
Comprehension	2
Studying	3
Assignments	2
Sum	23

on a pre-post basis, or as part of repeated assessments used to report progress to parents.

▼ **Guestimate: Rather than simply affixing "85% as determined by teacher observation" to every goal, guestimate what percentage of material/skill is currently mastered. Example: "_____ is able to comprehend 50% of grade-level reading material." This is not terribly accurate, but a guestimate of the present level of performance might give a better insight to annual goal performance.**

91. EMOTIONAL DISTURBANCE

Historically, it has been very difficult for the field to come to consensus on the definition of emotional disturbance, which has remained unchanged since 1977.[288]

The IDEA definition of emotional disturbance is based on criteria developed in California in the 1950s (by Eli Bower) and used in the first version of IDEA (P. L. 94-142).[289] In the IDEA regulations *emotional disturbance* is defined as a condition in which a child exhibits one or more of the following characteristics over a long period of time and to a marked degree that adversely affects a child's educational performance:

1. An inability to learn that cannot be explained by intellectual, sensory, or health factors.

2. **An inability to build or maintain satisfactory interpersonal relationships with peers and teachers.**

3. Inappropriate types of behavior or feelings under normal circumstances.

4. A general pervasive mood of unhappiness or depression.

5. A tendency to develop physical symptoms or fears associated with personal or school problems. (ii) Emotional disturbance includes schizophrenia.

Emotional disturbance is not always easily differentiated from other disabilities such as specific learning disabilities, ADHD and social maladjustment. If a student's behavior is intentional and undertaken with a specific purpose or consequence and in a willful manner, the behavior *might* be determined to be the result of social maladjustment rather than emotional disturbance. For example, a student who had been adjudicated for delinquent behavior (e.g., theft), the behavior (theft) could not be the basis for a determination of emotional disturbance. Emotional disturbance does not apply to students who are socially maladjusted unless it is determined that they have an emotional disturbance.

A key point in the above definition is that the condition must **adversely affect educational performance**. What happens if a child has emotional needs that fall within the realm of emotional disturbance (e.g., pervasive mood of unhappiness, or a cyclothymic disorder characterized by episodes of hypomania and minor depression) but educational performance is not affected? In this situation Section 504 would apply if a disability is determined, but the child does not need special education. For example, the child might need extensive counseling, but not specialized instruction.

As with all disabilities under IDEA, the disability must have an adverse affect on educational performance. For all disabilities, especially emotionally disturbance, adverse effect on educational performance goes beyond low standardized scores. An inability to participate in classroom activities, to interact with other students, or follow classroom rules might be viewed as an adverse effect on educational performance.

Think Behavior

This cannot be said enough: If you are the classroom teacher, the key to changing behavior is to think behavior. Identify specific behaviors, note when the behavior occurs, why the behavior occurs, or what preceded the occurrence of the behavior. To do this you don't need a special form, an aide to record behavior or special graphing tools. Use a calendar with room for notes to record the student's name and a very short description of the behavior and what happened before and after. Don't do this immediately, but set aside several minutes later in the day to record the event. If the event was particularly disturbing (e.g., a full-fledged temper tantrum with on-the-floor kicking, crying and screaming), writing a brief account is not only an excellent way to memorialize what happened but also a form of cheap therapy.

When recording behavior, don't confuse **behavior** and **labels**. A label of "emotional disturbance" is not the problem; the problem is the classroom behavior(s) that gave rise to the determination of emotional disturbance. A child first exhibits behaviors (or not), and these behaviors can result in a classification of emotional disturbance. For the classroom teacher behavior specificity is essential. Identify specific classroom behaviors and discuss these behaviors at the IEP meeting. What affects classroom performance? What prevents successful classroom participation?

Questions to Ask

What is the specific behavior?	
How frequently does this behavior occur?	
Is the behavior situational?	
Does the behavior involve specific students?	
Does the behavior involve school personnel?	
Does the behavior occur in nonacademic settings (e.g., bus, recess, lunch)?	
Does the behavior occur at home?	
What event precedes the behavior?	
What follows the occurrence of the behavior?	
What do you do following the behavior?	
What happens to the student?	
What interventions have been attempted?	
What accommodations are effective?	
What classroom supports will help address the behavior?	

92. MORE SOCIAL MALADJUSTMENT

The IDEA requires that during the determination of emotional disturbance, the evaluation team considers the possibility of social maladjustment because **"the term does not apply to children who are socially maladjusted."** However, under Section 504 social maladjustment would be a disability if a determination is made that the condition is a mental impairment that affects a major life activity. Such are the problems with social maladjustment. Sometimes a disability; sometimes not; sometimes used to excuse students from a disability determination; and sometimes misused, misunderstood, and simply a very confusing term. During the development of the regulations for IDEA several voiced the opinion that social maladjustment was not easily measured (or could not be measured), was not a valid term, and children who need special education have been denied these because the definition of emotional disturbance excludes children who are socially maladjusted.[290]

For the classroom teacher, the distinction between emotional disturbance and social maladjustment that results in criminal behavior is important from the standpoint of intervention. To highlight this point consider the fact that "the arrest rate for students labeled seriously emotionally disturbed who have been out school more than one year is 44 percent (Wagner, 1989), whereas it is between 3.9 percent and 4.7 percent for ages 16 to 24 (Federal Bureau of Investigation, 1987)."[291] One of the goals, special education services for secondary students, is to provide an effective transition from school to work, and a 44 percent arrest rate is hardly a ringing endorsement.

One logical solution to the problem would be to eliminate the "social maladjustment" clause from the definition of emotional disturbance. The Department of Education put its bureaucratic head in the D.C. sand and did nothing because "given the lack of consensus and the fact that Congress did not make any changes that required changing the definition, the Department recommended that the definition of *emotional disturbance* remain unchanged."[292] Ugh!

When school behavior is extremely disruptive as evidenced by antisocial behavior, bullying, disruptiveness, exploitiveness, fighting, rule-breaking, a determination of social maladjustment can provide the school with considerable disciplinary discretion. When the determining factor is social maladjustment, the solution is generally punishment, isolation, or removal from the school. If the determining factor is emotional disturbance, services and accommodations must be provided to mitigate the effects of the disability, in addition to the array of procedural safeguards available under IDEA.

The difference between emotional disturbance and social maladjustment is less than clear because no one is quite sure what in the world social maladjustment means. One approach is to equate social maladjustment with a conduct disorder or an oppositional-defiant disorder. The former is characterized by aggression to people (or animals), destruction of property and theft, and the latter by a student who is argumentative, refusing to comply with rules, annoying behavior (and easily annoyed), and a student who is often resentful and vindictive.

What to do? If a distinction can be made between emotional disturbance and social maladjustment, the distinguishing criteria are behaviors that are goal-directed, self-serving, and intentional. At the IEP meeting discuss these factors in relation to the behaviors that have given rise to the consideration of emotional disturbance as a possible IDEA disability category. Vermont has identified the following criteria for differentiating emotional disturbance and social maladjustment:[293]

A social maladjustment unaccompanied by an emotional disturbance is often indicated by some or all of the following:	
☐	Unhappiness or depression but not pervasive
☐	Problem behaviors are goal-directed, self-serving and manipulative
☐	Actions that are based on perceived self-interest
☐	Social and behavioral standards are understood but not accepted
☐	Negative counter-cultural standards or peers are accepted and followed
☐	Problem behaviors escalated during preadolescence or adolescence
☐	Inappropriate behavior only in selected settings
☐	Problem behaviors the result of encouragement by a peer group
☐	Behavior is intentional
☐	The student understands the consequences of behavior

The Vermont checklist can be useful but these criteria do not eliminate the possibility of emotional disturbance. The classroom teacher, the school, and certainly the student all benefit if a child with a disability receives appropriate special education services and accommodations.

The classroom teacher is often acutely aware of problems relating to school rules and conduct. Specific guidelines for the classroom teacher:

- Involve parents
- Be respectful to students
- Formulate classroom rules
- Identify positive and negative consequences
- Document instances of bullying, fighting, rule-breaking, etc.
- Address problems relating to school conduct at the IEP meeting
- If school conduct has been an issue, address the problem in the transition plan from school to work.

93. ADD/ADHD

(Other Health Impairments)

heightened alertness to environmental stimuli

The IDEA definition for **A**ttention **D**eficit **D**isorder (ADD) **A**ttention-**D**eficit **H**yperactivity **D**isorder (ADHD) is a subcategory of Other Health Impairments and reads

> *Other health impairment* means having limited strength, vitality or alertness, **including a heightened alertness to environmental stimuli, that results in limited alertness with respect to the educational environment,** that – problems such as asthma, attention deficit disorder or attention deficit hyperactivity disorder, diabetes, epilepsy, a heart condition, hemophilia, lead poisoning, leukemia, nephritis, rheumatic fever, and sickle cell anemia; and adversely affects a child's educational performance.[294]

For the classroom teacher this definition can be vague and difficult to understand. A "heightened alertness to environmental stimuli" might be the result of boredom, lack of motivation, disinterest, and so forth. Although primarily used by psychologists (and forever by lawyers...wouldn't you know) the fourth edition of the *Diagnostic Statistical Manual* (or DSM-IV for all you Court TV fans) provides more detailed criteria for determining ADHD on which the following checklist is based:

✓	DSM-IV Checklist for ADHD
☐	Careless mistakes in schoolwork
☐	Does give attention to detail
☐	Difficulty sustaining attention
☐	Difficulty organizing
☐	Often seems not to listen
☐	Often fails to follow instructions or finish tasks

☐	Often loses things necessary for tasks
☐	Avoids tasks requiring sustained effort
☐	Easily distracted by extraneous stimuli
☐	Often forgetful
☐	Fidgets
☐	Leaves seat without permission
☐	Difficulty engaging in activities quietly
☐	Talks excessively
☐	Blurts out answers
☐	Difficulty awaiting turn
☐	Interrupts others
Total Number checked from above	
☐	Some symptoms were present before 7, present in two or more settings, impairment in functioning, and are not better accounted for by another disorder.

ADHD: Classroom Tips

If a student's behavior in the classroom is disruptive or contrary to school/classroom rules, consider each of the following:

- **Attempt to understand what is rewarding and what is not**
- **Consider seating: (1) near the teacher, (2) away from the door or other outside distractions, (3) near children who are not disruptive**
- **Develop goals to increase periods of "sustained effort"**
- **Do not reward inappropriate behavior**
- **Ignore inappropriate behavior... within limits**
- **Reward appropriate behavior**
- **Focus on task completion**
- **Give more frequent quizzes/tests/assignments**
- **Incorporate more student participation in lessons**

- Provide an outline for lessons/presentations
- Provide clear and easily understood classroom rules
- Provide frequent feedback
- Structure material, content and lessons...use lots of structure
- Use a notebook for the child to record assignments
- Use large print (printed material and chalkboard)

94. BEHAVIOR AND MEDICATION

Medication cannot be a condition for school attendance.[295]

Children with disabilities in your classroom, as well as some children who might not be identified as disabled, might require medication. As the regular education teacher you should be aware of who requires medication, especially if medication must be administered during the school day. Also important is the need to monitor changes in behavior that might affect school performance. Take note of changes in behavior, and discuss these changes with the parents. Side effects associated with medication include appetite reduction, drowsiness, excessive staring among others, headaches, insomnia, irritability, moodiness, nervous tics, nervousness, sleep difficulties, stomachaches, unusual behavior.

So the school administrator suggests that little Tommy might have ADHD and, if so, Ritalin® is generally needed. No more. Because IDEA prohibits schools from requiring medication:

> **The State educational agency shall prohibit State and local educational agency personnel from requiring a child to obtain a prescription for a substance covered by the Controlled Substances Act (21 U.S.C. 801 et seq.) as a condition of attending school, receiving an evaluation under subsection (a) or (c) of section 614, or receiving services under this title.**[296]

Part VIII
Services

When must IEP services be provided: "As soon as possible following development of the IEP, special education and related services are made available to the child in accordance with the child's IEP."[297]

95. SPECIALLY DESIGNED INSTRUCTION

Make provision for supplementary services (such as resource room or itinerant instruction) to be provided in conjunction with regular class placement.[298]

Special education is provided by a special education teacher or a speech specialist if the instruction is necessary to adapt the content, methodology, or delivery of instruction (1) to address the unique needs of the child, and (2) **to ensure access of the child to the general curriculum,** so that the child can meet the educational standards of the school system that apply to all children.[299]

▼ **"Co-teaching" has many different meanings depending on the context in which it is used. Whether and how co-teaching is implemented is a matter that is best left to State and local officials' discretion.[300] (and, most importantly, to the regular classroom and special education teachers).**

Special education is defined as "specially designed instruction, at no cost to the parents, to meet the unique needs of a child with a disability, including (1) Instruction conducted in the classroom, in the home, in hospitals and institutions, and in other settings; and (2) Instruction in physical education. Speech-language pathology, travel training and vocation education can be "special education" if either entails specially designed instruction.

Special education is not synonymous with an educational placement outside of the regular classroom. Indeed, for every child with a disability the first placement considered is always the regular classroom. Because many services will be provided in the regular classroom, the regular classroom teacher must be part of the IEP planning process and have access to each child's IEP who participates in the classroom.

If special education is provided in the regular classroom, these services can be either provided directly, indirectly or both. **Direct services** mean that a certified special education teacher works with a child with a disability either individually, in a small group, or in a co-teaching or collaborative format (e.g., as a lead teacher). **Indirect services** include all support help that the special education teacher provides such as planning, consulting, modifying materials.

▼ Special education teachers should meet with
general education teacher teams to better
understand general curriculum so to better provide
that curriculum to all students with disabilities.

Resource Room Instruction

First and foremost, the resource room should be used to supplement the regular classroom. Resource room services can promote regular classroom participation if there is good communication between the regular classroom and
resource room teacher. The focus of resource room services is the general curriculum, and the resource room teacher's focus is regular classroom participation. This does not mean the resource room is simply a supervised study period
or a place where regular classroom homework is completed. The intent of the
resource room is to provide the specially designed instruction necessary for a
child to participate successfully in the regular classroom. The resource room
might be necessary to teach reading fluency skills; or instruction could be designed to teach mathematics skills that are required in the regular classroom.

Resource room services can vary between 21 percent to 60 percent of the
day in the resource room setting. The original intent of the resource room is to
support the regular classroom so that there must be planning between the regular classroom and resource room teacher for effective resource room instruction. Obviously, if a child is removed from the regular classroom for
resource room help, and that removal affects successful participation in the
general curriculum, the resource room might do more harm than good.

Direct Services

Collaborative teaching: The regular education teacher and special education teacher can collaborate by teaching separate groups, team teaching, or where
the regular or special education teacher assumes a supportive role. The IDEA
now allows the special education teacher to work with children who are disabled
and nondisabled so that the special education teacher might lead the overall
lesson and the classroom teacher provides diagnostic and individual help.

Services and Aids that Benefit All

For the costs of special education and related services, and supplementary
aids and services, provided in a regular class or other education related
setting to a child with a disability in accordance with the individualized
education program of the child, even if 1 or more nondisabled children
benefit from such services.[301]

Team teaching: This is especially useful when there are several children with disabilities in the regular classroom. In this situation the regular and special education teachers plan and teach as a team. Variations include lead and support teaching, co-teaching, and collaborative teaching.

Consultant teaching: This is the least restrictive special education service in the continuum of services. The role of the consultant teacher is to provide direct (e.g., team teaching, direct instruction, collaborative instruction) and indirect services to enable a child with a disability to succeed in the regular classroom. If a consultant teacher is used, be sure that the direct and indirect services are specified in the IEP. In other words, exactly how will the consultant teacher provide support to the classroom teacher and to the child.

Indirect Services

Indirect services include all the various supplemental aides and services that do not involve direct instruction. The classroom teacher should be aware of the types of supports and services available to help a child with a disability succeed in the classroom. Indirect services can include

- **Child Study Team support**
- **Consulting with specialists and school personnel**
- **Curriculum modifications**
- **Developing curriculum materials**
- **Grade level team meetings**
- **IEP Team meetings**
- **Parent conferences**
- **Parent contacts and support**
- **Planning and developing test accommodations**
- **Preparing assistive technology material**
- **Scoring tests**
- **Teacher planning**
- **Training and supervising aides**
- **Training scribes and readers**

96. RELATED SERVICES

The provision of related services such as counseling and speech/language services is one of the major areas in which schools fail to comply with the FAPE mandate.

In addition to special education, a child's IEP must specify necessary related services and additional supports *which are required for a child with a disability* to benefit from special Education.[302] If a child has a disability and **needs only a related service** such as speech or physical therapy and not special education, these services are provided under section 504 and not IDEA.

Related services can be provided in the regular classroom and must always be specified in the child's IEP. The regular classroom teacher should be aware of what related services are in a child's IEP, where these services are provided, and how the provision of these services might affect involvement in the general curriculum. A simple and obvious method for reducing classroom interruptions, especially during times when a child's other classroom needs are being met, is to include the regular classroom teacher in the scheduling process. At the very least the classroom teacher should be consulted before a child is removed from the regular classroom either for special education (e.g., resource room) or a related service.

Related services include the following:

• Achieving independence in the workplace	• Consulting with other staff members in planning school programs
• Administering psychological and educational tests	• Counseling and guidance of parents, children, and teachers regarding speech or language impairments
• Assisting in developing positive behavioral intervention strategies.	• Counseling regarding hearing loss
• Assisting in developing positive behavioral intervention strategies	• Counseling services
• Assisting parents in understanding the special needs	• Cued language transliteration services
• Audiology services	• Determination of needs for amplification
• Auditory training	• Diagnosis and appraisal of specific speech or language impairments
• Career development	• Employment preparation
• Community services	

- Evaluating the effectiveness of amplification.
- Group and individual counseling with the child and family
- Guidance counselors
- Hearing evaluation
- Interpreting services
- Language habilitation
- Leisure education
- Long cane or a service animal training
- Medical services for diagnostic or evaluation purposes
- Mobilizing school and community resources
- Obtaining, integrating, and interpreting information about child behavior and conditions relating to learning
- Oral transliteration services
- Orientation and mobility services
- Parent counseling and training.
- Physical and occupational therapy
- Planning and managing a program of psychological services
- Prevention of communicative impairments
- Providing parents with information about child development
- Psychological counseling for children and parents
- Psychological services
- Recreation and therapeutic recreation
- Referral for the habilitation of speech or language impairments
- Rehabilitation counseling
- School health services
- School nurse services
- Selecting and fitting an appropriate aid
- Sign language interpreting services
- Social work services in schools
- Specialized equipment (such as special or adapted buses, lifts, and ramps), if required to provide special transportation for a child with a disability.
- Speech and language pathology
- Speech conservation
- Speech reading (lipreading)
- Transportation services
- Travel training
- Using vision and distance low vision aids
- Vocational rehabilitation services

97. SUPPLEMENTARY AIDS AND SERVICES

Although the statue does not require 'mainstreaming' in every case, it is fundamental to the scheme and purpose of the Act that handicapped children be provided the same educational opportunity and exposure as those children who are not so disadvantaged.[303]

Supplementary aids and services' means aids, services, and other supports that are provided in regular education classes or other education-related settings to enable children with disabilities to be educated with nondisabled children to the maximum extent appropriate.[304]

Remember this phrase: **Supplementary Aids and Services**. This term is essential, is necessary, yet frequently misunderstood. Supplementary aids and services is the essence of what is generally considered the **mainstreaming requirement:** to provide aids and services to enable children with disabilities to be educated with children who are not disabled. This is the presumption that every child will be educated in the regular classroom. As per IDEA, there is no actual "mainstreaming requirement" but there certainly is a supplementary aids and services requirement.

> The court in *Greer v. Rome City School District* (p. 696) reasoned that the school must consider the whole range of supplemental aids and services, including resource rooms and itinerant instruction, before a placement outside of the regular classroom is considered.[305] In *Daniel v. State Board of Education* the court emphasized that mere token gestures were not sufficient to supplement the regular education curriculum.[306] And in *Oberti* the court understood how special education can have a segregative intent and that schools must "move beyond those systems, structures, and practices which tend to result in unnecessary segregation of children with disabilities."[307]

Supplementary aids and services are the basis for meeting the least restrictive requirement mandate. These services include any and all aids, services, and supports that might enable a child to succeed in the regular classroom.

▼ **The Supplementary Aids and Services Test: Only when the full range of supplementary aids and services are not successful can a child be removed from the regular classroom.**

Every child's IEP must specify special education, related services, supplementary aids and services and the supports that a child might need. Supplementary aids and services is sometimes confused during the development of the IEP as a unique group of services (or a service) that is somehow different from special education, related services and school supports. As indicated by the courts supplementary aids and services enables successful participation in the regular classroom and entails the **full range of services** which includes:

> **Full Range of Services**
> **(Supplementary Aids and Services)**
>
> **Special Education**
> **Related Services**
> **Supplementary Services**
> **Support Services**
> **Full Program Options**
> **Accommodations and Modifications**
> **Test Accommodations**
> **Assistive Technology**

After the IEP has been developed and when the child's placement is being determined, supplementary aids and services should be given first consideration. When special education is provided to a child in the regular classroom (e.g., by a consultant teacher), this is actually a supplementary aid and service that enables a child to be educated with nondisabled children. Other supplementary aids and services that might permit a child to be educated with nondisabled children include, in addition to special education, related services, supplementary services (e.g., a resource room), support services (e.g., consultant teacher services, aide, assistant teacher, parent tutoring), the availability of full program options, accommodations and modifications to the curriculum and tests, and assistive technology.

The list of possible supplementary aids and services is virtually endless in that any service, accommodation or support that enables a child to participate with nondisabled children falls within the category of "supplementary aids and services." Many supplementary aids and services rely either on the direct participation of the classroom teacher (e.g., co-teaching, collaborative instruction), or input from the classroom teacher involving the supplementary aid or service. For services such as assistive technology, the classroom teacher's expertise regarding the curriculum is often essential for outlining the content for the effective implementation of the assistive technology device or service. If a child uses a single-switch to participate in the general curriculum, someone must have expertise regarding the general curriculum to generate the appropriate computer content. To enable this type of participation involving the regular classroom curriculum the classroom teacher and technology specialist would need to collaborate and plan to develop an appropriate and effective assistive technology plan.

> ▼ **If a regular education instructor must devote all of her time to one handicapped child, she will be acting as a special education teacher in a regular education classroom. Moreover, she will be focusing her attentions on one child to the detriment of her entire class, including, perhaps, other, equally deserving, handicapped children who also may require extra attention.**[308]

98. TRANSITION SERVICES

Transition services help the student make the transition from school to post-school activities.

Transition services are included in a student's IEP which will be in effect when the student reaches the age of 16. Transition services are defined as meaning a coordinated set of activities that are designed to facilitate a student's transition from school to postsecondary activities. These activities include postsecondary, adult and vocational education, integrated and supported employment, adult services and independent living. Transition services also include instruction, related services, community experiences, the development of employment and other post-school adult living objectives; and the acquisition of daily living skills and functional vocational evaluation.[309]

▼ Client-centered transition plans: involve the student in the determination of transition services and post-school planning; involve the student in all planning and IEP meetings; involve the student in all transition activities that will affect his or her post-school future.

Transition and the Classroom Teacher

• Consider the postsecondary needs of students with disabilities.

• Help students understand postsecondary school options. For example, discuss the merits of two and four year schools, course and program selection, and admission processes.

• Help identify vocational areas of interest. For example, a two-year program as a medical technician might be discussed in a biology class.

• Devote time to career and postsecondary planning.

• Help generalize the use of technology such as doing an online job search.

- Discuss college placement tests and sources/procedures for obtaining test accommodations.

- If appropriate, incorporate useful postsecondary skills into the curriculum (e.g., writing a resume).

- Your participation in the IEP process could provide important insights toward the development of an effective transition plan.

- Read the transition plan, or the transition services specified in the IEP to understand the role, or potential role, of the classroom teacher.

99. CLASSROOM SUPPORTS

The regular education teacher of the child with a disability helps determine appropriate positive behavioral interventions and supports, and other strategies.

Classroom supports are essential for a child to achieve satisfactorily in the regular classroom. A statement of the program modifications or supports for school personnel must be included in every child's IEP in order to achieve annual goals, to be involved in and make progress in the general education curriculum, and to participate in extracurricular and other nonacademic activities.[310] Indeed, the focus of special education is not special education for the sake of special education but to achieve specific goals and to participate in the general curriculum. The following data from the 25th Annual Report to Congress indicates the various support services and accommodations used by one or more students to provide access to the general curriculum.[311]

Support System	(%)
Speech and language therapy	89
Occupational therapy	71
Family training, counseling, other support	56
Nursing service/health service	52
Psychological service	51
Physical therapy	51
Special transportation	50
Social work services	49
One-to-One paraeducator/assistant	49
Assistive technology service/device	45
Tutoring	43
Adaptive physical education	42
Service coordination/case management	41

Audiology/hearing service	37
Vision services	26
Communication service	17

In addition to the above, supplementary aids and services can be used to support the regular classroom teacher by providing direct special education services in the classroom, indirect services in the way of co-planning, and assist with the implementation of program modifications. Before the IEP meeting the classroom teacher should consider what the child needs to achieve successfully in the classroom, and then determine what supports are necessary for the child to achieve this success. Remember, the goal is not to occupy a child with busy work by means of a one-to-one aide but to enable a child to achieve as independently in the classroom. The ability of a child to achieve satisfactorily in the regular classroom without the help and general expertise of the classroom teacher is small. The regular classroom teacher must have support, and this support should be clearly articulated in the child's IEP.

Questions to Ask:

1. **Does the child need direct classroom teaching services?**
2. **Is planning time required for regular classroom participation?**
3. **Are test accommodations necessary?**
4. **Who will provide/supervise the accommodations?**
5. **Are curriculum accommodations necessary?**
6. **Does the child need aide support?**
7. **Does the child require an assistive technology device or training?**
8. **Does the child require a behavioral intervention plan?**

Peer Tutoring

Don't forget an essential component of classroom support: the nondisabled students in the classroom. Peer tutoring can be effective for providing additional opportunities to communicate, to interact, and solve problems. For the classroom teacher the key to peer tutoring is training, respect, and opportunity. Training can be as simple as in-classroom demonstrations showing what a tutor does regarding helping, allowing a tutee to respond independently and keeping track of progress. Effective peer tutoring requires respect between tutor and tutee. Finally, peer tutoring should be democratic in nature. Given the appropriate level of materials and difficulty, all children can be peer tutors.

100. REGULAR AND SPECIAL EDUCATION SUPPORT

Monitoring student progress is one of the most cited areas of regular classroom support for children with disabilities.

There are many classroom supports that can be used in the regular education classroom ranging from the easy-to-do "monitoring progress" to supports involving assistive technology services and devices.[312] As shown in the table below, monitoring progress is important in special classes and should be an area of support provided to regular classroom teachers. Other important areas of needed support for the classroom teacher include learning strategies, self-advocacy training and behavior management.

Table 15. Support Services in Regular and Special Education

Support	Classroom (%)	
	Regular	Special
Monitor progress	51.9	74.9
Teacher aides	27.5	53.9
Learning strategies	24.2	46.6
Peer tutor	22.9	21.3
Adult tutor	18.8	10.9
Books on tape	14.5	23.1
Self-advocacy training	14.1	7.2
Computer	11.2	18.9
Reader/interpreter	10.31	5.1
Behavior management	9.8	28.3
Special computer software	3.9	20.6
Communication aids	3.2	4.1
Special computer hardware	2.1	3.5

Self-advocacy Training

Self-advocacy training in the regular classroom is essential for developing independent skills, and generalizing these to postsecondary activities. Self-advocacy skills include

- **Decision-making skills**
- **Problem-solving skills**
- **Expressing needs**
- **Evaluating accommodations**
- **Self-management**
- **Self-assessment**
- **Assistive technology skills**
- **Self-ratings and behavior evaluation**
- **Self-evaluation of academic performance**

101. RESOURCE ROOM SERVICES

With regard to the commenter's question about whether moving a child from a self-contained classroom to a resource room would be a change of placement, we believe that it would be.[313]

The resource room was originally intended as a way to supplement a child who needed some extra help. Dunn described the resource room as a supplement to the regular classroom where a child receives "a small amount of extra assistance" and goes "only to use specialized equipment and to receive specialized instruction, either in a tutored situation or in a small group" (1963, p. 31). The purpose of the resource room has always been to supplement the regular classroom. However, the resource room is sometimes used to restrict access to the regular classroom or even the general curriculum. The misuse of the resource room support is exemplified by the self-contained resource room in which a child receives the majority of instruction in this misnamed alternative placement.

If there is no connection between the resource room and regular classroom, if the resource room encompasses or emphasizes a different curriculum than the general education curriculum, what exactly the resource supports will be unclear. The regular classroom and resource room teacher must share common ground in terms of curriculum and promoting regular classroom success.

When the resource room teacher works closely with the regular education teacher regarding the curriculum, progress, and enabling success in the regular classroom, this objective can be achieved. When the resource room is a separate placement, remote from the regular classroom in curriculum and goals, enabling regular classroom participation becomes even more difficult.

The regulations for P. L. 94-142 did not define Supplementary Aids and Services other than to "make provisions for supplementary services (such as resource room or itinerant instruction) to be provided in conjunction with regular class placement."[314] As stated in *Greer v. Rome City School District* (p. 696)[315]

before the school district may conclude that a handicapped child should be educated outside the regular classroom, it must consider whether supplemental aids and services would permit satisfactory education in the regular classroom. The

**school district must consider the whole range of
supplemental aids and services, including resource
rooms and itinerant instruction, for which it is
obligated under the Act and the regulations
promulgated there under to make provision.**

The change from a resource room as a placement that is designed to supplement the regular classroom to a special education placement was strengthened by the Office of Special Education Programs (OSEP) method for defining a resource room as one in which a child spends between 21 percent to 60 percent of the school day outside of the regular classroom. By the same token, a regular classroom placement entails 79 percent of the school or more in the regular classroom, and a separate placement as more than 60 percent of the school day outside of the regular classroom. If the school day is comprised of nine 40-minute periods, one period a day in a resource room would be a **regular classroom placement**, two to five periods a day in a resource room would be a **resource room placement**, and six to nine periods a day in a resource room or other settings outside of the regular classroom would be a **separate classroom placement**. If a resource room placement is defined as providing up to 60 percent of services, this would suggest the resource room provides far more than supplemental help.

The following table shows the number and percent of children served in resource rooms.[316] Specific learning disabilities account for over 67 percent of all children with disabilities in resource rooms. Surprisingly, there is a relatively large percentage of children in the mental retardation category (10.32%) who meet the resource room placement criteria (21–60%). Of course, some of these children are also in more restrictive settings, yet an effort is made to include children in the regular classroom often to some degree during the school day.

Table 16. Children with Disabilities in Resource Rooms

Disability	Children in RR	% of Children in RR	% of Child. With Disabilities	% of all Children
Specific Learning Disability	1,093,152	65.89%	18.65%	1.66%
Mental Retardation	178,635	10.77%	3.05%	0.27%
Emotional Disturbance	107,483	6.48%	1.83%	0.16%
Other Health Impairment	104,951	6.33%	1.79%	0.16%

Speech or Language Impair.	81,345	4.90%	1.39%	0.12%
Multiple Disabilities	21,312	1.28%	0.36%	0.03%
Orthopedic Impairment	15,996	0.96%	0.27%	0.02%
Hearing Impairment	13,357	0.81%	0.23%	0.02%
Autism	16,577	1.00%	0.28%	0.03%
Developmental Disorder	14,766	0.89%	0.25%	0.02%
Visual Impairment	4,350	0.26%	0.07%	0.01%
Traumatic Brain Injury	6,844	0.41%	0.12%	0.01%
Deaf-Blindness	303	0.02%	0.01%	0.00%
All	1,659,071	100.00%	28.30%	2.52%

There are no exact criteria when a resource room service changes from supplementing the regular classroom to replacing regular classroom services, but for a child who spends more than 50 percent of the day in a resource room the services provided are likely to replace rather than enable regular classroom participation.

The classroom teacher might regard the resource room as a place to get "extra help" while the special education teacher might look upon the resource room as a special education service that provides specially designed instruction apart from the regular classroom. The resource room is a place to receive that extra support, that supplements the regular classroom, but this does not mean that the resource room teacher is little more than a tutor. The role of the resource room teacher is to not only provide that "extra help" to enable regular classroom participation, but also to provide the specially designed instruction to achieve goals and to improve areas of need.

102. FEOG

(Full Educational Opportunity Goal)

I'm not sure how to pronounce this, but FEOG is extremely important for schools and teachers. Schools must ensure that children with disabilities have available the variety of educational programs and services that are available to nondisabled children. Programs and services that must be made available to children with disabilities include art, music, industrial arts, consumer and homemaking education, vocational education, physical education, special physical education (if necessary), and nonacademic and extracurricular services. [317]

All children are entitled to remedial services. If a child has a disability because of emotional disturbance, this does not preclude this child from receiving remedial reading or to participate in other school-wide programs.

> ## Full Educational Opportunity Goal (FEOG)
>
> 1. The State must have in effect policies and procedures to demonstrate that the State has established a goal of providing full educational opportunity to all children with disabilities, aged birth through 21, and a detailed timetable for accomplishing that goal.
>
> 2. The State must ensure that each public agency takes steps to ensure that its children with disabilities have available to them the variety of educational programs and services available to nondisabled children in the area served by the agency, including art, music, industrial arts, consumer and homemaking education, and vocational education.[318]

103. PARAPROFESSIONALS

Paraprofessionals and assistants who are appropriately trained and supervised can be used to assist in the provision of special education and related services under this part to children with disabilities.[319]

If a child with a disability has a full- or part-time aide, the aide must be supervised by the classroom teacher and/or special education teacher (or supervisor). The regular and special education teacher should discuss and collaborate on matters involving aides and paraprofessional. Aides and paraprofessionals are not independent of the classroom teacher, and the classroom teacher is "the" expert regarding the general curriculum.

Paraprofessionals and aides must be trained and supervised. For an aide in the regular classroom, the role is not to provide all instruction, to make all tasks easier, or to promote dependence. An aide is not licensed to ignore the general curriculum, or the overall goal of classroom participation. Every paraprofessional in the regular classroom should be aware that the goal for all children with disabilities is participation with nondisabled children; the goal is not the participation of the aide with nondisabled children.

▼ **The key word is "independence": do only what is necessary, and do not restrict opportunities for a child to participate in the curriculum or other school activities.**

No Child Left Behind

Under the No Child Left Behind (P.L. 107-110) act new paraprofessionals are to have (1) completed at least 2 years of college; (2) obtained at least an associate's; or (3) have demonstrated through a State or local academic assessment knowledge of, and the ability to assist in instructing, reading, writing, and mathematics. This requirement does not apply to a paraprofessional who provides services primarily to enhance the participation in programs by acting as a translator; or whose duties consist solely of conducting parental involvement activities.

The responsibilities of a paraprofessional can include being assigned

1. **to provide one-on-one tutoring for eligible students, if the tutoring is scheduled at a time when a student would not otherwise receive instruction from a teacher;**

2. **to assist with classroom management, such as organizing instructional and other materials;**

3. **to provide assistance in a computer laboratory;**

4. **to conduct parental involvement activities;**

5. **to provide support in a library or media center;**

6. **to act as a translator;**

7. **to provide instructional services to students.**

However, a paraprofessional may not provide any instructional service to a student unless the paraprofessional is working under the direct supervision of a teacher. But the paraprofessional

> **may assume limited duties that are assigned to similar personnel who are not working in a program supported with funds under this part, including duties beyond classroom instruction or that do not benefit participating children, so long as the amount of time spent on such duties is the same proportion of total work time as prevails with respect to similar personnel at the same school.**[320]

Paraprofessionals Planning

Just as an aide working independent of a classroom teacher in the regular classroom would be unacceptable, an aide assigned to a child with a disability without training or supervision is nonsensical. If an aide were given the responsibility to decide how a child with a disability participates in the curriculum, there would be no point to the development of an IEP, much less an IEP that was intended to promote involvement in the general curriculum. For every aide or paraprofessional working with a child with a disability, either on a part-time basis or as a one-to-one aide, a plan must be devised that articulates both training and supervision.

Paraprofessional Training

Aides must have a very clear idea of what is expected in terms of instruction, assessment, and providing accommodations. If an aide has scribe responsibilities, permissible scribe responsibilities must be articulated. For example, a scribe is not permitted to correct spelling, language or punctuation. If a paraprofessional is providing translating services, the fact that the language being used is not English does not mean that the translator can operate without training or supervision. For paraprofessionals in the regular classroom, whether working with the entire class or assigned to one child, the classroom teacher must assume at least some responsibility for this training and supervision.

What to Do?

1. **The classroom teacher determines the appropriate general education curriculum and not the paraprofessional.**

2. **Set aside time for paraprofessional training.**

3. **Show an interest in what the paraprofessional is doing (or not doing).**

4. **Provide feedback to the aide concerning performance.**

5. **Provide training for specific accommodations such as a scribe or reader.**

6. **Definitely provide training relating to any and all test accommodations.**

7. **Demonstrate what you want the aide to do (or not do).**

8. **Clearly demonstrate the concept of developing "independent student behavior."**

9. **Emphasize the need for student behavior and not paraprofessional help.**

10. **Emphasize independence.**

11. **Encourage participation in the general curriculum and classroom activities without help.**

Paraprofessional Supervision

In a regular classroom the classroom teacher provides the necessary supervision for classroom aides. For a child with a disability the classroom aide might provide either direct or indirect assistance as a result of being assigned to the overall classroom, being assigned primarily to assist child with disabilities, or being assigned as a one-to-one aides. For an aide assigned to the regular classroom, a child with a disability is entitled to assistance from that aide just as nondisabled children are entitled to assistance.

For aides specifically assigned to work with one or more children with disabilities in the regular classroom, shared responsibility for aide supervision is essential. The special education teacher will often provide training and supervision for specific tasks such as modifying the curriculum, classroom modifications, and specially designed instruction. However, the classroom teacher must be aware of what modifications are permissible and provide guidance and supervision relating to the general curriculum and classroom participation.

104. IN-SERVICE

If a child with extensive learning needs is to be assigned to your classroom, request in-service training to prepare yourself, classroom aides and other school personnel to better meet the needs of the child. The IDEA[321] provides considerable guidance and grants (read "money") for school personnel

- To ensure that those personnel have the necessary skills and knowledge, derived from practices that have been determined, through scientifically-based research, to be successful in serving those children.

- To encourage increased focus on academics and core content areas in special education personnel preparation programs.

- To ensure that regular education teachers have the necessary skills and knowledge to provide instruction to students with disabilities in the regular education classroom.

- To ensure that all special education teachers are highly qualified.

- To ensure that preservice and in-service personnel preparation programs include training in the use of new technologies, the area of early intervention, educational, and transition services, effectively involving parents; and positive behavioral supports.

- To provide high-quality professional development for principals, superintendents, and other administrators, including training in instructional leadership, behavioral supports in the school and classroom, paperwork reduction, promoting improved collaboration between special education and general education teachers, assessment and accountability, ensuring effective learning environments and fostering positive relationships with parents.

105. LEP AND DISABILITIES

*A child must not be determined to be a child with a disability
under this part if the determinant factor for that determination is
Limited English proficiency.*[322]

Limited English Proficiency (LEP) is a term used to describe a student "whose difficulties in speaking, reading, writing, or understanding the English language may be sufficient to deny the individual (1) the ability to meet the State's proficient level of achievement on State assessments; (2) the ability to successfully achieve in classrooms where the language of instruction is English; or (3) the opportunity to participate fully in society.[323] LEP students are also referred to as English-language learners (ELL).

▼ **Simple rule: ESL is not a disability. First understand ESL needs before attempting to understand disability needs. A child may have ESL needs, or disability needs, or ESL and disability needs.**

Limited English Proficiency can be complicated. A child may not only not speak English, but also have limited educational or instructional experience. English as second language is not a disability; nor is lack of instruction. Regarding specific learning disabilities, limited English proficiency cannot be the basis for a determination of this disability. What to do? **First**, consider factors that might indicate the existence of an explicit disability such as a visual or hearing impairment. Parents might have important information concerning the child but an interpreter will often be necessary to obtain this vital parent input. If the child has a disability such cerebral palsy, the disability and LEP must be addressed. If a child has cerebral palsy, is deaf or has a visual impairment, the disability may be relatively easy to identify. Limited English proficiency becomes more of an issue for high incidence disabilities such as specific learning disabilities, emotional disturbance and mental retardation (especially "educable mental retardation" or cases of retardation in the 50–75 IQ range). If a child's primary language is not English, poor reading might be the result of a lack of instruction, a reflection of English language skills, or a disability.

Second, determine academic skills in the child's native language. This can be difficult but be creative. Maybe an older student with a similar language background can develop one or two simple curriculum-based assessments, or assistance/volunteer can be sought in the community. For Spanish this is probably no problem, but Somali, Chinese, Hmong, and so on, gathering basic academic information in the child's native language might not be an easy task. For a child with a disability and ELL needs the classroom teacher, special education teacher and ESL specialist must use a team approach for meeting the child's language and content area needs.

Third, determine the child's ability to respond to instruction. This is especially important in that if a child is able to respond to instruction, in either English or the child's native language, this generally precludes the existence of a specific learning disability or at least indicates that the child should be given ample opportunity to demonstrate the ability to succeed in the classroom before a determination of a disability is made. Pennsylvania recognizes that "simply placing students in content area classes does not provide them meaningful access to content if they do not understand English. Teachers must adapt courses of study to meet student needs. Adapting coursework does not mean diluting or placing in lower grades for instruction."[324]

Fourth, consider cultural factors. For example, (and this I did not know) that "in Western cultures, when a student smiles knowingly at the teacher, it often indicates understanding. However, in many Asian cultures, it actually indicates confusion or frustration."[325] In Greece "no" is indicated by a "yes" type movement (head upward then backward movement). Asking a child whose native language is Greek whether he/she understands can be a tricky enterprise.

Fifth, do not ignore the student with a disability and/or ELL needs. What to do? Focus on basic interpersonal communication skills and academic language proficiency. Teach language and content. In the classroom use preteaching, emphasize key words, use cooperative learning, visual aids, participatory activities, outlines, extended time, and summarize content. Be respectful...always. Learn a few words of the child's native language. Visit the internet. I learned that "Yes" in Hmong is "Aws, and "No" is "Tsis." Ok, not only am I uncertain how to say "No" in Hmong, and I also read that saying "No" can be considered disrespectful so a student might respond "Yes, I don't understand." In any case, learning about a student's culture and language can be fun for you and the class.

Be aware that a child with an ELL student with a disability will have three areas of needs: disability, academic and language. An ELL student who is hard of hearing, deaf or blind will require all necessary accommodations to deal with specific disability needs; next, language needs must be considered; and finally a program must be provided to meet the academic needs of the student.

You are not expected to be an ESL/LEP/ELL instructor but you can provide a welcoming language environment and make attempts to include the child in all classroom activities. Oh, I stand corrected. A parent of a child with LEP needs can decline services in which case the school, and you as the classroom teacher, will be responsible for meeting the child's academic and language needs as best as you can.

NOTES

1. P.L. 108-446, 601(c)(5)
2. *Ibid.*
3. P.L. 108-446, 601(c)
4. See 601(c)(1)-(14)
5. EVANS v. THE BOARD OF EDUCATION OF THE RHINEBECK CEN-TRAL SCHOOL DISTRICT, 930 F. Supp. 83; 1996 U.S. Dist.
6. P.L. 108-446, 614(b)(5)(A)
7. P.L. 108-446, 601(c)(1)
8. 34 CFR 300.323(c)(1)
9. 34 CFR 300.323(a)
10. 34 CFR 300.226 Early intervening services.
11. From Public Law 107-110, Section 1208, the No Child Left Behind act of 2001.
12. P.L. 107-110, Section 1208(6)
13. P.L. 107-110. 1208(7)(C)&(D)
14. P.L. 108-446, 601(c)(9) Section 1.01
15. OBERTI v. BOARD OF EDUC., 995 F.2d 1204 (3rd Cir. 1993)
16. See 34 CFR 510.510 Resolution process
17. 34 CFR 300.517(a)
18. IDEA-1997, 34 CFR 300.350(a)
19. IN THE CIRCUIT COURT OF TAYLOR COUNTY, WEST VIRGINIA, JOHN DOE and JANE DOE, vs. MICHAEL WITHERS, and the TAYLOR COUNTY BOARD OF EDUCATION, a public corporation, CIVIL ACTION NO. 92-C-92
20. http://speced.uft.org/
21. P.L. 108-446, 612(d)(1)(B)(ii)
22. P.L. 108-446, 612(d)(3)(C), and 612(d)(4)(B)
23. 26th Annual Report to Congress, Vol. 2, Table 1–9. Children and students served under IDEA, Part B, in the U.S. and outlying areas, by age group, year and disability category: Fall 1993 through fall 2002, p. 25.
24. P.L. 108-446, 662(a)(4). PERSONNEL DEVELOPMENT TO IMPROVE SERVICES AND RESULTS FOR CHILDREN WITH DISABILITIES
25. P.L. 108-446, 612(a)(5)
26. 34 CFR 300.10
27. 34 CFR 300.308(b)(2)
28. 34 CFR 300.321(a)(3)
29. 34 CFR 300.320(a)(1)(i)
30. 34 CFR 300.320(a)(1)(i)
31. No Child Left Behind (NCLB) act (P.L. 107-10, Title I - Improving The Acade-mic Achievement of The Disadvantaged, Section 1111(b)(1)(D) STANDARDS

32. P.L. 108-446, 614(d)(1)(A)(i) Section 1.02
33. OBERTI v. BOARD OF EDUC., 995 F.2d 1204 (3rd Cir. 1993)
34. 700 F.2d 1058 (1983)
35. 458 U.S. 176, 210
36. P.L. 108-446, 614(d)(3)(C)
37. HUDSON v. ROWLEY, 458 U.S. 176(1982)
38. 25th Annual Report to Congress, page 53, Table 1–12, Percentage of Elementary and Middle School Students with Disabilities, by Age and Grade Level: 2001 Educational Outcomes for Students with Disabilities, How often are students with disabilities retained in grade?
39. Letter from UNITED STATES DEPARTMENT OF EDUCATION, OFFICE OF SPECIAL EDUCATION AND REHABILITATIVE SERVICES; To: Office of Special Education Programs, Ms. Patricia M. Lillie, Rebecca Felton, Ph.D, Learning Disabilities Association of North Carolina, Inc. http://www.dueprocessillinois.org/LillieFelton.html
40. P.L. 108-446, 612(a)(5)(A)
41. P.L. 108-446(a)(5)(A) Section 1.03
42. OBERTI v. BOARD OF EDUC., 995 F.2d 1204 (3rd Cir. 1993)
43. A memorandum from Special Education and Rehabilitative Services to State School Officers, January 12, 2001, http://www.dssc.org/frc/fed/JointAssessment Memo.final.pdf
44. 874 F.2d 1036 (5th Cir. 1989)
45. 874 F.2d 1036 (5th Cir. 1989), http://www.kidstogether.org/ct-danl.htm. Tip: Go to the library for a copy of this Court of Appeals case in the Federal Reporter (second series) if the internet copy is difficult to read.
46. 874 F.2d 1036 (5th Cir. 1989)
47. 874 F.2d 1036 (5th Cir. 1989)
48. 874 F.2d 1036 (5th Cir. 1989)
49. 950, F.2d 688 (11th Cir. 1991)
50. Data from Figure 1-36, 25the Annual Report to Congress, Percentage of Students with Disabilities Ages 13 Through 17 Included in the Regular Classroom 100 Percent of the Time, by Disability: 2002 (from *NLTS2 School Survey*)
51. Roncker v. Walter, 700 F.2d 1058 (1983), p. 1063. Section 1.04
52. Oberti v. Board of Educ., 995 F.2d 1204 (3rd Cir. 1993)
53. DANIEL R.R. v. STATE BD. OF EDUC., 874F.2d 1036 (5th Cir. 1989)
54. DANIEL R.R. v. STATE BD. OF EDUC., 874F.2d 1036 (5th Cir. 1989)
55. 34 CFR 300.116(b)(2)
56. From Wikipedia, the free encyclopedia, http://en.wikipedia.org/wiki/Inclusive _classroom
57. 46550 Federal Register / Vol. 71, No. 156 / Monday, August 14, 2006 / Rules and Regulations, p. 46550.
58. CLYDE K.; Sheila K., Plaintiffs-Appellants, v. PUYALLUP SCHOOL, Defendant-Appellee, 35 F.3d 1396, 94 Ed. Law Rep. 707,6 A.D.D. 102, Decided Sept. 13, 1994.
59. 25th Annual report to Congress, Table AB9

60. P.L. 108-446, 614(d)(1)(B)(ii)
61. P.L. 108-446, 614(d)(3)(C)
62. P.L. 108-446, 614(d)(4)
63. 34 CFR 300.323(d)
64. P.L. 108-446, 614(c)(1)(a)
65. P.L. 108-446, 601(c)(1)
66. U.S. Supreme Court HENDRICK HUDSON DIST. BD. OF ED. v. ROWLEY, 458 U.S. 176(1982) 458 U.S. 176 BOARD OF EDUCATION OF THE HENDRICK HUDSON ENTRAL SCHOOL DISTRICT, WESTCHESTER COUNTY, ET AL. v. ROWLEY, BY HER PARENTS, ROWLEY ET UX.
67. 34 CFR 300.116(e)
68. 34 CFR 300.116 Placements.
69. Brown V. Board of Education, 347 U.S. 483 (1954)
70. P.L. 108-446, 601(c)(1)
71. Daniel R.R. v. State Board of Education, United States, Court of Appeals, 1989, 874 F.2d 1036 (5th Cir.)
72. See 43 CFR 300.115 Continuum of alternative placements
73. Daniel R.R. v. State Board of Education, United States, Court of Appeals, 1989, 874 F.2d 1036 (5th Cir.)
74. Oberti v. Board of Education, 789 F.Supp. 1322 (D.N.J. 1992), p. 1333.
75. 34 CFR 300.116(e)
76. See 34 CFR 300.116 Placements
77. 34 CFR 300.116(c)
78. 34 CFR 300.116(d)
79. 34 CFR 300.117
80. 34 CFR 300.116(e)
81. Table 2-2. Students ages 6 through 21 served under IDEA, Part B, by educational environment and state: Fall 2002
82. These rankings are based on data from the 25th Annual Report to Congress. See Figures 1-42 to 1-46 Percentage of SEELS (The Special education Elementary Longitudinal Study) Students 6–12 who Scored in the 0 to 20 percentile range.
83. Co-Teaching: Are Two Heads Better Than One in an Inclusion Classroom? by Millicent Lawton, Harvard Education Letter's Research Online. http://www.edletter.org/past/issues/1999-ma/coteaching.shtml
84. 26th Annual Report to Congress, Table 1-3 and C-8
85. See http://thechp.syr.edu/italy.htm
86. Hoover Institution, Education Next, Autism and the Inclusion Mandate, Ann Christy Dybvik, 2004, No.1
87. 26th Annual Report to Congress, Table 1-3
88. 34 CFR 300.308(c)(12)
89. Source: Brain Injury Association of America, http://www.biausa.org/Pages/causes_of_brain_injury.html
90. Source: Brain Injury Association of America, http://www.biausa.org/Pages/causes_of_brain_injury.html

91. 34 CFR 300.8(c)(9)
92. 34 CFR 300.8(c)(7)
93. Microsoft online has an excellent collection of free clip art at http://office.microsoft.com/en-us/clipart/download.aspx
94. 34 CFR 300.5
95. 34 CFR 300.308(c)(13)
96. http://www.afb.org/Section.asp?SectionID=6&TopicID=22&DocumentID=808
97. Permission to use the National Braille Press logo and Braille Alphabet Card kindly granted by the National Braille Press.
98. Source: National Braille Press, http://www.nbp.org/ic/nbp/braille/literacy.html
99. Eligibility of Blind and Other Physically Handicapped Persons for Loan of Library Materials through the National Library Service for the Blind and Physically Handicapped (NLS). http://www.loc.gov/nls/eligible.html
100. 34 CFR.308(c)(2)
101. http://www.socialsecurity.gov/disability/professionals/bluebook/Childhood Listings.htm
102. P.L. 108-446, 615(a)
103. IDAHO Special Education Manual, 2001, Bureau of Special Education, Idaho State Department of Education, Section 4. Prereferral Activities, p. 23.
104. Operating Standards for Ohio's Schools Serving Children With Disabilities 3301-51-01(N), http://www.ode.state.oh.us/exceptional_children/children_with_disabilities/operating_standards/New/33015101.pdf
105. Special Education In North Dakota, Guidelines: Evaluation Process, North Dakota Department of Public Instruction, Bismarck, ND, 1999
106. Rules of the Alabama State Board of Education, State Department of Education, Chapter 290-8-9 Special Education Services, 290-8-9-.02, P. 490, http://128.146.206.233/glarrc/Resources/PDFs/StateRegsPDF/ALser702.pdf
107. Utah State Board of Education Rules, (2000), II©(4), p. 15.
108. WAC 392-172-104 Referral procedures–Time line.
109. Regulations Governing Special Education Programs for Children with Disabilities in Virginia (2002), 8 VAC 20-80-56. Eligibility.
110. Rules of Alabama State Board of Education, 290-8-9-01(3)(a)
111. A Guide to the Admission, Review and Dismissal Process, Division of Special Education, Texas Education Agency (2002), p. iv.
112. IDAHO Special Education Manual, 2001, Bureau of Special Education, Idaho State Department of Education, p. 16.
113. 8VAC20-80-52. Referral for evaluation. http://leg1.state.va.us/cgi-bin/legp504.exe?000+reg+8VAC20-80-52
114. P.L. 108-446, 614(a)(1)(B) REQUEST FOR INITIAL EVALUATION.
115. Illinois Administrative Code, 226.110(b)
116. Massachusetts 603 CMR 28.04(1)
117. REGULATIONS OF THE COMMISSIONER OF EDUCATION Part 200.4(a)(1)

118. SUPP. NO. 00-4 SPECIAL EDUCATION SERVICES 290-8-9-.01(3)(b) 290-8-9-.01(3)(g)
119. P.L. 108-446, 601(c)(1)
120. Federal Register / Vol. 70, No. 118 / Tuesday, June 21, 2005 / Proposed Rules, p. 35802
121. HR 108-77
122. P.L. 108-446, 614(b)(5)
123. IMPROVING EDUCATION RESULTS FOR CHILDREN WITH DISABILITIES ACT OF 2003, Report 108-77 for IDEA.
124. Hudson v. Rowley 458 U.S. 176 (1982).
125. Hudson v. Rowley 458 U.S. 176 (1982). See http://caselaw.lp.findlaw.com/scripts/getcase.pl?navby=search&linkurl=&graphurl=&court=US&case=/us/458/176.html
126. KENNETH LOGUE and GRETCHEN LOGUE, parents and legal guardians of Noah Logue, a minor, Plaintiffs - Appellants, v. UNIFIED SCHOOL DISTRICT NO. 512, SHAWNEE MISSION, Defendant - Appellee. Nos. 97-3087, 97-3112, UNITED STATES COURT OF APPEALS FOR THE TENTH CIRCUIT, 1998 U.S. App. LEXIS 16280; 98 Colo. J. C.A.R. 3865, July 16, 1998, Filed.
127. U.S. Supreme Court HENDRICK HUDSON DIST. BD. OF ED. v. ROWLEY, 458 U.S. 176(1982) 458 U.S. 176 BOARD OF EDUCATION OF THE HENDRICK HUDSON ENTRAL SCHOOL DISTRICT, WESTCHESTER COUNTY, ET AL. v. ROWLEY, BY HER PARENTS, ROWLEY ET UX.
128. P.L. 108-446, 614(d)(3)
129. Senate Report for IDEA, November 3, 2003
130. P.L. 108-446, 613(d)
131. *Ibid.*
132. A GAO report on how the Department of Education monitors noncompliance, September, 2004, http://www.gao.gov/new.items/d04879.pdf
133. IDEA-1997, 34 CFR 300, Appendix A, Extent to Which Child Will Participate With Nondisabled Children
134. IDEA, 34 CFR 300, Appendix A. I. Involvement and Progress of Each Child with a Disability in the General Curriculum
135. Public Law 93-112 and amended by Public Law 102-569 in 1992.
136. P.L. 108-446, 601(c)(1)
137. See 34 CFR 510.510 Resolution process
138. P.L. 108-446, 615(d)(1)
139. P.L. 108-446, 615(d)(2)
140. P.L. 108-446, 615(b)(1)
141. P.L. 108-446, 615(b)(6)
142. 34 CFR 300.504
143. P.L. 108-446, 615(c)(1)
144. P.L. 108-446, 614(a)(1)(C)(i0
145. Federal Register / Vol. 70, No. 118 / Tuesday, June 21, 2005 / Proposed Rules, p. 35799

146. 34 CFR 300.506
147. P.L. 108-446, 601(c)(8)
148. P.L. 108-446, 612(a)(16(A)
149. 34 CFR 300.15
150. P.L. 108-446, 614(c)(1)(B)(i)
151. P.L. 108-446, 614(b)(2)(A)(ii)
152. PR 34 CFR 300.304(c)(6)
153. P.L. 108-446, 614(b)(2)(A)
154. 68698-9, Federal Register / Vol. 68, No. 236 / Tuesday, December 9, 2003 / Rules and Regulations, Department of , Education, 34 CFR Part 200, Title I–Improving the Academic, Achievement of the Disadvantaged; Final Rule
155. P.L. 108-446, 601(c)(1)
156. 25th Annual Report to Congress. See Figures 1–31 of SEELS (The Special education Elementary Longitudinal Study).
157. P.L. 108-446, 614(d)(A)`(VI)(aa)
158. See 34 CFR 300.304
159. See 614(a)(2)
160. P.L. 108-446, 608(b)
161. Idaho Special Education Manual (September, 2001). Bureau of Special Education, Idaho State Department of Education, Section 5, p. 11.
162. 34 CFR 200.12(b)(4)
163. 34 CFR 200.13(c)
164. P.L. 108-446, 612(a)(16(C)(ii)
165. http://www.isbe.state.il.us/ils/ela/word/goal1.doc and http://www.isbe.state.il.us/assessment/pdfs/API_reading_0506.pdf
166. 34 CFR 300.302
167. P.L. 108-446, 614(a)(1)(E) Rule of construction.
168. P.L. 108-446, 615(c)(1)
169. 200.4, REGULATIONS OF THE COMMISSIONER OF EDUCATION, PART 200–STUDENTS WITH DISABILITIES.
170. 25th Annual Report to Congress, Table 1-4, Volume 1
171. 34 CFR 300.307(a)(3)-(4)
172. 34 CFR 300.307(a)(1)-(3)
173. 34 CFR 300.309(a)(1)
174. 34 CFR 300.309(b)
175. 34 CFR 300.309(b)(2)
176. 34 CFR 300.309(b)
177. 34 CFR 300.309(2)
178. 34 CFR 300.309(b)(1)
179. 34 CFR 300.309(a)(1)
180. 34 CFR 300.309(b)(2)
181. 34 CFR 300.309(a)(2)(ii)
182. P.L. 108-446, 601(c)(5)(A)
183. 34 CFR 300.8(c)(11)
184. 26th Annual Report to Congress, Table 1-3

185. 34 CFR 300.8(c)(3)&(5)
186. National Institute for Literacy, see http://www.nifl.gov/partnershipforreading/publications/reading_first1fluency.html
187. National Reading Panel Report, *Teaching Children to Read*, International Reading Association, 2002, p. 12.
188. Reading for Understanding, RAND Reading Study Group, Office of Education Research and Improvement, 2002. see http://www.rand.org/pubs/monograph_reports/MR1465/MR1465.pdf
189. P.L. 108-446, 614(a)(1)(A)
190. 34 CFR 300.306(a)
191. 34 CFR 300.111(d)
192. 34 CFR 300.8(c)6
193. http://www.aamr.org/Policies/faq_mental_retardation.shtml
194. 34 CFR 300.8(b)
195. 25th Annual Report to Congress, data from Table AB8
196. Racial Disparities in Median Age at Death of Persons With Down syndrome–United States, 1968–1997, http://www.cdc.gov/mmwr/preview/mmwrhtml/mm5022a3.htm
197. From the 25th Annual Report to Congress, data from Table AA15, Racial/Ethnic Composition (Number) of Students Ages 6–21Served Under IDEA, Part B by Disability, During the 2001–02 School Year
198. P.L. 108-446, 601(c)(12)
199. HUDSON v. ROWLEY, 458 U.S. 176(1982)
200. 34 CFR 300.324(b)(2)
201. 34 CFR 300.321
202. 34 CFR 300.321(b)
203. P.L. 108-446, 614(d)(1)(C)(i)
204. Senate Report 108-185, November 3, 2003
205. OBERTI v. BOARD OF EDUC., 995 F.2d 1204 (3rd Cir. 1993)
206. see 34 CFR 300.324(a)(3) and 324(b)(3)
207. 34 CFR 104.1
208. Human Immunodeficiency Virus (HIV) can result in Acquired Immune Deficiency Syndrome (AIDS)
209. 29 U.S.C. 794(a)
210. 34 CFR 104.4(b)(2)
211. Section 504, Title 29–LABOR, CHAPTER 16–VOCATIONAL REHABILITATION AND OTHER REHABILITATION SERVICES, SUBCHAPTER V–RIGHTS AND ADVOCACY, Sec. 794. Nondiscrimination under Federal grants and programs
212. SCHOOL BOARD OF NASSAU COUNTY, FLORIDA, ET AL., v. ARLINE, SUPREME COURT OF THE UNITED STATES, *480 U.S. 273; 107 S. Ct. 1123; 94 L. Ed. 2d 307*, Argued December 3, 1986. Decided March 3, 1987
213. 692 F. Supp. 1286; 1988 U.S. Dist.
214. see Federal Register / Vol. 71, No. 156 / Monday, August 14, 2006 / Rules and Regulations, p. 46746.

215. M.L., a minor v. FEDERAL WAY SCHOOL DISTRICT (387 F.3d 1101)
216. From Senate Report 108-85, November 3, 2003 to accompany S. 1248.
217. P.L. 108-446, 614(d)(1)(C)(ii)
218. A letter from Congress (January 20, 1998) to the U.S. Department of Education (Richard Riley) expressing concerns over the proposed regulations for IDEA-1997 being developed by the Office of Special Education Programs (OSEP).
219. P.L. 108-446, 614(d)(3)(D)-(F)
220. see the Federal Register / Vol. 70, No. 118 / Tuesday, June 21, 2005 / Proposed Rules 35821
221. Sacramento Unified School District v. Rachel H., 14 F.3d 1398 (9th Cir. 1994)
222. 34 CFR 300.323(d)
223. P.L. 108-446, 614(d)(1)(A)(i)
224. Greer v. Rome City School District, 956 F.2d 1025 (11th Cir. 1992)
225. P.L. 108-446, 614(d)(2)(B)
226. Section 636
227. 458 U.S. 176 (1982)
228. EVANS v. THE BOARD OF EDUCATION OF THE RHINEBECK CENTRAL SCHOOL DISTRICT, 930 F. Supp. 83; 1996 U.S. Dist.
229. P.L. 108-446, 614d(1)(A)(i)((II)
230. From 1the 1999 regulations for IDEA 1997 (Appendix A, #4)
231. Questions and Answers, Michigan Merit Curriculum, High School Graduation Requirements, Michigan Department of Education, November, 2006. see http://www.michigan.gov/documents/mde/faq7_178599_7.pdf
232. 26th Annual Report to Congress, V. 1, Table 1-23
233. See 26th Annual Report to Congress, 1-24
234. 26th Annual Report to Congress, Table 1-22
235. 25th Annual Report to Congress, Section II, p. 357, Table AD2, Number of Students with Disabilities Exiting Special Education by Age Year, During the 2000–2001 School year
236. 26th Annual Report to Congress, Table 4-2
237. 29 USC 722(b)(2)(B)
238. See Table 1-20 from the 25th Annual Report to Congress
239. DECLASSIFICATION–STUDENTS WHO LEAVE SPECIAL EDUCATION, A Special Topic report from the Special Education Elementary, Longitudinal Study, p. 8, Prepared for: Dr. Lisa Holden-Pitt, Office of Special Education Programs, U.S. Department of Education, SRI Project P10656 SEELS, September, 2005, p. 7. see http://seels.net/designdocs/SEELS_Declass_FINAL.pdf
240. John P. Lind and Detlev L. Lind, Achives of General Psychiatry, 1961, 4, 331–339 (In Leonard P. Ullman and Leonard Krasner, Case Studies in Behavior Modification, Holt, New York, 1966.
241. 26th Annual Report to Congress, C. 2, Tables 1-4, 1-5 and 1-6.
242. 34 CFR 300.305(a)(2)
243. 34 CFR 300.305(e)

244. 34 CFR 300.305(e)(3)

245. DECLASSIFICATION–STUDENTS WHO LEAVE SPECIAL EDUCA-TION, p. 2.

246. 34 CFR 300.320(a)(6)(i)

247. 34 CFR 104.12

248. 26th Annual Report to Congress, Figure 1-32 SEELS school program survey, 2001. SEELS is funded by the Office of Special Education, U.S. Department of Education. SEELS is The Special Education Elementary Longitudinal Study, a six-year study from 1999–2005.

249. 34 CFR 300.116(e)

250. 34 CFR 300.160

251. Massachusetts Comprehensive Assessment System (MCA) 2005 update, Requirements for the Participation of Students with Disabilities in MCAS, p. 13.

252. Test Access & accommodations for Students with Disabilities, The University of the State of New York, The State Education Department, Office of Vocational and Education Services for Individuals with Disabilities, October 2003, Updated September 2005.

253. Alabama Student Assessment Program Policies and Procedures for Students of Special Populations, Bulletin 2003, No. 11, Ed Richardson, Alabama State Department of Education, Montgomery, Alabama, P. 7.

254. http://www.pen.k12.va.us/, STUDENTS WITH DISABILITIES: Guidelines for Testing in the Virginia State Assessment Program *(NORM-REFERENCED TESTING)*

255. Amanuensis refers to an individual who copies from dictation. For example, a student might require an aid to record responses for essay-type tests where the task is content-based rather than an exercise to evaluate writing skills.

256. American Diabetes Association (ADA) and the Disability Rights Education and Defense Fund, Inc. (DREDF). P. 6, see http://www.dredf.org/504/504-plan-2004.pdf

257. *Ibid.*

258. Council of Administrators of Special Education (CASE). (1992). Student access: a resource guide for educators. Section 504 of the Rehabilitation Act of 1973. ERIC Document #349 769

259. 34 CFR 104.35(c)(2)

260. 34 CFR 104.33(b)

261. Virginia Department of Education's Sample IEP Form

262. PR 34 CFR 300.309(b)(2)

263. The Effects of Test Accommodation on Test Performance: A Review of the Literature. Stephen G. Sireci, Shuhong Li, and Stanley Scarpati, University of Massachusetts Amherst. See http://www.education.umn.edu/NCEO/OnlinePubs/TestAccommLitReview.pdf

264. From Burns, E. (1998). *Test Accommodations for Students with Disabilities.* Charles C Thomas: Springfield, IL.

265. *Test Access and Accommodations for Students with Disabilities*, The University of the State of New York, The State Education Department, Office of Vocational and

Education Services for Individuals with Disabilities, October 2003, Updated September 2005. See http://www.vesid.nysed.gov/specialed/publications/policy/testaccess/guide.htm

266. California High School Exit Examination (CAHSEE) Scribe and Sign Language Guidelines, http://www.cde.ca.gov/ta/tg/hs/documents/scribeguide.doc

267. http://www.gpc.edu/cds/Deaf_and_Hard_of_Hearing.html#Interpreter Guidelines

268. see http://www.rid.org/124.pdf INTERPRETING IN EDUCATIONAL SETTINGS (K–12)

269. American Printing House for the Blind, Large Print: Guidelines for Optimal Readability and APHont™ a font for low vision http://www.aph.org/edresearch/lpguide.htm

270. Senate Report 108-185, Senate Report for IDEA, November 3, 2003

271. 34 CFR 300.530(f)(1)(i)

272. P.L. 108-446, 614(d)(3)(C)

273. HONIG v. DOE, 484 U.S. 305 (1988)

274. 34 CFR 300.530(a)

275. HONIG v. DOE, 484 U.S. 305 (1988)

276. 34 CFR 300.530

277. 26th Annual Report to Congress, Vol. 2, Table 5-3.

278. *Ibid.*, Vol. 2, Table 5-1

279. 25th Annual Report to Congress, 2000-01 SEELS data, Volume 1, Section 1, p. 40-41. see http://www.ed.gov/about/reports/annual/osep/2003/25th-vol-1-sec-1.pdf

280. Based on data from the 25th Annual Report to Congress, Table AE1.

281. Federal Register / Vol. 70, No. 118 / Tuesday, June 21, 2005 / Proposed Rules, p. 35823.

282. P.L. 108-446, 615(k)(6)(A)

283. 34 CFR 300.310(a)

284. P.L. 108-446, 614(c)(1)(A)(iii)

285. P.L. 108-446, 615(k)(5)

286. P.L. 108-446, 300.310 Observation

287. Federal Register / Vol. 71, No. 156 / Monday, August 14, 2006 / Rules and Regulations, p. 46579.

288. Federal Register / Vol. 71, No. 156 / Monday, August 14, 2006 / Rules and Regulations, p. 46550.

289. P.L. 108-446, 300.8(b)(4)(i)

290. Federal Register / Vol. 71, No. 156 / Monday, August 14, 2006 / Rules and Regulations, p. 46549.

291. The Education of Students with Disabilities: Where Do We Stand?, National Council on Disability September, 1989, p. 32.

292. *Ibid.*, p. 46550

293. Vermont Department of Education – State Board of Education Manual of Rules and Practices, Special Education, SPECIAL EDUCATION 2360 8/29/2003, page 32, 2362(h)(2)

294. 34 CFR 300.8(b)(9)
295. 34 CFR 300.174
296. P.L. 108-446, 612(a)(25)(A)
297. 34 CFR 300.323(c)(2)
298. 34 CFR 300.115(b)(2)
299. 34 CFR §300.38(a) Special education.
300. Federal Register / Vol. 71, No. 156 / Monday, August 14, 2006 / Rules and Regulations, p. 46561.
301. P.L. 108-446, 613(4)(A) (i)
302. Related services are explained in the regulations at 34 CFR 300.34
303. Hawaii v. Katherine D., 727 F.2d 809 (1983)
304. P.L. 108-446, 602(33)
305. 950 F.2d 688 (11th Ctr. 1991)
306. 874 F.2d 1036 (5th Ctr. 1989), p. 1048.
307. Oberti v. Board of Education, 789 F.Supp. 1322 (D.N.J. 1992), p. 1333.
308. DANIEL R.R. v. STATE BD. OF EDUC., 874F.2d 1036 (5th Cir. 1989)
309. 34 CFR 300.42
310. P.L. 108-446, 614(a)(d)(1)(A)(i)(IV)
311. Table 1-11 Percentage of schools reporting the use of support services by one or more student with disabilities: 1999–2000
312. 26th Annual Report to Congress, Figure 1-33, SEELS school program survey, 2001.
313. Federal Register / Vol. 71, No. 156 / Monday, August 14, 2006 / Rules and Regulations, p. 46644.
314. IDEA-1990, 34 CFR 300.551(b)(2)
315. 950 F.2d 688 (11th Ctr. 1991)
316. 26th Annual Report to Congress, Table F-2. Students ages 6 through 21 served under IDEA, Part B, by educational environment and state: Fall 2001 and Table C-8. Estimated resident population ages 6 through 21, by race/ethnicity and state: 2002.
317. See 34 CFR 300.107-110
318. See 34 CFR 300.109 and 34 CFR 300.110
319. 34 CFR 300.156(b)2)(iii)
320. NCLB, "SEC. 1119. QUALIFICATIONS FOR TEACHERS AND PARA-PROFESSIONALS.
321. SEC. 662. PERSONNEL DEVELOPMENT TO IMPROVE SERVICES AND RESULTS FOR CHILDREN WITH DISABILITIES.
322. 34 CFR 300.306(b)(1)(iii)
323. 20 USC 7801, Title IX, General Provisions, 9101"(25)(D)
324. http://www.pde.state.pa.us/k12/cwp/view.asp?A=11&Q=45272 Basic Education Circulars (Pennsylvania Code) Educating Students With Limited English Proficiency (LEP) and English Language Learners (ELL), 22 Pa. Code §4.26, Pennsylvania Department of Education
325. See Teaching Today at http://www.glencoe.com/sec/teachingtoday/education upclose.phtml/24

REFERENCES

Burns, E. (1998). *Test Accommodations for Students with Disabilities*. Springfield, IL: Charles C Thomas.

Burns, E. (2001). *Developing and Implementing IDEA-IEPs: An Individualized Education Program (IEP) Handbook for Meeting Individuals with Disabilities Education Act (IDEA) Requirements*. Springfield, IL: Charles C Thomas.

Burns, E. (2003). *A Handbook for Supplementary Aids and Services: A Best practice and IDEA Guide "to Enable Children with Disabilities to be Educated with Nondisabled Children to the Maximum Extent Appropriate."* Springfield, IL: Charles C Thomas.

Burns, E. (2004). *The Special Education Consultant Teacher: Enabling Children with Disabilities to be Educated with Nondisabled Children to the Maximum Extent Appropriate*. Springfield, IL: Charles C Thomas.

Burns, E. (2006). *IEP-2005: Writing and Implementing Individualized Education Programs*. Springfield, IL: Charles C Thomas.

Council of Administrators of Special Education. (1992). *Student access: a resource guide for educators. Section 504 of the Rehabilitation Act of 1973*. Albuquerque, NM: Author. ERIC No. 349 769.

Dunn, L.M. (1968). Special education for the mildly retarded–Is much of it justifiable? *Exceptional Children, 35*, 5–22.

Friend, M, and Bursuck, W. (1996). *Including Students with Special Needs: A Practical Guide for Regular education teachers*. Boston: Allyn and Bacon.

Iwata, B.A., Dorsey, M.F., Slifer, K.J., Bauman, K.E., Richman, G.S. (1982). Toward a Functional analysis of self-injury. Reprinted in *Journal of Applied Behavioral Analysis*, 1994, *27*, 197–209.

Johnson, G.O., and Kirk, S.A. (1950). Are mentally handicapped children segregated in the regular grades? *Exceptional Children, 17*, 65–68 and 87–88.

Love, Harold D., (1972). *Educating Exceptional Children in Regular Classroom*. Springfield, IL: Charles C Thomas.

National Council on Disability (2000). *Back to school on civil rights: advancing the Federal commitment to leave no children behind*. 1331 F Street, NW, Suite 1050, Washington, D.C.

New York State Education Department, Regulations of the Commissioner of Education, Part 200, 200.4(a)(1)(vi), January, 1998.

Rena B. L. and Doorlag, D.H. (1983). *Teaching Special Students in the Mainstream*. Columbus, OH: Charles E. Merrill Publishing Company.

Rothstein, L. F. (1995). *Special Education Law* (2nd ed). New York: Longman.

Smith, T., Polloway, E., Patton, J., & Dowdy, C. (1995). *Teaching Children with Special Needs in Inclusive Settings*. Boston: Allyn and Bacon.

Twenty-fourth Annual Report to Congress on the Implementation of the Individuals with Disabilities Education Act, U.S. Department of Education, 2002, Washington, D.C.: See http://www.ed.gov/about/reports/annual/osep/2002/index.html.

Twenty-fifth Annual Report to Congress on the Implementation of the Individuals with Disabilities Education Act, U.S. Department of Education, 2002, Washington, D.C. See http://www.ed.gov/about/reports/annual/osep/2003/index.html.

Twenty-Sixth Annual Report to Congress on the Implementation of the Individuals with Disabilities Education Act, U.S. Department of Education, 2002, Washington, D.C. See http://www.ed.gov/about/reports/annual/osep/2004/index.html.

INDEX